D1271914

The Scar That Binds

The Scar
That Binds

*American Culture
and the Vietnam War*

Keith Beattie

NEW YORK UNIVERSITY PRESS
New York and London

NEW YORK UNIVERSITY PRESS
New York and London

Library of Congress Cataloging-in-Publication Data
Beattie, Keith, 1954–
The scar that binds : American culture and the Vietnam War / Keith
Beattie
p.   cm.
Includes bibliographical references (p.) and index.
ISBN 0-8147-1326-2 (acid-free paper)
1. Vietnamese Conflict, 1961–1975—United States.   2. Vietnamese
Conflict, 1961–1975—Influence.   3. United States-Civilization—1945–
I. Title
DS558.B4   1998
959.704'3373—dc21   97-45456
                                        CIP

New York University Press books are printed on acid-free paper,
and their binding materials are chosen for strength and durability.

Manufactured in the United States of America

10 9 8 7 6 5 4 3 2 1

For my mother and father

Contents

Acknowledgments

The support I received during the years spent researching and writing *The Scar That Binds* can now, finally, be gratefully acknowledged. First and foremost, I would like to thank Roger Bell, head of the School of History at the University of New South Wales, Sydney, Australia, for his helpful comments on various drafts of this work and for his encouragement throughout its writing. *Many* thanks. Rick Berg, Michael Clark, Peter Ehrenhaus, David James, Susan Jeffords, and John Carlos Rowe generously responded to my ideas on this topic during the early months of 1991. Richard Pascal, Jim Gilbert, and, in particular, Harry Haines assisted with extremely productive responses to an initial draft of the work. I am indebted to Andrew Martin for providing me with a galley copy of his book dealing with representations of the Vietnam War. J. William Gibson offered important observations during our long-distance correspondence. Andrew Ross and George Lipsitz have also been supportive of the project.

Morris Dickstein kindly commented on a published version of "The Healed Wound" (*Australasian Journal of American Studies* 9, 1 [July 1990]: 38–48) during the fourteenth biennial Australian and New Zealand American Studies Association (ANZASA) conference, Sydney University, July 1990. A different version of this paper was presented at the "Narrative and Metaphor Across the Disciplines" conference, University of Auckland, July 1996. Papers based on Part 2, "The Vietnam Veteran as Ventriloquist," were presented at the fifteenth ANZASA conference, Flinders University, Adelaide, July 1992, and the seventh Australian History and Film conference, Australian National University, Canberra, November 1995. An earlier version of Part 3 was presented at the sixteenth ANZASA conference, Melbourne University, April 1994. I am indebted to the audiences on these occasions for their positive criticisms. An expanded version of the paper delivered at the History and Film conference is forthcoming in an edited collection of papers to be published by the Australian National Film and Sound Archive, Canberra. A version of "The Voice of the Veteran" appeared in the journal *Media International Australia* (May 1996): 14–28. My thanks to Jeff Doyle on this occasion. The staff and postgraduate students of the School of History at the University of New South Wales offered valuable comments in response to presentations of earlier versions of my work. I would especially like to thank Chris Dixon and Sean Brawley for their contributions during these presentations.

At Massey University, New Zealand, I'd like to thank Roy Shuker for his friendship and for his insights into all aspects of the mutable field known as culture; Kerry Howe for his sage advice to keep going; John Muirhead for the books; Lynne Coates for her help with the intricacies of word processing; and the members of the editorial collective of *Sites: A Journal of South Pacific Cultural Studies*, including Allanah, Anne-Marie, Avril, Brennon, Gregor, Henry, Jeff, Keith, Robyn, and Roy.

The staff of the Circulation Desk at Bancroft Library, University of California, Berkeley; the Interlibrary Loans Unit, University of New South Wales Libraries; and the Film Loans Unit of the National Library of Australia provided assistance.

Louise and Michael Thake were always there, for which I'm always grateful.

My thanks to Niko Pfund, director of New York University Press, and to managing editor, Despina Papazoglou Gimbel.

I would also like to thank Nick Sebastian for permission to reproduce his photograph on the cover of this book.

A lifelong debt of gratitude is owed to Julie Ann Smith—for a world of reasons that a simple acknowledgment such as this cannot possibly encompass.

Introduction

It had come to this. Two presidents from two different political parties had spoken, as if in unison, on what was once a fiercely contentious topic. During his presidential inaugural address, George Bush pronounced that "the final lesson of Vietnam is that no great nation can long afford to be sundered by a memory."[1] Speaking at the Vietnam Veterans Memorial in 1993, President Bill Clinton stated, "Let [the war in Vietnam] not divide us as a people any longer."[2] In the two statements "Vietnam" is foregrounded as a rupturing presence within American culture while *at the same time* it is used to evoke the need for unity. Both quotations connote a single object: the desire for totality achieved through the erasure of the divisions associated with the war. Within the strategies that function to achieve this end, the notion of unity is constructed as an uncomplicated and coherent condition critically necessary for the common good.

Another American president, Ronald Reagan, repeated on a number of occasions the contradiction sketched here in his evocations of the impact of the Vietnam War upon U.S. culture. When formally accepting the Vietnam Veterans Memorial on behalf of the nation, Reagan referred to the "scars" suffered by those who served in Vietnam and made reference to those who had "strong opinions on the war." Having alluded to protest stemming from the war, Reagan went on to argue that it was time to "move on, in unity," thereby rhetorically relegating a divisive experience to the past and presenting social unity as a condition necessary for America's progress into the future.[3] Four years later, again speaking at the Wall, as the Vietnam Veterans Memorial has become known, Reagan referred to the "memories of a time when we faced great divisions here at home." The existence of these memories became the occasion to stress what he defined as a "profound truth about our nation: that from all our divisions we have always eventually emerged strengthened."[4] According to Reagan, then, the existence of divisions within the United States foregrounds the profound and indisputable truth of strength through unity that is the real history of the nation.

American presidents have not been the only ones to represent the impact of the Vietnam War in terms of a contradiction involving social division, on the one hand, and a presumed cultural unity, on the other. Certain interpretations of the Vietnam Veterans Memorial, for example, have stressed its function in circulating a memory of the mortally wounded soldier; yet equally as popular, if not more so, have been references to the Wall as an object that brings Americans together by healing the wounds of war. The practice of healing is the erasure of the memory and the "scarring" effects of the divisive impact of the war in the presumption of an America reunited in the wake of the Vietnam War. The film *The Deer Hunter* (1978) depicted the human toll of the war on small-town, working-class America while seeking closure in a final scene in which the damaged characters unite to sing "God Bless America"—an action that, in the absence of any directorial sense of irony, is a reaffirmation of the ties between them as individuals and as members of the nation. The novel *In Country* (1987) establishes the deleterious effects of the war upon the lives of a number of characters only to conclude with the three central characters united at the Vietnam Veterans Memorial, which is defined in the novel as a site that functions to foster social integration.[5] In the novel *Indian Country* (1987) a Vietnam veteran who has alienated his family as a result of his violent and psychotic responses to his service in Vietnam is eventually healed of the psychological wounds of war through reunion with his family.[6] In such television series as *Magnum, P.I.* (1980), *The A-Team* (1983), and *Riptide* (1984) military service in Vietnam features as an experience that unites the otherwise marginalized characters to one another and to other Vietnam veterans. In time it was the status as group player that allowed these characters to reunite with society. The message of the film *Platoon* (1986)—that "we did not fight the enemy, we fought ourselves"—suggests that social cohesion will obviate the need for war. The television series *Tour of Duty* (1987) and *China Beach* (1988) used the war as a device to evoke social divisions between Americans that weekly were displaced within the affirmation of group loyalty and unity.

Within each of these examples the assertions of disruption and division that are central to representations of the impact of the war upon the United States are eroded and contradicted within a widespread and continual ideological operation that has functioned to reinstate the notion of cultural, social, and political collectivity and holism. Michael Herr identified the contradictory nature of the experience of the Vietnam War when he wrote that the word "Vietnam" signified the best and worst of experiences, which he summarized as "pain, pleasure, horror, guilt, nostalgia." However, through processes of revision and rearticulation such an awareness of contradictions has been transformed into a different set of meanings. "Vietnam . . . we've all been there," Herr concluded.[7] As the personal pronoun of collectivity—*we*—intimates, the connotations of division inherent in the word "Vietnam" have been replaced with an imaginary holism. "Vietnam," once the sign of social segmentation and political divisions, has been appropriated as a site for the representation of unity. It is this paradox—the impact of the war defined as both rupture and union, and how the former collapses into the latter—that is the general object of analysis within this study.

As this outline suggests, this book examines American culture. It is not a book about the Vietnam War and its representations. There is little mention here of the seemingly endless stream of texts dealing with the battles and in-country trauma of America and Americans in Vietnam. Critical work continues in this crowded field of study—the films, novels, poetry, memoirs, and military and diplomatic histories of the war have all received critical attention. What such studies emphasize is that the texts of the war can provide useful opportunities for those wishing to study American culture. Andrew Martin's *Receptions of War* (1993) perceptively illustrates this point. Martin studies representations of the war as a way of commenting upon "the process through which an unpopular war has come to be received in popular culture."[8] His study differs from many within the field through its focus on texts drawn from film, fiction, and written history. Typically, studies of the representation of the war have incorporated only one or two of these categories as the objects of analysis (notably film and fiction). In these studies the method of separating written texts from visual texts tends to contain meanings within form. In opposition to such categorization, an interdisciplinary approach permits the tracing of common meanings across the arbitrary boundaries of textual categories. An effective study in these terms is Susan Jeffords's laudable *The Remasculinization of America: Gender and the Vietnam War* (1989).[9] Aspects of Jeffords's analysis have contributed to certain features of my study, although no attempt has been made to duplicate her method of employing representations of the war as a way of exposing patriarchal beliefs and values.

In contrast to the proliferating studies concerned with representations of the war as a combat experience, *The Scar That Binds* opens and examines an unexplored critical space through an analysis of representations of the effects, traces, presences, and legacies of the war in Vietnam upon and within the culture of the United States. The focus on texts dealing with the impacts of the war, as opposed to representations of the war itself, provides a cogent and unique impression of the place and function of "Vietnam" within U.S. culture. An interdisciplinary approach is adopted in this study as an aspect of a method that seeks to reveal historical and ideological conditions in the wake of the war. Specifically, the aim of interdisciplinarity is to render a more detailed impression of the context that is post–Vietnam War U.S. culture than is achievable through an analysis of texts of a single discipline. In keeping with an interdisciplinary focus, this study traverses and is informed by perspectives from the areas of historiography, political theory, literary theory, sociology, communications, and cultural studies. The need to confront this wide interpretative terrain is the result of the demands of examining what is said about the impact of the war in texts drawn from various fields, including film, written and oral history, literature, and journalism. The focus reveals a unique and detailed historical record that includes the antiwar movement, the role and place of the Vietnam veteran, definitions and perceptions concerning the war years of "the 6os," and varieties of national commemoration and historical revisionism, among other topics. Although this study involves texts from a number of areas, no attempt has been made to undertake an encyclopedic coverage of all documents dealing with the cultural impact of the war—the task of the bibliographer differs from the form of interpretative critique pursued here. Nor does the analysis necessarily seek to offer a detailed explication or a close reading of individual texts.

This study of contemporary American culture recognizes that political and economic structures set limits on individual and collective agency and the production of cultural meanings, inscribing those actions and meanings with varieties of unstated presuppositions. Thus, the analysis is not only concerned with what is said. Unarticulated positions inform the paradox of segmentation and unity and add crucial dimensions to the topics and issues available within a variety of textual representations. Accordingly, the task is to address hidden textual meanings that typically remain unsaid.[10] The interrogation of concealed meanings pursued within this book takes the form of a decoding and critique of the operation of what I call the ideology of unity.

Certain terms within this phrase require explication. As it is used here, "ideology" refers to mental frameworks or categories that people use to define and interpret experience; it consists of simple yet meaningful concepts and images of "practical thought" that are reproduced as coherent and universal interpretations of everyday reality.[11] In turn, the assumptions are informed by common sense. Commonsense explanations and conceptions do not rest on logic or argument; rather, they appear to be spontaneous or preconceived notions that are widely shared. As such, common sense "*feels* . . . as if it has always been there, [a] sedimented, bedrock wisdom . . . , a form of natural wisdom," as the cultural theorist Stuart Hall has noted.[12] The ideology of unity shares the general characteristics of ideology by directing commonsense forms of everyday interpretation toward a specific end. The ideology of unity represents the commonsense notion that an essentialized form of social, cultural, and political unity is necessary to the good of all Americans. On a basic level the ideology operates through expressions that, having passed into cliché, are taken for granted as common sense. Expressions such as "unity is strength," "unity is power," "united we stand; divided we fall," and "out of many, one" validate unity and function to delegitimate contradictory or oppositional voices. To be outside the union, that is, to refuse or contest the ideology of unity, is to risk being marginalized as alien, unmanageable, dangerous, anarchic, even unpatriotic. It is with the assistance of such powerful rhetorical and social supports that conceptions of homogeneity and uniformity are naturalized within the culture.[13]

Culture is the site of the generation of meaning. It is a determining, productive, and open field through which experience is constructed, defined, and interpreted. Culture involves the shared lifestyles, personal dispositions, beliefs, values, codes, and language of a small group or a society. Reference to shared meanings does not imply that meanings are common, or inherent, to a specific culture nor does it suggest the absence of conflict in the reproduction of meaning. The field through which meaning is constructed and circulated is not quiescent or static—it is a space characterized by contending definitions leading to the emergence of dominant meanings and concepts.

Throughout its history America has used this space to express and defer to supposedly nonpoliticized concepts of national and cultural unity. The continued evocation of the notion of holism in the specific context of the impact of the Vietnam War highlights the particular effectivity of "Vietnam" in the perpetuation of cultural conceptions of unity and exposes the shortcomings of the common claim that the war ruptured the existing ideological structure. The assessment of rupture recognizes only one side of the Vietnam paradox. The other side of the paradox, the one traced in this book through a focus on the operation of the ideology of unity, demonstrates that fundamental ideological and mythological patterns were not destroyed by the war in Vietnam. The notion of unity, a basic ideological premise historically ingrained within U.S. culture, survived the war.[14] Indeed, aspects of what *Time* magazine has called "The War That Will Not End" remain in the culture precisely because they provide a unique vehicle for the representation of cultural unity.[15] The depiction of the impact of the war as a crisis within American culture has reinforced and legitimated calls for an ameliorative response in the form of the necessity of cultural unity. The continued deployment of the ideology of unity underlines the fact that the impact of the war—believed to be profoundly disruptive—has in practice been the central focus for the assertion of the notion of unity.

There is a crucial issue at stake in the representation of unity that belies the seeming neutrality of the category. The ideology of unity analyzed here functions to negate a simple fact, namely, that the United States is a culture structured by divisions, diversities, and differences. The notion of a differentiated culture—a multiculture—is ignored by an ideology that reduces cultural and political complexity to a unified whole. The paradox of division and unity features a contest between differing conceptions of the effects of the war and varying perceptions of the structure of U.S. culture that are mediated by the force of an ideology that emphasizes cultural indivisibility and collectivity. The continual slippage away from cultural division and difference toward cultural unity that results from this mediation foregrounds the central issue at stake in the paradox: the denial of difference within U.S. culture.[16] The specific aim of this study, then, is to examine the ways in which the ideology of unity operates and produces effects within and through representations of the impact upon American culture of the Vietnam War, and to suggest that the privileging of the seemingly natural notion of unity displaces and denies cultural relations of difference. By exposing the operations of the dominant ideology of unity, I affirm the existence of cultural difference within the United States. I hope that the denaturalization of the ideology of unity undertaken here will invite further interrogation of cultural unity, leading to a broader understanding of the United States as an hierarchically organized multiculture.

The critique undertaken within this study of the signs of the ideology of unity operating within American culture revealed three dominant meanings structured within metaphor within a range of texts: the "wound," the "voice" of the Vietnam veteran, and "home." I refer to these decoded dominant meanings as "strategies of unity," a term used to evoke the specific work and material effects of the ideology of unity within U.S. culture since the late sixties. The first strategy, identified as *"The Healed Wound,"* concerns the encoding of the ideology of unity within a powerful and widespread metaphor. The divisive impact of the war in Vietnam upon American culture has commonly been defined as a "wound," while reconciliatory efforts have been termed "healing." An examination of these positions reveals that the wound is cultural division, a longstanding characteristic of U.S. culture though one that was widely attributed to have resulted from the impact of the war. Through the circumlocutions surrounding the Vietnam War this condition was commonly expressed as impotence. The erasure of division and difference in the "healing" of the disabling wound resulted in unity and attendant perceptions of cultural reinvigoration and strength. The healing outcome was predicated in part on the denial—or forgetting—of the memory of the war and matters stemming from U.S. involvement in Vietnam. The healing process operated across a wide cultural terrain, specifically at the level of the individual and the community as synecdochic expressions of the need to heal the nation. A healed nation results in unity and consensus and the inscription of the status quo. The centrality within popular and critical interpretations of the metaphor of healing the wounds and scars of the Vietnam War positions the trope as the dominant strategy studied here. Aspects of other strategies examined in this study interact with and contribute to features of "healing the scars of war" while advancing and enlarging a number of unique positions that contribute to the work of negotiating, and overcoming, the paradox associated with the impact of the Vietnam War on American culture.

The second strategy, referred to as *"The Vietnam Veteran as Ventriloquist,"* encodes the "truth" of unity within representations of the American veteran of the war in Vietnam. Early representations of the male veteran depicted him as an inarticulate psychopath incapable of effective communication, and hence functionally "silent." Subsequently, however, the intersection of a number of factors resulted in altering the veteran's speaking position. The first factor in this process involved the critical project in which the Vietnam War was defined as unique. The unique war, it was argued, needed a form of representation capable of revealing the truth of the war. The result of this conception was the denigration of conventional written histories, which were deemed incapable of adequately representing the war. This conclusion reflected the exclusionary notion that only those who experienced the war could adequately describe its truth. Participation—"having been there"—became the crucial indicator of the truthfulness of accounts of wartime experience. The outcome of the interrelated set of assumptions was that the male veteran's experience of the war in Vietnam positioned him as the sole legitimate domestic spokesperson of the essential truth of the conflict. Ironically, having been accorded a central speaking role, the veteran's heavily mediated voice was heard to speak only of unity. Compounding the irony surrounding the representation of the veteran, it was through his pronouncements on the topic of cultural integration and union—and not as a result of his war service—that the veteran, in the final phase of apotheosis, was represented as a hero. The denial of the veteran's agency implicit within this conclusion is, however, actively contested within the process of "talking back"—a consideration of forms of representation in which the veteran is heard to speak in a variety of voices.

The final strategy, titled *"Bringing the War 'Home,'"* concerns the assertion of unity defined in terms of "home." The notion of home was reworked and realigned across a twenty-year period, beginning in the late Sixties when sections of the antiwar movement sought to "bring the war home." This radical position was subsequently revised within commonsense assumptions emphasizing home as a condition devoid of contest and opposition. Similarly, representations during the early to midseventies depicting the repatriation of the war with the veteran were revised during the latter half of the seventies within cultural characteristics that functioned to recuperate the "violent" or "sick" veteran within the unity of the therapeutic family. During the eighties the notion of a consensual, convivial "home" was reinforced within the nostalgic agenda of the Reagan administration, while in the late eighties home was represented as a feature of the war in Vietnam and of the American home front. The transferability of home reinforces the notion that home is not a place but a set of homogenizing definitions inscribed within the culture.

The three strategies referred to here are understood to represent different strands of the same ideological discourse and to operate simultaneously throughout the period covered in this book. The years that mark the temporal boundaries of the analysis are defined by the release dates of the first and last texts selected as central to this study: 1968 to 1989.[17] Within this period the height of the ideological assertion of unity is understood to coincide with the years of the Reagan presidency. During these years, as with the entire period covered here, unity is interpreted as a project operating through ideologically structured signifying practices to produce a specific outcome. Political theorist Michael Ryan has argued that a reality different to that presented in dominant depictions of American political life and American society would be created if representation "addressed the multiplicity of contiguous social parts instead of pretending to give a substitute for an imaginary whole."[18] Unfortunately, there is one major hurdle to overcome before this issue can be confronted: the ideology of unity. This study demonstrates the depth and breadth to which this ideology is inscribed within representations of the impact of the Vietnam War, and the effects of that inscription. The divisions exposed by the war are negated, difference is elided, unity prevails—America is no longer asunder. Or so the ideology of unity would have us believe.

1

The Healed Wound

We can find no scar,
But internal difference   —Emily Dickinson

The healing process mobilises potent symbolic
resources, for in attempting to redress the breaches
caused by illness, however these are perceived, healers
everywhere manipulate symbolic media which identify
physical with social order.   —Jean Comaroff

It is inescapable: an object of war is to wound. War is blood, war is body fragments, war is the dismemberment of the body—though not the body's absence. Mortally wounded bodies are present on the battlefield in a display that attests to the dreadful power of war. Censorship, however, attempts to obscure this fact by concealing the presence of the injured, wounded body. In the case of the Gulf War, Pentagon censorship functioned to deny the essential object of the conflict. In this war there was no shortage of information relating to the deployment of weapons, the nature of these weapons, their capabilities and their cost to the U.S. taxpayer. This information was replete with intricate diagrams and even on-board video cameras to illustrate the effectiveness of the weapons. The so-called Nintendo war[1] took the spectator to the point of impact, to the heart of "hard" targets, while steadfastly refusing to expose the "soft" targets of Iraqi bodies. Early in the air war Vietnam veteran General Norman Schwarzkopf was quoted as saying: "I have absolutely no idea what the Iraqi casualties are, and I tell you, if I have anything to say about it, we're never going to get into the body-count business."[2] The callous disregard for the Iraqi dead and suffering was sublimated through reference to the deservedly criticized body count of the Vietnam War, thus turning the "refusal to count" into "the crowning virtue of a higher morality, of a humanist revulsion against the quantification of death."[3]

Military censorship of the wounded body permitted Americans to view the war in the Persian Gulf as a conflict without wounds or blood. Another veteran of Vietnam, Colin Powell, called it a clean win even though it has been estimated that Iraqi dead over six weeks of combat was *double* that of U.S. casualties during a decade of war in Vietnam.[4] The illusion fostered by censorship of a theater of operations devoid of blood legitimated military objectives and guaranteed the unrestricted use of an overdetermined firepower. Thus, along with lines drawn in the sand, censorship of images of the injured body became a matter of military strategy.

Paul Fussell has pointed out how the wounded, dismembered body has long been absent from representations of battle. "In the popular and genteel iconography of war . . . from the eighteenth- and nineteenth-century history paintings to twentieth-century photographs, the bodies of the dead, if inert, are intact." Fussell exemplifies this observation by referring to a popular and widely distributed collection of photographs published as *Life Goes to War* (1977). The dismembered body fails to appear in even the bleakest images in this anthology of photographs from World War II. Although depicted as severely wounded, Allied troops were not "shown suffering what was termed, in the Vietnam War, traumatic amputation: everyone has all his limbs, his hands and feet and digits."[5] In Fussell's description, as in innumerable accounts of the conflict in the Persian Gulf, the war in Vietnam features as a point of contrast. In one critical respect the war in the Gulf was not another Vietnam, nor was the war in Vietnam a replaying of World War II—the difference lay in the fact that the Vietnam War preserved the fact of war by maintaining the visibility of the injured or disfigured body.

A brief perusal of virtually any collection of photographs of the war in Vietnam reveals a gallery of images of injury and pain. Indeed, some of the most widely circulated images of the war concern the injured body: Buddhist monks immolating themselves; Nick Ut's photograph of a scarred and badly burned Vietnamese girl, Kim Phuc, running along a road near her napalmed village; Ron Haeberle's photographs for *Life* magazine of the dead at My Lai; Eddie Adams's photograph of General Nguyen Ngoc Loan's execution of a suspected Viet Cong insurgent during Tet 1968. The sheer visible presence in newspapers, newsmagazines, and televised images of physically and mortally wounded U.S. soldiers served to painfully reinforce the notion that the meaning of this war was wounding and injury.

Wounding further touched the American conscience through the fact that during and after the Vietnam War Americans were unavoidably confronted with physical disability in the form of seventy-five thousand permanently disabled veterans, and in excess of fifty-eight thousand mortally wounded soldiers.[6] The overwhelming presence of wounding so impressed itself upon the popular imagination that injury and wounding ascended to dominance as *the* framework for representing and interpreting the distressing political, economic, social, or psychological consequences of the war in Vietnam for U.S. culture.[7]

The definitional processes that constructed the impact of the war as a "wound" were extended and reinforced through widespread use of the word "healing" to refer to postwar attempts to confront and overcome the consequences of the war. The *New York Times Magazine*, for example, referred to the war's lingering domestic impact as "the wound that will not heal," and *Time* magazine used this phrase as a headline on a number of occasions to specify postwar situations within the United States.[8] Other journals described the effects of the war as a "trauma" and then proceeded to postulate the fate of "the healing nation."[9] Similarly, the Vietnam Veterans Memorial in Washington, D.C., is commonly referred to as the "wall that heals the wounds of war,"[10] and a succession of American presidents have spoken of the need to heal the wounds inflicted by America's involvement in Vietnam. President Johnson expressed the need to "heal" the divisions in American culture, especially those created by the war. Speaking in 1975, President Ford, quoting Lincoln, talked of "bind[ing] up the nation's wounds" and he entitled his post–Vietnam, post-Watergate memoir *A Time to Heal* (1979). In a major message to Congress in October 1978, President Carter spoke of the obligation to "forgive" Vietnam-era draft resisters as part of the process of "healing [the] wounds [of war]."[11] More recently President Clinton, speaking at the Vietnam Veterans Memorial, also quoted Lincoln in a reference to the need to "bind up" the wounds resulting from the war in Vietnam.[12]

The metaphor of the wound has pervaded not only written and spoken accounts but also visual representations, as in a cartoon by David Levine that depicts President Johnson revealing the scar from his gall-bladder operation in the shape of the map of Vietnam.[13] The metaphor—primarily in the form of a wounded veteran—has been central to various films seeking to represent the effects of the war on the U.S. home front. The depth to which the metaphor has penetrated various discourses is evident in the fact that in addition to journalism, political rhetoric, and film, the metaphor is also present in a number of written histories. One historian drew attention to the metaphor by making it the title of his text: *The Wound Within: America in the Vietnam Years, 1945–1975* (1974), and other authors have frequently employed the terms "wound" or "trauma" in accounts of the war years.[14] For example, Walter Capps, in *The Unfinished War: Vietnam and the American Conscience* (1990), makes a number of references to the trauma inflicted by the Vietnam War. Capps asserts that the trauma issued from tragedy, which he describes as "a dramatic event with an ending that was inevitably unhappy because integral elements eluded successful resolution. . . . Viewing [the war in Vietnam] as tragedy, we can identify ways in which we are accommodating trauma."[15]

Capps continues to juggle terms by referring to the "trauma we call Vietnam."[16] Capps's use of the metonym "Vietnam" to refer to the effects of the Vietnam War reflects various uses of the word "Vietnamization" to signify the impact of the war. In *The Wound Within*, Alexander Kendrick stated that as "the war accentuated the negative in the theses and antitheses of American life, Vietnam became increasingly Americanized [and] America became increasingly Vietnamized."[17] Four years earlier David Halberstam had written of "the Vietnamization of America," perhaps using the phrase for the first time to refer to situations on the U.S. home front.[18] Continued widespread use of "Vietnam" or "Vietnamization" in place of the word "wound" in references to the U.S. domestic scene during and after the war would have resulted in the promulgation of the name of a country, and an experience, many felt best forgotten. A revision and reorientation of terms resulted in the continued preeminence of the paradigm of the "wound" and its corollary "healing" as a method for interpreting the impact of the war.

With reference to this paradigm, it has been argued that a "fundamental therapeutic tool [is] a set of codes" for reordering perceptions disrupted by illness or "wounding."[19] In the following part the metaphoric language responsible for circulating specific codes is critiqued to reveal the cultural complexity of, and the meanings inherent within, the wound/healing mode of interpretation. Mary Douglas has argued that the symbolism of healing (and it is not doing violence to the definitions to say that this applies equally to metaphoric interpretations) "would not be complete without examining the whole context in which symbols are gen-

erated and applied."[20] The context in this case is that of post-\
American culture as revealed through the language of its textu\
ucts. Context is foregrounded here as a critical concept in historical and
cultural research. Texts, however, remain the source of contextual disclosure. A critical reading of the texts within this part reveals the predomi-
nance of the discourse of healing and the hegemony of a "healed" subject
and culture. Nevertheless, the revelation of hegemony through reading
need not abet "healing." Reading is an act of criticism, not collaboration;
the same reading also reveals competing and contradictory approaches to
healing. In this way, Douglas's injunction to consider the context within
which healing takes place leads to an awareness of contest. Indeed, the
two features identified here—context and contest—inform the critique
undertaken in this study.

Within what follows it is revealed that the "wound" represents cultural division characterized as a stereotyped version of difference defined
as "impotence." Contrary to common assumptions, the war in Vietnam
did not cause the "wound." Rather, the war exposed the existence of
"wounds" already present within American culture. Healing, in contrast,
is cultural unity defined as empowerment. Healing the wounds exposed
by the war demanded, as a first step, a forgetting of the war and associated issues (defeat in the war, the country of Vietnam, and guilt related to
the war). Such denial was a necessary precondition for the imposition of
consensus and unity. To achieve this object, healing has operated across a
variety of sites, including those of the individual, the community, and the
nation. Each site is far from arbitrary and is a reflection of the concerns
of the various texts, yet each intermediary site is expressive of the need to
heal the nation. If the nation is healed, so too are the other related cultural sites.

Habeas Corpus and Common Sense

Lakoff and Johnson in their respected text on metaphor state that
"human *thought processes* are largely metaphorical. . . . Metaphors as
linguistic expressions are possible precisely because there are metaphors
in a person's conceptual system."[21] A type of essentialism is operating
here in which it is assumed that specific patterns of thought are immanent
within the human subject. According to the authors of this statement,
thought structures language. The position adopted within this study in-

verts such an essentialist notion and maintains that conceptualization and experience are ordered through language.[22] This structuralist perception is extended within Foucault's suggestion that language and discursive formations are implicated with forms of cultural authority and power.[23] Once the debilitating impact of the war in Vietnam is defined as a wound, healing that wound becomes imperative for the health of the culture. In this way the wound metaphor determines, or demands, specific responses and impressions. Metaphors, then, are not passive; they do not merely clarify descriptions.

The ubiquity within language of bodily metaphors positions them as central to cultural processes of meaning and understanding. Douglas suggests that the prevalence of bodily metaphors in daily discourse is a result of the fact that the body provides a convenient repertoire of symbols (or metaphors) for the construction of a functional image of culture and society.[24] Indeed, the body as an image of the social, moral, and political order appears in a number of disciplines. Further, metaphors derived from the body inform daily interpretations of experience. It is common to speak of a "body of knowledge" and its central canon, or *corpus*. The body of evidence often has to be fleshed out. We speak of the body politic, which can be lively or dormant, depending upon the actions of individual members and the rule of the head of state. Certain fluids of the body—blood, sweat, tears, bile, milk—figure in diverse ways within the language. Blood, for example, provides a variety of interpretative expressions. The disastrous stereotypes of "race" are based in part on the metaphors of "pure" and "mixed" blood.[25] Ill feeling is bad blood; fear makes the blood run cold; anger makes the blood boil; a miser is bloodless; a vicious attack is bloodthirsty; an unrestrained attack is a bloodbath.

However, there is another side to the use of the body as a way of theorizing, reflecting, and constructing experience. The discursive body is a framework through which cultural conditions are naturalized and acquire the status of immutable truth. Habeas corpus, being in possession of the body, is thus a valuable tool in the process of cultural legitimation. Extending this understanding, Foucault has shown how hegemonic culture helps maintain its dominance through its management of the human body.[26] Manipulation of the language of the body is a much more subtle form of control. In the case of the wound and healing metaphors, the language of the body encodes a specific worldview that replicates the conditions of unity beneficial to the maintenance of a hegemonic culture. With the circulation of the wound metaphor, the (injured) flesh becomes *the word*—the final arbiter of the condition of postwar culture.

This observation is reinforced in David Cooper's discussion of the work of metaphor. In a commentary on Roland Barthes's *Mythologies*, Cooper argues that the various "symbols, clichés, and fetishes" that Barthes has studied "might be more accurately entitled 'metaphors'" and applies this perception to the analogous functioning of metaphor by quoting Barthes to the effect that "the very principle of myth is . . . [to] transform history into nature." Cooper adds that Barthes is here rephrasing the observation that metaphor "predominantly tends to represent the relatively more 'cultural' in terms of the more 'natural,' such as referring to states as families or organisms. . . . "[27] The effect of this process "is for people to treat as fixed and natural things which are historically contingent and for which human agents are responsible." In support of this assertion are those metaphors in which economic problems are portrayed as illnesses. An example of this practice is inflation described as a cancer, a condition "that is, of economic life itself and not a product of bad management."[28]

It is the natural, taken-for-granted, self-evident quality of the wound metaphor that permits it to enter into *common sense*. Common sense has grown accustomed to presenting (ahistorical) assumptions as natural. "It is precisely its . . . 'naturalness,' its refusal to be made to examine the premises on which it is founded, its resistance to change or correction, its effect of instant recognition . . . which makes common sense . . . *unconscious*."[29] As a result of the uncontested, unconscious, assumptions of common sense, it is impossible to learn from the construct "*how things are*: you can only discover *where they fit* into the existing scheme of things."[30] In this way, the world constructed by common sense does not "make sense." It "consists of all of those ideas which can be tagged onto existing knowledge without challenging it."[31] The constant repetition of the metaphors of common sense ("time is money," "inflation is a cancer," "the wound created by the war in Vietnam") transforms them into clichés. Having been repeated until it is accepted in this unexamined form, a "metaphor is fully hegemonic, it is common sense in performance as an ideological practice."[32]

As a commonsensical, ideological, and hegemonic interpretation, the repetition of the wound metaphor results in the reinforcement of a particular view of U.S. culture that is at once ahistorical and yet made to appear totally natural. By drawing on its common(sense) association with the body, the wound metaphor posits a unified culture as fixed and natural and implies that before the infliction of the unhealthy wound the United States had been such a culture. This conclusion incorporates a third order of signification associated with the wound metaphor. On one level, that of denotation, a wound refers to a cut or gash in an individual's body. On another level, that of connotation, it refers to a deleterious situation within the culture. On yet another level, the ideological level, these meanings are rewritten such that the term points to the existence of a "healthy," unified culture that has momentarily been disrupted from outside. The comment that "connotations and myths fit together to form a coherent pattern or sense of wholeness"[33] is ironic in the case of the third level of the wound metaphor. The wholeness referred to here results from the coalescence of connotations into a web of dominant meanings that is ideology. In the case of the wound metaphor, wholeness refers to the cultural unity that ideology serves to reinforce. The credibility of this interpretation, however, rests on the equation that a "healthy" culture is one that is unified. The equation is validated in the recognition that the unhealthy wound has predominantly been interpreted as "impotence," a traumatic condition that displaced contending conditions of physical and mental impairment to express cultural division.

The Wound That Dare Not Speak Its Name

Representations of the register of the war on the (cultural) body have taken various forms, chief among them being paraplegia, a condition that has proven to be enduringly popular as a way of evoking the crippling effects of the war. Luke Martin (Jon Voight) in *Coming Home* (1978), Steve (John Savage) in *The Deer Hunter* (1978), and Ron Kovic (Tom Cruise) in *Born on the Fourth of July* (1989), all bear the effects of the war in this way. Equally as popular in evoking the impact of the war has been the "sick vet" image,[34] a stereotype based on the notion of a mental wound that, until relatively recently, was beyond categorization. The veteran was said to be "crazy" or, more clinically, to suffer from stress or delayed stress. The veteran, like the rest of the population, was afflicted with a certain malaise as a result of the war. The namelessness, the inability to specify adequately the nature of the mental wound, was finally overcome in 1980 when the diagnosis by the American Psychiatric Association officially determined that the disturbed veteran was suffering from "post-traumatic stress disorder."[35]

The effect of this diagnosis was equivalent to a cure for the veteran's mental condition: the veteran was no longer "crazy." The outcome proved the adage that to name a thing is to have power over it. Yet the power of the war to inspire consternation within U.S. culture could not be ignored or readily dismissed through labeling. In fact, the wound that the war exposed resulted in circumlocution—as if naming the wound would overpower those who did so, giving some credence to the suggestion that silence was a legacy of the war. The elocutionary taboo surrounding the wound is exemplified in the film *The Big Chill* when the veteran Nick (William Hurt) rebuffs the sexual advances of his female friend by asking, "Did I ever tell you what happened to me in Vietnam?" No elaboration is forthcoming yet, contextually, the inference is clear. The war in Vietnam, "the war that dare not speak its name,"[36] produced an unspeakable wound: impotence.

The wound that is impotence carries with it many of the definitions of a physical wound (bruise, injury, hurt). In addition, the wound as impotence affects the will as much as the body. Impotence in this sense is a loss of power, a psychic trauma. Given these considerations, any analysis that foregrounds the wound exclusively in terms of either its physical, or mental, effects denies the complexity of the wound. The cultural utility of the various meanings implicit within the wound is reflected in the fact that the metaphor has been circulated in a variety of contexts. For example, the Fisher King of Arthurian legend was said to have been struck in battle by a javelin that "wounded him through the two thighs."[37] Hemingway's Frederic Henry of *A Farewell to Arms* (1929) is injured in his legs and thighs by an explosion on the Italian front during the First World War.[38] A number of post–World War II films deal with the problems of readjustment facing veterans suffering various wounds—including blindness (*The Pride of the Marines*, 1945), the loss of hands (*The Best Years of Our Lives*, 1946), and paraplegia (*The Men*, 1951)—in ways that attest to the wounding force of the "historical trauma" that was World War II.[39] Implicit within each reference is the suggestion that the specific wound is a form of male lack or impotence.[40] Such representational repetitions have rendered the metaphor into cliché where its meanings have passed unexamined. Clichés demand to be interrogated. There are subtle ideological messages encoded within references to the wounding effects of the Vietnam War that can be understood only through attention to the ways in which references to impotence are reproduced within a range of texts.

The wound is borne by the veteran Tom Hudson in Bobbie Ann Mason's novel *In Country* (1987) and, Mason implies, it also affects her character Emmett Hughes, who is incapable of maintaining a relationship with his onetime companion, Anita.[41] Similarly, in Mason's "Big Bertha Stories" (1990) the main character, a Vietnam veteran, is berated by his wife: "You've still got your legs, even if you don't know what to do with what's between them anymore."[42] In Robert Stone's novel *Dog Soldiers* (1976), the erstwhile journalist John Converse is rendered impotent after being fragmentation-bombed in Cambodia. Back in San Francisco, Converse visits a friend, Douglas Dalton, who fought in the Spanish Civil War. During a discussion of his predicament Converse mentions Charmian, his contact for the heroin he has smuggled into the United States. Dalton concludes from the discussion that Converse is in love with Charmian and underlines his own impotence when he says: "That's all over for me . . . since the Jarama." In Stone's novel the Vietnam War reporter and the veteran of the Spanish Civil War both bear the marks of war in the form of a common wound.[43] In the film *Cutter's Way* (1981) it is implied that the multiple amputee Alex Cutter (John Heard) can no longer sexually satisfy his wife, Mo (Lisa Eichhorn), who seeks solace with Cutter's pointedly named friend, Richard Bone (Jeff Bridges). Further, Cutter's missing limbs evoke the suggestion of castration, which lurks behind the implication of impotence in many of these examples. In *Dispatches* (1978) Michael Herr summarizes the various meanings outlined here when he refers to the castrating "wound of wounds, the Wound."[44]

Within these examples the war in Vietnam is the ostensible cause of the wound suffered by the central protagonist. However, an available alternative reading points to the fact that war may not be the prime causative agent of impotence. An intimation of the variant reading appears in the fact that the wound creates a dichotomy between those who bear the wound (veterans of the Vietnam War) and the rest of society. The wound-based distinction between veterans and others in society suggests that division ("us" and "them") is the result of the wound; yet in other contexts a slippage occurs whereby division is not the outcome of the wound—it is the wound. Here, the wound defined as impotence is linked to cultural division, which is stereotyped as a bipolar construction of difference. Although veterans are the obvious bearers of the wound, the implication of the slippage is that all Americans are wounded by the existence of difference. In this equation the traditional connotations of impotence as a lack of power are expressed in the notion that the United States is rendered powerless by the existence of difference exposed by the war. In this way, impotence is not directly attributable to "the war." The cause of the wound involves a curious anatomy whereby castration and impotence result from a stab in the back.

Stab Wounds

The "stab-in-the-back" legend holds that certain domestic groups were responsible for defeat of the U.S. military in Vietnam. In effect, the myth maintains that selected home front groups betrayed America and turned the country into a "pitiful, helpless giant," as Richard Nixon suggested. Norman Podhoretz underlined the reference to a lack of power implicit within the myth when in 1985 he asserted that the result of the betrayal was U.S. impotence.[45] According to the legend, a number of culprits were to blame for this lamentable state of affairs. In the same way that many Germans after the First World War blamed their country's loss of the war on the civilians who signed the Treaty of Versailles, many Amercians in the wake of the Vietnam War blamed Vietnam-era civilian leaders for military defeat. The position is reflected in the results of a poll conducted by the *New York Times* in 1985 that revealed support for the notion that "military leaders should be able to fight wars without civilian leaders tying their hands."[46] According to the proponents of the stab-in-the-back thesis, the media also contributed to this defeat. President Nixon excoriated "the liberal press" for subverting the people's support for "wars of the Vietnam type . . . in the defense of freedom and our own country."[47] Discussing U.S. "impotence," Podhoretz censured the antiwar movement and the press for "assuming that almost anything an American spokesman or indeed any Western leader said about anything was probably untrue."[48] Podhoretz and other new revisionists attempted to shift guilt for the war from those who instigated and pursued it to those who opposed it. The denigration of the antiwar movement through the propagation of the stab-in-the-back thesis is exemplified in William Westmoreland's idea that "a misguided minority opposition . . . masterfully manipulated by Hanoi and Moscow" led to American defeat in Vietnam.[49]

The stab-in-the-back thesis was perpetuated by the genre of the "return-to-Vietnam" films, in which an inefficient civilian bureaucracy and a weak-willed government are responsible for losing the war and for abandoning American prisoners of war in Vietnam. Also implicated in both processes, typically, are liberals, the press, and generally those at home who no longer care about the unfinished business of the war. Where executive action is found wanting, these films propose individual intervention as the answer to repatriation for those Americans still held captive in Southeast Asia. The popularity of these arguments among certain members of the audience is reflected in part in the number of films in this category. Throughout the late seventies and during the eighties the genre grew to include, among others, *Good Guys Wear Black* (1977), *Uncommon Valor* (1983), *Missing in Action* (1984), *Missing in Action II: The Beginning* (1985), *Rambo: First Blood, II* (1985), *P.O.W.: The Escape* (1986), and *Braddock: Missing in Action III (1988)*.

Rambo is notable among these texts for its concentration of generic elements and its success at the box office. The film resonates within culture in a multitude of ways, and the opening lines have been the source of endless quotation and misquotation. At the beginning of the film Colonel Trautman (Richard Crenna) visits Rambo (Sylvester Stallone) in military prison and promises him a reprieve if he will accept a mission to return to Vietnam. Rambo responds with the question "Do we get to win this time?" The plural pronoun is addressed directly at the audience, filling the cinema with an attitude of accusation: "Who are 'they' that wouldn't let 'us' win last time?"

In *First Blood* (1982), the first film to feature the character of John Rambo, the antiwar movement had been implicated in this betrayal, specifically in Rambo's fierce verbal attack on the "maggots" who protested him at the airport on his return from Vietnam. However, there is another category of victimizer and betrayer lurking behind Rambo's comments. The antiwar movement was not the only social movement active during the sixties. The women's movement and the civil rights movement were both aspects of cultural struggle during the Vietnam War years. Susan Jeffords has noted that "while much that happened during the war ... helped to further the development of both women's and civil rights movements, it is also clear that both of these political movements had begun well before 1964, with the first large U.S. troop commitment to Vietnam." According to Jeffords, "It is thus possible to read the war ... as being a response to challenges by women and men of color to the validity and sufficiency of systems that ensured white male power, a response that was shaped in terms of the sole remaining stable space of power: the arena of warfare."[50] In this cogent interpretation, Vietnam was where America went to reassert and reassure a contested (white) masculinity.

The loss of the war suggests that this project was not concluded in Vietnam and hence it had to "come home" to America where the struggle to (re)assert a threatened white masculinity in the face of "assaults" by the women's movement was conducted in various places within the culture. Robert Bly, in the widely reproduced essay "The Vietnam War and the Erosion of Male Confidence," asserted that "women came out of the Sixties and Seventies with considerable confidence in their values, but men lack this clarity and belief."[51] The same suggestion occurred elsewhere. John Wheeler argued that "masculinity went into eclipse during the Vietnam era, while women's causes and femininity came into ascendancy."[52] It can be inferred from Bly and Wheeler that women's confidence was gained at the expense of men. Reinforcing this suggestion, Bly's essay signaled the beginning of a men's movement aimed at retrieving masculine pride and power felt to have been eroded or lost during the war years of the sixties. The post–Vietnam "war against women"[53] also attempts to renovate structures of masculinity and patriarchy perceived to have been damaged during the war years by the putative threat posed by women. The outcome of the various representations of female threat is a common image in which "child or woman, wife or mother, [the] female cuts men to ribbons or swallows them whole. She travels accompanied by . . . damaged men suffering from nameless wounds."[54]

The viability of the notion of feminine threat during the war years was reinforced by representations of female perfidy on the home front. In keeping with the representations of earlier wars, women on the home front during the Vietnam War were depicted in diverse ways as having betrayed the fighting male.[55] In one case, the pacifist message of the slogan "Girls Say Yes To Boys Who Say No" was reinterpreted as an attempt to subvert the masculine (war) ethos. Elsewhere in the culture the alleged scorn that Vietnam veterans received on their return from the war was translated into an assault on masculinity. An example of this process is contained in the bitter yet popular song "Ruby, Don't Take Your Love to Town" (1969) in which the paraplegic male veteran, who did not start "that crazy Asian war" yet who nevertheless was duty-bound and "proud to do [his] patriotic chore," is contrasted with his wife, who is represented as unfaithful and uncaring. As the wife walks out and slams the door, as she has slammed it "one hundred times before," the veteran dreams of revenge: "If I could move I'd get my gun / and put her in the ground."[56] While murder is a standard response in popular song to female infidelity ("Hey, Joe," 1969, sung by Jimi Hendrix, is one example), the act of murdering a spouse who has been unfaithful while the husband was overseas fulfilling his "patriotic chore" gains an especially virulent resonance in the dominantly masculine domain of popular culture.

Images of women betraying the U.S. fighting man and the systems of warfare that reinforced white male power were extended within a number of postwar texts dealing with the war in which women of color are represented as posing a special threat to U.S. soldiers. The killing of a female Vietnamese sniper in Kubrick's *Full Metal Jacket* (1987) is one manifestation of a form of representation that positions women of color as targets of a savage white-male retributive fantasy, which in turn contributes to a cultural pattern that Susan Jeffords has called the "remasculinization of American culture."[57] In clear and direct ways the representations of the links between women and the war reveal aspects of central cultural anxieties surrounding the conflict, and gender. However, while women have been implicated within the process of betraying the U.S. fighting male—an emasculating process—the loss of potency cannot be reduced to the role of women. The ideological efficacy of the films that replicate the stab-in-the-back theme is their refusal to name names. It is this tactic, also employed by Reagan, that suggests the real cause of impotence.

"Us" and "Them"

During his presidency Ronald Reagan refused to name directly those "responsible" for defeat. Typically, he evoked the issue of culpability through circumlocution and innuendo. An example of Reagan's use of these rhetorical devices is a comment he made at the Vietnam Veterans Memorial in 1982: "We're beginning to understand how much we were led astray [during the Vietnam era]," he said, simultaneously raising the question of blame yet refusing to specify those responsible.[58] Reagan's comment privileges "us" and constructs difference in terms of a dichotomy between "us" and an unrepresented "them." The privileging of "us" in this construct begs the crucial question, who are "we"?

Reagan the populist and the populist films articulating the betrayal theme exploit a particular ideological position. According to Ernesto Laclau, populist ideology equates "we" with "the people" and contrasts the latter to the power bloc.[59] This is and has been the function of populism: to speak to and for the interests of what has euphemistically been termed the grass roots, the popular classes or, more specifically, the working class. Both Ronald Reagan and Margaret Thatcher presented themselves in the populist vein by articulating certain desires and fears of "the people" in ways consistent with the formations studied in the late fifties by Richard Hoggart. In *The Uses of Literacy* (1957), Hoggart offers an accessible discussion of what he identifies as the "us/them" dichotomy implicit within definitions of "the people."[60] According to the sources quoted by Hoggart: "'They' are 'the people at the top,' 'the higher ups,' the people who ... call you up, tell you to go to war [and] ... 'aren't really to be trusted.'" "Us," by contrast, means the group that stands together, those who are "all in the same boat," and for whom "unity is strength."[61]

The operation of the definitions of "us" and "them" within representations of the war and its impact on the United States demonstrate that healing occurs among "the people"—veterans and nonveterans, vocal antiwar protestors and silent supporters of the war, whites and blacks. Indeed, a feature of the construction of unity within such representations is that government bureaucrats are demonized as the cause of the war while "the people" are represented as unified against them.

This situation exposes a crucial paradox implicit within the definitions. "Our" identity as the group that stands together is defined in opposition to "them," yet the differentiating dichotomy also threatens "our" ability to be united. Difference, the quality that establishes unity within "the people," must be denied. "We" can be unified only if difference does not intrude upon the realm of the people. In this way the "us/them" dualism *represents a stereotyped form of difference as a wounding presence that renders "us" impotent.* The operation of the ideology of unity "resolves" the paradox through a recognition of the wounding presence, only to subsume and elide that recognition (thereby regaining national strength) within and through the assertion of unity referred to as healing.

Healing

In terms of the application of the metaphors of the wound and healing, the wound is defined as difference resulting in impotence; healing refers

to the empowering qualities of unity. Healing in its various forms addresses division across a number of sites, and at each site the United States
is made strong as it is healed. Healing is the legitimation of long-standing
conditions, the denial of change, and the silencing of the voices of difference.

For the healing metaphor to gain currency in post–Vietnam discourse,
a change was required of the terms used to describe the ill effects besieging the body politic. Historically, as Susan Sontag has pointed out, analo-
gies for cultural disruption based on infectious diseases such as syphilis
and tuberculosis were replaced by those based on cancer—with the physical effects of cancer often described in military metaphors. Accordingly,
cancer cells do not multiply, they are "invasive," with carcinogenic cells
mounting "assaults" on the body's "defenses."[62] The wound metaphor
reversed the situation by describing the effects of a war in bodily terms.
This innovation begs the question of why the metaphor changed from one
of disease to one of physical impairment. In a specific and overt way the
presence of thousands of physically and mortally wounded veterans no
doubt foregrounded the notion of wounding in post–Vietnam War America. In addition, the popularity of the wound metaphor can be traced to
its ability to perform an interpretive function unavailable to metaphors
based on a virus or cancer. Neither a viral infection nor cancer automat-
ically implies healing; instead, each tends to suggest chronic illness. Alternatively, a wound evokes a healthy body—one that has been surprised
by a wound that will eventually disappear, allowing a healed and healthy
(cultural) body to re-emerge.

In this way the establishment of the wound metaphor predetermined
the appearance of the healing metaphor, while the popularity of healing
as a metaphor referring to cultural unity was abetted by the existence
within the culture of a therapeutic discourse. According to historian
Christopher Lasch, American culture in the seventies, the period when
healing was ascendant, was characterized by an intense concern with the
self and the body. Lasch contended that during this period a therapeutic
outlook displaced religion and threatened "to displace politics as well" as
the "organizing framework of American culture." To Lasch, Americans
hungered not for personal salvation "but for the feeling, the momentary
illusion, of personal well-being, health, and psychic security."[63] Philip
Rieff claimed that the need for "psychic security," which had given rise to
psychoanalysis, allowed for "the triumph of the therapeutic" attitude in

the seventies.[64] The historian Jackson Lears, however, felt that "neither Rieff nor Lasch . . . quite grasped the full historical complexity of the therapeutic world view." Lears argued that both authors "tend to tie [the therapeutic outlook] too closely to psychoanalysis and other formal therapeutic regimens. . . . Actually the therapeutic world view was less a formal regime than a way of life embraced by people sometimes only dimly aware of psychiatry."[65]

Bellah and his colleagues exemplified Lears's perception in their analysis of individualism in late-twentieth-century American life. They argued that "a language influenced by therapy" was used by Americans in the seventies to articulate thoughts on family, work, community, and society.[66] Although Bellah and his colleagues mentioned psychoanalysis as a reason for the rise of the therapeutic as a major mode of thinking about the self and society, they tended to follow Lears in tracing the popularity of therapies and the roots of the therapeutic discourse to the late nineteenth century. Within this period, according to Lears, the therapeutic mode was "not simply imposed" on the population by the "helping professions" but stemmed from "the effort to reconstruct a coherent sense of identity in a culture which was rendering all identities . . . vaporous and unreal. . . . [A] sense of selfhood . . . had grown fragmented."[67] Similarly, in the late twentieth century the discourse of healing has flourished within a culture wounded by exposure to the existence of multiple identities—a culture fragmented into multiple positions. According to the logic of the metaphoric language of cultural unity, these positions represent damaging wounds that demand to be healed.

However, the process of cultural curing is complicated by the fact that healing typically involves a regimen. Healing is prescriptive. "Take three tablets daily," "Keep the leg raised," "Do not eat red meat" are all palliative directives. In 1948 the sociologist Lawrence Frank suggested that a "sick society" required the same therapy a doctor provided a patient, "enabling him to revise his 'past' . . . and escape from its coercion."[68] Frank's prescription foreshadowed circumstances within post–Vietnam War American culture in which healing was achieved through a revision of the past. In this case, amnesia was not deemed a form of dysfunction; rather, it was a necessary and healthy precondition for overcoming the wounding impact of the war. In U.S. culture in the wake of the Vietnam War, memory was enjoined to fail so that healing could be achieved.

Vietnamnesia

The cultural manifestations referred to as healing contributed to a pattern whereby "society remembers less and less, faster and faster."[69] Indeed, healing was explicitly facilitated by an absence of any need to confront the political, moral, or social issues surrounding the war and its impact on U.S. culture. Devoid of their cause, these issues became ahistorical aberrations, and as such they not only could be but *had* to be forgotten. The result of this process is a form of amnesia defined as a "motivated forgetting"[70] of the war and its effects on the United States.

Official views that sought to erase the public memory of the war were especially prominent immediately after the "fall" of Saigon. An early attempt to seek consensus through forgetfulness is evident in President Ford's speech at Tulane University on April 23, 1975. "The war is finished as far as America is concerned," he asserted. "These events, tragic as they are, portend neither the end of the world nor America's leadership in the world."[71] Secretary of State Kissinger foreshadowed Ford when, during the final week of the war, he argued that while the United States "should never have been [in Vietnam] at all," the issue was now irrelevant—"now [the war is] history."[72] Immediately after the war ended Kissinger stated that "what we need now in this country . . . is to . . . put Vietnam behind us and to concentrate on problems of the future."[73] In 1980 William Westmoreland, who had been chief of staff of the army in Vietnam, declared that "the war is history now. We don't worry about that."[74] In early 1989, during his inaugural address to the nation, President George Bush argued that "surely the statute of limitations [on the war's legacy] has been reached," and urged Americans to forget the disruptive memory of "Vietnam."[75] The various nostrums to forget signal the end of the war on two counts: the willful effacement of memory erodes the effects of the war, and it translates into a form of death for all those who participated in the war. "The dead," as one veteran faced with these assertions put it, "are not only buried but they never existed, there never was a war."[76]

Erasure of the plain and indisputable fact that the United States lost the war in Vietnam begins with simple definitions such as the characterization of the outcome of the war as a tragedy. Defeat, as Walter Benjamin knew, possesses the potential to change a nation if it is willing or able to confront the fact of defeat.[77] Such potential is denied in the application of euphemisms that obscure defeat, rewriting it as tragedy or, in Reagan's terms, as victory. In 1985 Reagan asserted: "[T]he truth of the matter is that we did have victory. We continue to talk about losing [the Vietnam War]. We didn't lose that war. We won virtually every engagement."[78] Reagan's comment placed him at the center of history, the site of memory, from where he asserts the veracity of his claim ("the truth of the matter"). The correlative of Reagan's rewriting of memory is the revision of the history of the war in a way that endorses the win position—the notion that the war in Vietnam could have been won "if only we had thrown a little more fire in the lake one more time,"[79] a position evident in the so-called new scholarship of the war.[80] Certain authors have attributed defeat, or what is typically labeled "failure," to a mixture of factors, including restraints on the exercise of military power, an unworthy South Vietnamese ally, and a stab in the back from a media biased against the war effort.[81]

A modification of these arguments occurs in what Jerome Slater has called the "pragmatic revisionist" approach, a term he applied to a number of narrative and interpretative histories, including *America in Vietnam* by Guenter Lewy (1978), *The Irony of Vietnam* by Gelb and Betts (1978), and Harry Summers's *On Strategy* (1982), among others. Central to these texts is the assumption that "a different mix of means (particularly less reliance on excessive military power and more on socio-economic reform) might have brought a different result [to the war]."[82] Other aspects of this position include the argument that "although the war may have been a mistake and the manner in which it was fought counterproductive, it was not therefore immoral or unjustified ... especially since the terrible events in Indochina since the communist victories there provide a retrospective justification for the war."[83]

There is a common element uniting these texts beyond conservative attempts to legitimate arguments through recourse to assertions of objectivity and veracity. The premise that underlines these texts is not the common, though itself naive, question motivating historical analysis: "What happened?" Instead the mode of investigation encoded in the "new scholarship" is directed by the question "What if?" In this way the proponents of the win position ignore certain outcomes, the most obvious being, of course, that the United States was militarily defeated in Vietnam. The need to reassert this fact is indicative of the corruption of history wrought by the win thesis. Nevertheless, the history of the war in Vietnam does not involve only the struggle of history and memory against forgetting. Foucault noted that the "battle for and around history" seeks to stifle interpretations of the past and "also to propose and impose on people a framework in which to interpret the present."[84] Consistent with Foucault's insight, the outcome of the war is ransacked for lessons that, according to the methods of the new revisionists, become paradigms for the present and, even more crucially, the future. Forgetting defeat in the war is necessary for the perpetuation of conditions and attitudes required for pursuing further military intervention in the future. According to military historian Harry Summers, "The quintessential 'strategic lesson learnt' from the Vietnam War is that we must once again become masters of the profession of arms."[85] Here, as Noam Chomsky argued in a different relation, "The only judgement that Clio is permitted to hand down is a judgement of tactics: Could we have won? Other questions might be imagined. Should we have won? Did we have the right to try?"[86] Such questions are disregarded in a conclusion that contributes toward, and stems from, the willful forgetting of the historical outcome of the war.

The denial of military defeat underlines the limits of healing. Healing is a process that affects only the United States. The American need to be healed has ignored the marginalized international community that is Vietnam and has refused to accept the memory of the wars in Vietnam, Cambodia, and Laos presented by the arrival in the United States of Indochinese refugees. For decades the influx of refugees from communist countries reinforced conceptions of the United States as a haven for (anticommunist) political exiles and a moral beacon in the world, conceptions that have been contested and contradicted by the arrival of refugees from Southeast Asia: "[S]ince Southeast Asians are . . . linked to a war in which the United States suffered defeat, they are the first refugees from communism who are ambivalently received as symbols of the decline of the United States as a military and moral force in the world."[87] In certain cases, the functional response in the United States has been to marginalize or exclude or forget these people. Related to this response was America's refusal to confront Vietnam's postwar financial plight; a situation that has altered, to a degree, as a result of the lifting of the economic blockade against Vietnam. In the decade after the war the refusal to recognize Vietnam's war-related problems was evident in the special issues of newsmagazines produced to mark the tenth anniversary of U.S. defeat in Vietnam. "Almost without exception," Alexander Cockburn noted, the magazines found it "impossible to discuss the central aspect of the war: what Americans did in Vietnam before 1975. This is a closed book, along with the memory of the nearly 3 million Vietnamese the Americans managed to kill."[88]

The widespread denial of the impact of the war on Vietnam continued beyond 1985. In 1988 the journalist James Fallows, writing in the *Atlantic Monthly*, exemplified the ongoing refusal to acknowledge the devastation wrought by the war on Vietnamese society. After a brief visit to Vietnam as part of a group tour, Fallows concluded that the effects of the war on Vietnam were negligible, adding that "the Vietnam War will be important in history only for what it did internally to the United States."[89] Presumably, Fallows failed to see, or ignored, the deforestation of the Vietnamese countryside as a result of massive chemical spraying, the continuing birth defects as an outcome of the spraying, the large number of orphaned children, the parlous state of the Vietnamese economy, and the continued political instability in the region, notably in Cambodia. Noam Chomsky underlined the ethnocentrism of Fallows's comment when he observed that the conclusion was similar to a "German liberal saying that it is now clear that the Holocaust will be important in history mostly for what it did, internally, to Germany, not what difference it made to the Jews."[90]

The dominant movement to deny or forget the effects of the war on Vietnam represented through these examples has been addressed within U.S. culture in various ways. More astute observations than Fallows's have come from U.S. veterans returning to postwar Vietnam. The written accounts of their journeys reflect the authors' common need to confront the past and to understand the society they first encountered during the war.[91] The authors are acutely aware of the problems facing Vietnam; indeed, many are motivated by a desire to provide aid and assistance to Vietnamese people affected by the war. The general impression gained from this increasing body of work is that of *rapprochement*. These narratives, then, are in direct opposition to the motives for returning to Vietnam presented in texts that cynically exploit the notion that American prisoners of war (POWs) are still held within Vietnam and that others remain missing in action (MIA). Centrally implicated in this category are cinematic representations of the "return trip,"[92] including the films *Uncommon Valor* (1983), *Missing in Action I, II, III* (1984, 1985, 1988), *Rambo* (1985), *P.O.W.: The Escape* (1986), and *Operation Nam* (1985). Further texts in this category include J. C. Pollock's best-selling novel *Mission M.I.A.* and a series of novels by Jack Buchanan featuring a former Green Beret, Mark Stone, who "has only one activity that gives meaning to his life—finding America's forgotten fighting men, the P.O.W.'s the government has conveniently labeled M.I.A.'s, and bring them back from their hell on earth."[93]

Textual representations utilizing the myth of the POW/MIA typically contribute to the revisionist desire to win the war. Vietnam becomes the last frontier in a violent confrontation with a ruthless communism, the outcome of which, as a result of American military victory, will retrieve lost American pride and commitment. The contemporary permutation of the frontier myth adopts basic elements from the mythical features of the frontier narrated in the late nineteenth century by the historian Frederick Jackson Turner. According to Turner's thesis, the existence of the free land of the frontier permitted the realization of those features (most notably individualism) that imbue and reinforce American democracy. Specifically, Turner defined the frontier as the "meeting point between savagery and civilization,"[94] thereby positioning the American Indian as the mysterious and dangerous Other. Narratives of captivity in the New World, beginning with Puritan stories of whites being taken prisoner by Indians, fed the fear of savagery on the frontier. Myths of the frontier and captivity intersect in the POW/MIA narratives in which the Vietnamese are cast as the threatening Other stalking the last sealed frontier.

The very real danger inherent in the promulgation of these myths is reinforced in the assessment that they contributed in part to America's decision to intervene in Vietnam. Located throughout the discourse of the Vietnam War are references to the myth of the frontier as conscious or unconscious justification for America's military involvement in Asia. In literature, Norman Mailer, Michael Herr, and Arthur Kopit, among others, referred to the frontier myth in order to explain America's involvement in the war.[95] The short-lived genre of the so-called Vietnam western, which included the films *The Wild Bunch* (1969), *Soldier Blue* (1970), *Little Big Man* (1971), and *Ulzana's Raid* (1972), drew parallels between the slaughter of the Native Americans and the murderous destruction of the Vietnamese population.[96] In 1972, Frances FitzGerald commented upon the depth to which the language of the myth ("conquest," the "triumph of light over darkness," and of "civilization over brutish nature") prevailed "quite unconsciously" among American officers and government officials in descriptions of the war against the North Vietnamese.[97] Richard Slotkin has noted the similarities in his monumental studies of the frontier myth, and John Hellmann has studied reconfigurations of the frontier myth within the context of an examination of a number of American myths informing and influencing perceptions of the Vietnam experience.[98] Similarly, the social historian Richard Baritz has analyzed the beginnings of the frontier myth in the Puritan approach to nature and the original inhabitants of the North American continent as a method of understanding the ideological justifications for U.S. war policy in Vietnam.[99]

In the context of the attendant dangers of a postwar proliferation of myth within the "return trip" representations, it is curious to find, in a different context, calls for the repair of public myth. In 1982, the historian William McNeill sought to assure the place of myth in American culture by proposing the reinvigoration of mythic patterns of thought, and in 1980, historian James Oliver Robertson supported the functional role of myth within the culture as a method of maintaining cultural cohesion.[100] In "The Structural Study of Myth" Claude Lévi-Strauss argued that myths are narratives that a culture employs in attempts to explain contradictions that it cannot otherwise resolve.[101] This attempt invariably involves a confrontation with the past as the point of origin of the contradictions. Yet, as Theodor Adorno has pointed out, "coming to terms" with the past does not necessarily imply "a serious working through of the past, the breaking of its spell through an act of clear consciousness."[102] Adorno's perception is validated in relation to the mythical appropriation of "Vietnam" in which public memory is perverted and abstracted within the myths of the past recoded and reconstructed in the present.

In opposition to the process of forgetting implicated in certain assessments of post–Vietnam War U.S. culture is the unmediated memory of the destruction wrought by the Vietnam War. This memory has the potential to subvert the explanations presented within myth and metaphor. However, as Foucault noted, memory is not translated directly into a legitimate record of the past. Representations based on individual memory must contend with a diversity of forms that represent history.[103] The resultant struggle between contending interpretations of the past is waged across the entire field of culture. "Vietnam" has formed a central site in this struggle with the ability and the authority to define the outcome of the wound in the balance.

The dominance of the interpretation referred to as healing is the erasure of the painful memory of war. A successful critique of the ideology of healing exposes the ways in which power is situated within and, worked through, a wide range of representations concerned with the impact of the conflict in Vietnam. The range of representations is not a united front mobilized by a conspiratorial power. References to "elites' preferences for turning the past into myths that promote uniformity and stability,"[104] for example, reduce ideological operations to purposive interventions by elites, thereby failing to specify the subtle and complex ways in which myths and ideology are reproduced. Ideological represen-tations are located in various places within the cultures of the United States—including the popular media, the academic discourses of written history and criticism, and everyday language—and together these cul-tures involve a number of participants in the reproduction of the partic-ular worldview referred to as healing. The result is that healing operates on more than one level within the culture. The individual, the community, and the nation, each of which is examined here, are all constructed within textual representations as sites of healing.

The Personal Imperative

On one level the healing process is personal. It involves the individual, specifically the veteran, and the veteran's characteristic wound. The man-ifestations of the veteran's wound were, on two counts, anomalous and thus especially in need of treatment. First, the veteran's wound of impo-tence, or even more severely of castration, came to suggest that the wounded veteran was incapable of any sort of intercourse, sexual or so-cial. The dysfunctional Vietnam veteran became a pariah whose only means of asserting himself and his masculinity was through violence. This issue is exemplified in Alex Cutter's violent outbursts in the film *Cutter's Way* (1981), and is typified in the orgiastic explosion of mayhem that is the finale to *Taxi Driver* (1976). In another way, the visible presence of the veteran's wound in the form of a loss of limbs or the inability to use limbs marked him as an outcast in popular representations by placing him outside the so-called cosmetic culture. The features of this experience can be contextualized through reference to the characteristics implicated in what Christopher Lasch labeled the "culture of narcissism." Lasch ar-gued that during the seventies the United States was dominated by the character type he described as "excessively self-conscious," "constantly searching for flaws and signs of decay," and "haunted by fantasies . . . of eternal youth."[105] The cosmetic culture has exploited the personal moti-vations created by a consumer culture in which "the closer the actual body approximates to the idealized images of youth, health, fitness and beauty, the higher its exchange-value."[106]

The advertising industry plays a particular role in support of the cos-metic culture by deliberately fostering a preoccupation with physical ap-pearance, and a range of rewards are allocated to those who pay attention to their appearance. The result is that "bodily imperfections" carry "penalties in everyday interactions."[107] Codes within the cosmetic culture are preoccupied with what Naomi Wolf calls "the beauty myth,"[108] a web of meanings evident in a widespread obsession with diets, "fitness," and fashionable clothes, the increasing sales of perfumes, and a growing reliance on plastic surgery. The privileging of "wholeness" within the cosmetic culture has resulted in the exclusion of anyone who is less than whole. In this way the physically disabled have been discriminated against for failing to meet the demands manufactured within the cosmetic culture. The result of physical disability has been social distancing in the form of marginalization or exclusion. Physical difference based on impairment is rarely represented on film, for example, and on those occasions when it is depicted, the physically disabled are typically characterized as criminals, demons, comics, or victims.[109]

The display of the veteran's wound contradicted the cultural emphasis on holism within the cosmetic culture of the seventies, thus marking the veteran for recuperation and incorporation into the cultural collectivity. By continuing to represent the veteran as wounded, the hegemonic culture failed to exploit the full possibilities of healing. In this way the healing imperative inflicted upon the veteran issued from a culture that stressed the need for healing. In relation to the veterans' "healing need," psychologist Robert Jay Lifton perceived that those who attended the sessions he organized for veterans had two aspirations: "healing themselves while finding a mode of political expression."[110] It has been concluded from this assessment that the "two goals were actually inseparable. Without some form of political-social expression there could be no healing of . . . wounds."[111] However, it could have been deduced from the dominant representations that the inverse was also true: without healing there could be no politics. Specifically, the veterans' bodies intersected with a "healing need" to reinforce the power of unity within an expression of what can be termed a cultural politics of healing.

Nowhere is this process more evident than in the film *The Deer Hunter* (1978). Steven (John Savage) returns after the war to a Veterans Administration hospital missing both his legs and an arm. When he is visited by Michael (Robert De Niro), he insists that he does not want to go home. Michael ignores Steven's pleas and literally drags him back to his wife and friends. Having successfully found and retrieved Steven, Michael returns to Vietnam in an attempt to repatriate Nick (Christopher Walken). However, in his narcotized and deranged state, Nick will not be persuaded to return to America. Nick's psychic wound is, notably, far more significant than Steven's physical wounds. As if underlining or targeting the site of his malaise, Nick shoots himself in the head while playing the fatal game of Russian roulette. Nick's death reveals the only alternative available to those who refuse to be healed of their wounds within a reunited group of friends.

The conclusion was reinforced in the film *Coming Home*, released the same year as *The Deer Hunter*. The malaise suffered by the Vietnam veteran Bob (Bruce Dern) is evident in symptoms that manifest themselves as an unwillingness or an inability to be reunited with his wife, Sally (Jane Fonda). Beyond the healing reach of his wife's open arms, Bob drowns himself. Bob's fate is contrasted to the visibly wounded Luke (Jon Voight), a paraplegic, who does return "home." Luke's reintegration is marked by the fact that it is possible to forget that his injuries preclude him from walking and sexual intercourse. Film critic Lawrence Suid has noted that "viewers often miss the reality that Voight [sic] is impotent, expecting him to jump out of his wheelchair *a la* Dr. Strangelove and yell, 'Jane [sic], I can walk! I can make real love!'"[112] The same kind of transformation that sees Sally changed from a repressed housewife to a liberated woman takes hold of Luke, who, it has been observed, "goes from a violently embittered, self-pitying, totally dependent cripple into a well-adjusted, emphatic, politically and sexually active handicapped person."[113] Such a well-integrated figure is unlikely to suggest the crippling effects of the war. Luke becomes, instead, emblematic of the therapeutic power of reunion.

Much more problematic, in terms of a complete "healing," is the experience of Ron Kovic (Tom Cruise) in Oliver Stone's film *Born on the Fourth of July* (1989). Although the emphasis within this film is upon recuperation and reincorporation, the vision of a fully rehabilitated Kovic is disrupted by the graphic foregrounding of the excremental and excessive aspects of the wound in scenes set in a V.A. hospital. To a certain degree, Kovic resists reincorporation. His antiwar activism, for example, is a sign of his resistance to the reconciliatory aspects of healing. However, the ending of the film moves away from resistance toward an intimation of the notion that "strength" resides within social collectivity. In contrast to Kovic's autobiography, which ends where it began, by emphasizing Kovic's wounding,[114] the film ends with Kovic's appearance at the 1976 Democratic National Convention. Kovic's move into mainstream party politics and the enthusiastic reception he receives on his way to make a speech at the convention, suggest reconciliation. Indeed, such a conclusion is consistent with a number of Stone's other films (*Salvador*, 1986; *Platoon*, 1986; and *Wall Street*, 1987) in which the naive central character undergoes a personal transformation resulting in a form of inclusion back into "the world."

Beyond the field of popular film the cultural emphasis on healing the veteran's wound through a form of cultural integration was evident in legal attempts to specify the wounding effects suffered by Vietnam veterans exposed to the defoliant Agent Orange. The veterans' Agent Orange case stressed the need for compensation as the outcome of the legal process. Compensation refers to making amends for something missing or removed. The object of compensation, then, is to restore a subject to wholeness. Similarly, medical science is predicated on the presumption that it can perform restorative work on the body. The two patterns, financial compensation and medical restitution, interrelated in legal moves within the Agent Orange case to seek a solution to issues of bodily health. The Dow Chemical Company, one manufacturer of the defoliants used in Vietnam, argued that the chemical was benign and as such it was not the cause of any of the health problems befalling Vietnam veterans.[115] Throughout the early eighties the object of the class action case brought by veterans against a number of companies responsible for manufacturing the herbicide was to arrive at a legal definition and ruling—and in this way, a diagnosis—that would identify the cause of the veterans' wound. In turn, the (legal) "diagnosis" would function as the starting point for determining levels of compensation for afflicted veterans. The out-of-court settlement by the defendant companies precluded such a court-based diagnosis, thus denying veterans a formal acknowledgment of their wounds.[116] In this case the veterans' wound proved excessive, in the sense that it resisted legal and political moves to establish a definition that would lead to redress for the wound. Elsewhere in the culture, however, formal processes of medical definition and diagnosis provided the basis for the healing of the veterans' (mental) wound.

In 1980, the third edition of the American Psychiatric Association's *Diagnostic and Statistical Manual of Mental Disorders* redefined the veteran's psychological wound as "post-traumatic stress disorder" (PTSD).[117] With this diagnosis the wounded Vietnam veterans were no longer outsiders marginalized by authority—they were, instead, the focus of incorporation through the healing aegis of authority. PTSD identified the symptoms to be treated for the full recuperation of the veteran and provided an opportunity to relegitimize the veteran's relation to officially defined forms of authority. Such authority was once the soldier's problem: sending him to war, causing him to fight a guerrilla war with inappropriate tactics, and abusing him with inadequate health care on his release from military service. In certain ways, however, this history was rewritten as (medical) authority reconstructed itself as the Vietnam veteran's ally through its definition of PTSD, which provided the cure to specific problems affecting him.

The emphasis on reintegration within areas as diverse as the cosmetic culture, film, and legal and medical definitions reflects the dominant need to interpret the effects of the war in Vietnam in ways consistent with cultural drives toward unity and incorporation. Wounds were denied or refigured within and through textual contributions to an image of U.S. culture as a healthy and attractive place devoid of any suggestion of wounds. The result of the intersection of the cultural movements stressing holism and well-being and filmic representations of healing was the reproduction of the commonsense notion that unity is a healthy, desirable condition. In this realm wounds are not only out of place, they are actively resisted.

Rituals of the Community

The trials and tribulations of the wounded male veteran compelled him to go forth with the healing word. The religious connotations of this imperative are integral to a number of interpretations of the veteran's postwar role. As one commentator noted: "The healing of the terrible personal and social wounds of Vietnam . . . is at heart a religious and theological enterprise, whether or not it is couched explicitly in those terms."[118] William Mahedy undertakes this enterprise in his text *Out of the Night: The Spiritual Journey of Vietnam Vets* (1986), making it explicit in his interpretation of the function of veterans centers, storefront locations for the counseling of Vietnam veterans. For Mahedy, the centers are "spiritual centers" and "places of genuine healing" that lead to "the formation of real community."[119] "Spirituality," "community," and "healing" are the words Mahedy uses in relation to the centers. Within the religious framework adopted within a number of post–Vietnam War texts, the veteran performs his rite of healing as a spiritual exercise of specific benefit to the community. The relationship between the community and healing from the war defined in religious terms is suggested by Walter Capps in *The Un-finished War* (1990) when he comments: "In more communities than most people realize the vet centers have come to assume some of the roles of neighborhood religious communities," and the counselors in these centers perform "the work of confessors, serving as unordained priests."[120] The procedure for healing that the veteran undertakes within these centers, led by counselors who are unofficial religious instructors and therapists, can be summarized by the terms Mahedy used frequently in connection with the centers: "confession" and "communion."

The role of confession, or testimony, in the healing process is expressed in the idea that in veterans centers "burdens shared become burdens lifted, and life begins anew."[121] According to Capps, this is especially rel-evant to the Vietnam veterans since they are "[s]till carrying the heaviest burdens of the war."[122] Social reintegration, without which "there could be no genuine healing," demands that veterans publicly articulate their stories as a way of bringing a "change in the society that sent them to war."[123] The other aspect of healing undertaken within the veterans centers—"help[ing] people become functional"—is achieved through communion, or fellowship with other Vietnam veterans: "A veteran com-munity forms around a Vet Center. Its style and ethos resemble the ca-maraderie of the combat zone. Commitment, genuine concern, and affection for each other are hallmarks of one's newfound 'unit.'" Mahedy concludes that confession and communion erase "the wounds of war" and result in "spiritual reintegration".[124]

This method of achieving healing is recirculated and reinforced within John Wheeler's populist text *Touched with Fire* (1984). Wheeler extends confession beyond the veterans and makes it applicable to society as a whole. He feels that only by sharing the "experience of the Vietnam era" will Americans, not only veterans, "break down the divisions" among themselves leading "to healing and a stronger country." The divisions Wheeler refers to are multiple: they exist between those who went to Viet-nam and those who did not, between men and women, and within the "self divided from self."[125] Echoing Mahedy, Wheeler argues that these divisions will be "healed" only through "confession" (overcoming the silence that supposedly surrounded the war) and "communion," what Wheeler calls "ties."[126]

In *The History of Sexuality* (1977), Foucault argued that the ritual of confession operating within the institutions and disciplines of medicine, religion, education, and law occurs in the context of a relationship of power, "for one does not confess without the presence (or virtual presence) of a partner who is not simply the interlocutor but the authority who requires the confession, prescribes and appreciates it, and intervenes in order to judge, punish, forgive, console, and reconcile. . . . "[127] The issues of authority, power, and punishment raised within Foucault's conceptualization of the confessional process are absent from accounts that propose confession as a healthy response to the impact of the war. Further, the easy assurances of the efficacy of confession proposed by interpretations within the "religious paradigm" are belied in Foucault's emphasis on the role of mediation in the confessional process. Questions of access to print and electronic media capable of translating individual confessions into forms of national salvation are not addressed in simple assertions of the beneficial aspects of confession.

Ignoring such issues, Capps, like Wheeler and Mahedy, interprets confession as an unproblematic and functional cultural act. He declares that neither "Eden" promised by the new religious faiths nor "Armageddon" and the beliefs of the religious right epitomized by such people as Jerry Falwell and the so-called Moral Majority provide an adequate solution to the problems spawned by the war. In chapter 8 of *The Unfinished War*, "The Healing Process," Capps characterizes the combat veterans in their acts of confession and community within the veterans centers as the only people to have achieved practices capable of collective healing.[128] Within this emphasis Capps fails to mention varieties of veterans' confessions occurring outside the veterans centers, such as the "Winter Soldier Investigations" convened in Detroit in early 1977 by Vietnam Veterans Against the War as a forum for veterans to attest to "American war crimes" committed in Vietnam.[129] Capps's refusal to acknowledge such forms of confession is significant. Healing, for Capps, is meant to be apolitical. He overlooks the fact that the notion of collective guilt underlying his call for a societal mea culpa serves a political function by exonerating the actions of those in power. However, within the terms of his argument, the spurious notion of collective guilt is consistent with what he sees as the presence of a widespread loss of innocence engendered by the impact of the war. According to Capps, "After [the experience of this war], assumptions of innocence could never be the same again. No clear-eyed, wide-open sense that as Americans, we are here to make the world a better place. No vigorous sense of trust and confidence. No Billy Budd. No opportunity for undiminished heroism. No new or recent esteemed warriors. No John Wayne."[130]

Despite this assertion, there have been few signs of a readiness to deal with postwar guilt or responsibility. In 1975, *Time* magazine dispensed of the question of guilt by stating that "there cannot be an infinite cycle of ... recrimination and guilt. The U.S. has paid for Viet Nam many times over."[131] Two years later, in March 1977, President Carter argued that America did not owe Vietnam a debt since "the destruction was mutual."[132] The pattern of denying guilt, as opposed to widespread confessions of guilt, continued as the dominant cultural response to the war in Vietnam. In this way, Capps's declaration of the end of innocence was myopic. Capps's statement originally appeared in 1982, in the first edition of his book. To have let it stand, unaltered, for the second edition of the work (1990) ignores the many examples that contradict the argument. John Wayne is dead, but it was cancer and not the war in Vietnam that killed him. The ideal of personal and national innocence survived Vietnam and, further, the war has become a site for the recuperation of the attendant myths of the warrior and heroism. John Wayne was replaced by John Rambo, who has been supported by a host of cultural heroes who are all Vietnam veterans: Sonny Crocket of *Miami Vice* (1984), Magnum of the eponymously named television series (1980), the members of *The A-Team* television series (1983), Martin Riggs of the *Lethal Weapon* film series (1987, 1989, 1992), Oliver North, Colin Powell, Norman Schwartzkopf.[133]

The end of heroism and militarism signaled by Capps was translated into a call for the end of wayward military intervention that has been reinterpreted as *support* for continuing military actions. "No more Vietnams!" is encoded with the implicit message that "this time we'll get it right." Far from the end of innocence and soldiery, the war in Vietnam is rewritten as a negative correlative against which future military action is measured. "Getting it right"—which not only underwrote but in some senses legitimated the invasion of Grenada and support for the Contra rebels in Nicaragua—also resulted in an upsurge in the rhetoric of Allied righteousness as headlines valorized all aspects of victory in the Persian Gulf. To the victorious, then, go the rights to assert innocence. Guilt is irrelevant in the presence of actions that are interpreted as totally justified. The culture industries capitalized on the allied victory in the Gulf War by manufacturing a new breed of warriors for the screen. *The Sands of Iwo Jima* (1949) has already been replayed in the desert sands of the Persian Gulf in the lamentable film *Desert Shield* (1991).

Contrary to the existence of what has been called a "seller's market for guilt" infusing post–Vietnam War American culture,[134] there has been little change to the viability or circulation of the myth of innocence. The denial of guilt that supports the myth has been manifest in interpretations of the United States as the victim of the war, a construct that extends the revision or forgetting of the history of the war.[135] Indeed, "Vietnamnesia," the authoritative repression of the war, interacts dialectically with the notion of innocence: maintaining innocence requires the denial of the war, and the denial of the war allows for innocence to be maintained. The dialectic received support as a result of Reagan's election to the presidency and his upholding of the inviolate myth of innocence. His revision of the "meaning" of the war (based on an enforced forgetting of alternative memories) was legitimated in its most powerful manifestation through reference to the American dead in Vietnam. Reagan implied that to contest his conclusion was to discredit the "memory of 50,000 [*sic*] young Americans who died" in the war. To remember the dead meant promulgating the myth of innocence by not "giv[ing] way to feelings of guilt as if we were doing something shameful [in Vietnam]. . . . [I]t's time," he insisted in August 1980, that "we recognize that ours was, in truth, a noble cause."[136] With these statements Reagan employed a not particularly subtle rhetorical maneuver: in the name of remembering (the dead) he recuperated the myth of national innocence and its implicit aspects of forgetting guilt and healing the community. The assertion of innocence is not only willful amnesia, it also functions to assure communal unity.

Reagan frequently defined unity, specifically the union of the localized community, in terms of an idealized and idyllic innocence. His television campaign advertisements featuring neighborhood scenes of "Morning Again" in America, and the frequent references within his speeches to everyday folk in the community were employed in a way that constructed the community as a state of grace. In exploiting the association of innocence and community, Reagan deferred to a tradition that extends back to the Puritan myth of the founding white communities as islands of virtue among a sea of savagery. Popular representations in particular have renovated and reworked the relationship of the community and innocence. Within film, for example, neighborhood community has frequently been depicted as the place of naive ideals (as in *Meet Me in St. Louis*, 1944), while the virtuous member of the small town frequently has her/his values tested and finally reaffirmed through contact with a corrupt city (the paradigmatic example is *Mr. Smith Goes to Washington*,

1939). The notion of pre–Vietnam War and hence prelapsarian "inno-cence" is evoked in the film *American Graffiti* (1973) through its setting in a small California town of the early sixties. Presented as the wellspring of benevolence, the community is a place of caring and healing, a refuge from the painful experience of the world.

Despite its appeal, the need for community possessed the potential to reveal the limits of healing. As Bellah and his colleagues hinted in their study of community in Reagan's America, "the tremendous nostalgia . . . for the idealized 'small town'" suggested the "fear that there may be no way at all to relate to those who are too different."[137] The suggestion was lost in the discourse of healing from the divisive war. Instead, the con-structions of interiority/exteriority, inclusiveness and exclusiveness upon which unity is based continued to define the absence of difference. To be included in the community is to be healed and innocent. In contrast, the wounded outsiders are those who bear the marks of difference as the traces of culpability. A guilty, damaging difference, then, must be contin-ually marginalized or denied in the relentless assertion of community.

The National Allegory

The affirmation of unity and the denial of difference referred to as heal-ing was massively extended in its most ambitious phase—the healing of the nation. As a completely amorphous entity, the nation needed to be sit-uated within a specific site that would provide a focus for the discussion and evocation of national healing. With its completion, the Vietnam Vet-erans Memorial in Washington, D.C., became a feature that was quickly appropriated as the representational focus of the "nation" and its need to be healed of the wounds of war. A deluge of texts soon represented the memorial in the language of healing. The most notable example in these terms is *To Heal a Nation* (1986), a book written by Jan Scruggs, the orig-inator of an idea of a memorial to veterans of the Vietnam War.[138]

The healing function of the memorial was reinforced by definitions that interpreted the black wall as a symbol of national rejuvenation and vigor. The strength that supposedly results from healing was expressed by President Reagan during a speech in which he formally accepted the memorial on behalf of the nation. Reagan, who was fond of references to fictional characters, on this occasion alluded to Hemingway's Frederic

Henry, a character who was familiar with the wounds of war and believed that it is possible to be made "strong at the broken places."[139] According to Reagan:

> The Memorial reflects as a mirror reflects.... And as you touch it ... you're touching ... the reflection of the Washington Monument or the chair in which great Abe Lincoln sits.... It's been said that these memorials reflect a hunger for healing. Well, I do not know if perfect healing ever occurs. But I know that sometimes when a bone is broken, if it's knit together well, it will in the end be stronger than if it had not been broken.[140]

The reconstruction that Reagan points to suggests the reimposition of the enduring order of things stretching back to Lincoln and Washington, and with this suggestion Reagan's speech exposes the central aspect of healing: the legitimation of unity as an essential characteristic of the status quo.

Within the dominant interpretation, reproduced in Reagan's colloquially styled comments, the memorial is permitted to speak only of healing, and within this framework all other articulations are viewed as potentially divisive and derided as political. An example of this process of exclusion can be found in the rules of the design competition for the memorial that stressed the absence of politics and emphasized healing. Those wishing to submit designs were instructed: "The memorial will make no political statement regarding the war or its conduct. It will transcend those issues. The hope is that the creation of the memorial will begin a healing process, a reconciliation of the grievous divisions wrought by the war."[141] The banishment of politics and the aggressive foregrounding of the memorial's healing function denied or precluded alternative ways of understanding or interpretation capable of informing the memory and legacy of the war.

Given the desire for reconciliation implicit in healing, and the continued stress put upon the apolitical function of the memorial, it is ironic that the memorial was, from its inception, surrounded by often bitter acrimony and politics. The design itself provoked a well-documented conflict of interests.[142] Many of those who disputed the winning design did so on the grounds that the completed memorial would fail to evoke healing because it was not, in effect, a *traditional* monument. A number of figures associated with the memorial's construction, including Ross Perot, who helped fund the design competition, objected to the final proposal. Perot's objections were partially met in Reagan's acceptance speech, in which he reinterpreted the memorial as a reflection of nearby traditional monuments. More specifically, those who were dissatisfied with the memorial were assuaged, to a degree, through a compromise in which a life-size bronze statue of three Vietnam War combat soldiers was installed near the memorial. Ironically, this addition reinvoked and refocused criticisms of memorial designs. Maya Lin, the designer of the Wall, called the statue "trite," and its sculptor, Frederick Hart, rejoined by calling the memorial "contemptuous of life."[143]

The existence of such debates subverts the notion that the Wall is unequivocally a site of unity. Contending positions not obsessed with unity have reinterpreted the memorial's function by focusing on the names etched into its black marble slabs. To many interpreters the names evoke mortal injury, the "main purpose and outcome of war," in the words of Elaine Scarry.[144] Within this focus, the powerful connotative effect of what Maya Lin called the "sea of names"[145] has the potential to redirect the meaning of the memorial away from unity toward sorrow and loss. Indeed, grief motivated many of the contributions to the memorial fund, and inevitably the expression of sorrow, or attempts to relieve it, raised other questions. One donor to the memorial fund, a woman from Michigan, "saw the soldiers [who fought in Vietnam] as courageous, but victims of 'needless sacrifice.'" One man sent funds as a way of expressing his response to a "war [he] hated and [for] the friends and the loved ones [he] lost."[146] Statements on the war and its effect, such as "The waste," "Such a waste," "Oh God, the waste," are frequently repeated at the memorial.[147] The notion of a despised and disruptive war evoked within these comments contests the easy assumptions of healing and redirects attention to questions concerning the legitimacy of the war. The grief and anger motivating many comments at the Wall possess the ability to reproduce what has been called in a different memorializing context, "mourning *and* militancy."[148] The names, then, have been and continue to be crucial in attempts to stabilize the meaning of the memorial. It is within the lavish media and textual attention given to the memorial at the level of the names that the task of asserting the notion of national healing is replicated in subtle ways.

The simple unadorned list of names on the Vietnam Veterans Memorial is a variation of generic designs of memorials to war dead. The emphasis on patriotic symbols and signs of national "sacrifice" found among many memorials to the dead of earlier wars was consciously contradicted in Maya Lin's focus on the names in a memorial devoid of statements and flags (the compromise between contending interpretations of the function of the memorial included the installation of a flagstaff at the memorial site and the addition of a brief inscription to the memorial itself). The Vietnam Veterans Memorial privileges the names, thus foregrounding the presence of those American men and women who died in Vietnam.

A list of names, it is asserted, was central to the original concept of a memorial. According to an apocryphal account, Jan Scruggs, the founder of the memorial fund, awoke in the night after earlier in the evening having seen the film *The Deer Hunter*. Scruggs envisioned a "memorial to all the names of everyone killed [in the war]."[149] Ironically, the notion that a film influenced Scruggs's decision to create a Vietnam veterans memorial is echoed in the fact that certain filmic representations have prominently featured the names on the Wall. Typically, the memorial is seen briefly in long-shot, and then the camera pans slowly over the names in close-up.[150] A television commercial has exploited the frequently reproduced scenes of people touching the names in its depiction of a child reaching to the names as the voice-over refers to "the touch, the feel, the fabric of our lives."[151] Touching the names, taking rubbings of the engraved outlines of the names, and leaving mementos at the place of the names have for many people become ritualized parts of the process of visiting the memorial. One observer has noted that "pictures of this touching have often appeared in the media. The pictures convey healing,"[152] thus implicating media in the reproduction of the notion of healing.

Without mediation the act of touching the names on the memorial would remain a personal experience untranslated to the rest of America. The interventions of the media transform the personal into the national, the denotative into the connotative, the literal into metaphor. Within this transformation the simple act of touching the memorial, an action that can carry a variety of personal meanings, is conflated with the nation's apparent desire to be healed. In this way the mass media construct, to quote Fredric Jameson out of context, a "national allegory" in which "private individual destiny" represents a symbolic, or metaphoric, narrative of the condition of the entire culture.[153]

Similarly, within and through the mediation of printed textual responses to the memorial, the individual identities of those whose names appear on the memorial become the focus of a healing or healed nation. An example of the allegorical process operating through the appropriation of the names on the Wall is located within Bobbie Ann Mason's novel

In Country (1987), a work that pays particular attention to various names. Brand names, for example, litter almost every page, reflecting the commercial culture's obsession with mass-produced products, and the issue of names as a reflection of identity is introduced with the central character, Samantha Hughes, who is known as Sam. Through the privileging of a female character, Mason presents the opportunity to represent the feminine in its "multiplicity."[154] However, as Mason's story progresses, the realization of this opportunity is lost as the masculine character returns to the plot. Previously lacking any motivation, Sam's uncle, Emmett, devises a plan for members of the family to visit the Vietnam Veterans Memorial and in enacting this plan Emmett gradually grows to dominate the narrative.

Sam's mother advises that on arrival at the memorial Sam should "look at the names. You'll see all those country boy names, I bet you anything. Billy Gene and Freddie Ray and Jimmy Bob Calhoun . . . you look at those names and tell me if they're not mostly country boy names."[155] The stereotypical interpretation of these names as those of "country boys" is contradicted within the narrative itself. The inhabitants of the southern rural township of Mason's Hopewell have names such as Tom Hudson, Lonnie Malone, and Ed McMahon. Significantly, each of these characters is white. "Race" is absent from Hopewell, a curious omission, given the history of the towns of the South, and also a perplexing absence in a novel that seeks to criticize constructions of difference. Such qualifications determine that the names on the memorial are not necessarily those of "country boys"—but they are those of white males. Within *In Country* the memorial becomes a black wall for white people.

The denial of "race" in Mason's narrative is paralleled in the process of erasure of the feminine that began with the privileging of Emmett's role. The denial culminates at the memorial, where Sam finds the name of a soldier, "Sam Hughes," killed in Vietnam. Sam's journey toward self-knowledge ends in the obliteration of her identity in that of a (white) male soldier. Constantly denied access to information concerning the war because of her gender, Sam is eventually admitted to the "mystery" of Vietnam through the agencies and identities of men. For Sam, the price of healing from the war is the abandonment of identity, resulting in what David Rodowick has called the "universalization of subjectivity as maleness."[156] Mason writes: "[Sam] touches her own name. How odd it feels, as though all the names in America have been used to decorate this wall."[157] The multiplicity of the United States is reduced to a collectivity of white males that Sam's name helps her enter. In this country, Sam's name is a contraction of sameness.

The stereotyping and denial of identity and the construction of union evidenced in Mason's novel is also apparent in an article written by William Broyles, Jr., for *Newsweek* magazine. The report deals with the candlelit vigil and recitation of the names of the Vietnam War dead held in the National Cathedral to coincide with the 1982 dedication of the Vietnam Veterans Memorial. Broyles's interpretation of the names encodes a variety of stereotypes embedded within the national allegory:

> Names. Jose K. Brown. Sai G. Gew. Glenn F. Cashdollar. Kenyu Shimabukuru. Famous L. Lane. Witold J. Leszczynski. Thomas L. Little Sun. Salvatore J. Piscitello. Max Lieberman. Savas Escamilla Trevino. Billy Joe Lawrence.
>
> For 56 hours they read the names in the Gothic confines of the National Cathedral. Rhythmic Spanish names. Tongue-twisting Polish names, guttural German, exotic African, homely Anglo-Saxon names. Chinese, Polynesian, Indian and Russian names. They are names which reach deep into the heart of America, each testimony to a family's decision, sometime in the past, to wrench itself from home and culture to test our country's promise of new opportunities and a better life. They are names drawn from the farthest corners of the world and then, in this generation, sent to another distant corner in a war America has done its best to forget.[158]

Broyles reproduces the myths of the center and periphery upon which constructions of otherness are based. The United States is, as Marita Sturken notes, positioned at the center of the world and all other parts of the globe are the "farthest corners."[159] Only the Anglo-Saxon names are "homely," the true reflection of "the heart of America." The "other" names are stereotyped in accordance with prejudicial images of marginalized nations. Africa and Africans are "exotic." Spain is the land of dance and melody, as exemplified in "rhythmic Spanish names." "Guttural German" names is a construction reminiscent of Sylvia Plath's disparaging and intentionally malicious reference to the German language spoken by her father as a glottal "barbed-wire snare."[160] Within Broyles's rewriting of identity, assumed generic cultural traits are presented as natural and traditional.

Tradition, according to Raymond Williams, is "a deliberately selective and connecting process which offers a historical and cultural ratification of a contemporary order." Williams also noted that the "selective tradition" is "at once powerful and vulnerable." "Powerful because it is so skilled in making active selective connections, dismissing those it does not want," vulnerable because "the selective version of a 'living tradition' is always tied, though often in complex and hidden ways, to explicit contemporary limits and pressures."[161] The ratification of selected representations of identity and unity encountered in Broyles's interpretation of names is contested by the "pressures and limits" imposed within the culture by the politics of identity. Identity politics represent the idea that personal and collective identities—based on "race," region, religion, class, gender, and sexual preferences—can infuse and structure the practice of political experience. Such a politics exists and functions in the form of new social movements, including the modern women's movement, the gay movement, Jesse Jackson's Rainbow Coalition and its variants, and the green movement.[162] Despite the emphasis on "newness" in the term used to describe these formations, such movements are not historically unique or novel. Many of the features present within the new social movements are indistinguishable from features in earlier social movements based on aspects of identity. The difference is a matter of degree and elaboration: the new social movements have consciously foregrounded coalitional practices aimed at realizing the slogan the "personal is political."

Identity and coalitional politics seek to establish the validity of relational identities, as opposed to an identity fixed in the pejorative images exhibited in Broyles's work. The operation of a politics of identity resists dominant messages of cultural unity that ridicule or deny the existence of difference. An effective (counter)memory of personal identities capable of contesting the stereotyping of individual experiences is maintainable, then, only outside the national allegory of healing. The contrast between the existence of difference and the dominant metaphor of healing does not result in stasis. Competing forces struggle for dominance in a contest in which, to quote Walter Benjamin, "*even the dead* will *not* be safe"[163] from being continually conscripted to articulate the need for national unity. If the struggle is lost, the Wall would cease to be a memorial, a site of memory. It would become, instead, a monument—a place of tradition marking the massive reconstruction of experience that is encoded in healing.

The Unhealed

The outcome of the struggle over the imposition of "healing" is far from guaranteed. Historically, a number of texts have sought to resist the negative force of assertions of healing/unity. The film *Cutter's Way* (1981), while still relying on the convention of the wounded veteran, is one of the very few films to deal with the wounding impact of the war without referral to the dubious qualities associated with healing. The multiple amputee Alex Cutter (John Heard) of the film's title is motivated by a desire to avenge a girl's murder. The murderer, according to Cutter, is a wealthy industrialist, Cord (Stephen Elliott). For Cutter, Cord's culpability does not stop with the murdered girl. "Cord's responsible," Cutter insists, "he and his type. It's never their ass that's on the line." Cutter's desire for revenge extends to include those in power who sent him to a debilitating and wounding war while they remained safely insulated from the war and its effects. In the film's final scenes Bone (Jeff Bridges), holding the dead Cutter's gun, accuses Cord of killing the girl. Cord's answer is the rhetorical question "What if it was?" This ambiguity is maintained in the scene that follows: immediately the screen whites out and a gunshot is heard, leaving the audience to suspect that Bone has shot Cord. The uncertainty that surrounds Cord's part in the murder is reflected in the lack of certainty that Bone has pulled the trigger on Cord. If the "drive to narrative closure in Hollywood films tends to 'tame' alternate views and reaffirm dominant ones,"[164] then the intentionally ambiguous ending of *Cutter's Way* militates against a conclusive reading.

While the ending fails to support dominant views, it also fails to categorically dispute them—it neither confirms nor denies. However, the film unequivocally maintains the suggestion that culture is composed of a number of different positions, summarized within the reconfiguration of the terms of "them" and "us" ("it's never *their* ass that's on the line"). In addition, Cutter's outburst hints at the fact that this division is longstanding. Historically, one group has managed to insulate itself from the effect of the war and similar disruptions ("it's *never* . . . "), a position that underlines the enduring existence of class and power differences within the culture.

Interestingly, *Cutter's Way* anticipated issues subsequently raised and reworked in the film *Rambo* (1985). The latter film's presentation of the stab-in-the-back thesis is a rewriting of the position presented in *Cutter's Way* that contends that the (working-class) U.S. soldier was betrayed through the very act of having been sent to Vietnam.[165] Similarly, the rearticulation of the "us" and "them" dichotomy in *Rambo*—in which "us" is a unified collectivity rallied against those who are different—is an attempt to revise the wounding class-based cultural divisions established in *Cutter's Way*.

Cutter's outburst at those whose bodies are never "on the line" has since resonated within the culture in a number of important ways, most conspicuously as a yardstick of the patriotism of Republican vice-presidents and Democratic presidents. Specifically, however, Cutter's indignation implicates not patriotism but the role of class in deciding who is sent to war. The fact that Vietnam was a class-based war is an issue that is rarely raised with effect within representations of themes surrounding the war.[166] The failure of texts to come to terms with the class basis of the war is exemplified in the opening scenes of *The Deer Hunter* in which Cimino attempts to represent the working-class experiences and ethnic backgrounds of the characters who will go to war. As the film critics Leonard Quart and Al Auster argue, Cimino's perspective fails to depict a class and "a culture and identity that is both alive and able to fight its own battles . . . without charismatic heroes to aid them." Instead, "His workers live in a time warp, politically unconscious and passive men and women" living a life "without dissatisfaction, anger or restlessness—a working class that has no hunger for success or mobility but is totally satisfied and complacent about both the virtues and limitations of life."[167] The final scene of the film forgoes analysis of the ways in which class and ethnicity were reconfigured in support of the war by simplistically asserting that patriotism is the only solution to the damaging effects of the conflict.

In contrast to this conclusion, but finally no less satisfactory in its representation of issues related to the war, Stone's 1990 film version of Ron Kovic's 1977 memoir *Born on the Fourth of July* attempted to dispel the move from class to patriotism by representing the disastrous impact wrought by chauvinistic myths on Kovic's working-class background. Here too, however, closure involves ignoring images and issues of class and restating those of patriotism and nation in scenes involving Kovic's reassessment of American ideals, and his eventual affirmation of the processes of democratic electoral politics.

The themes of birth and patriotism evident in the title of Kovic's memoir were, ironically, repeated in the title of Bruce Springsteen's song "Born in the U.S.A." (1984). Springsteen attempts to confront issues of class as they intersect with the veteran's experience in descriptions of a working-class hero who is sent to Vietnam after getting into "a little hometown jam." Returning to the United States, the veteran, unemployed and ignored by the Veterans Administration, reflects on the irony of a lost American war and the disruption in its wake on the lives of those around him. Despite the critical stance implicit in lyrics that emphasize class and loss, the chorus—repeated shouts of the line "Born in the U.S.A!"— made the song open to appropriation as an anthem of jingoistic expression. Refusing and resisting such an expression, the video filmed by John Sayles that accompanied the song's release anchored the verbal images of the lyric to powerful visual images of working-class life. The video features shots of a happy childhood in a working-class neighborhood, high school photographs, and a wedding, followed by images of cars for sale, welfare lines, soldiers in Vietnam, and a Vietnamese child. The final segment features graves at Arlington Cemetery and men working in a welding plant. The ironic contrast created by the words of the chorus and scenes depicting the connection between the war and its effects on members of the working class dispels any sense of facile patriotism.

The divisive impact of the war present in texts such as *Cutters' Way* and Springsteen's song had earlier been registered in Robert Stone's novel *Dog Soldiers* (1976) through the presence of three kilograms of heroin smuggled into America from Vietnam. As the novel registers the effect of the heroin on the lives of various characters, the reader is toured through an America that mocks the dominant myth of healing/unity. Indeed, the failure of community, of the center to hold, is a theme that runs throughout Stone's work. In his first novel, *A Hall of Mirrors* (1968), a character announces: "If somebody ever tells you, Geraldine, that they need you, you tell them to buy a dog."[168] In *A Flag for Sunrise* (1983) Holliwell, a liberal anthropologist, delivers a narcotized lecture on the parlous state of U.S. culture: "Underneath it all, our secret culture, the non-exportable one, is dying. It's going sour and we're going to die of it. We'll die of it quietly around our own hearths while our children laugh at us."[169] In his next novel, *Children of Light* (1986), the central character's schizophrenia becomes a reflection of the divided condition of the United States referred to by Holliwell.[170] In *Outerbridge Reach* (1992), Owen Browne, a veteran of the war in Vietnam, muses upon an "imagined country, a homeland that could function as both community and cause.... Browne felt his own country had failed him in that regard. It was agreeable to think such a place might exist.... But no such place existed."[171]

Pursuing the misanthropic theme in *Dog Soldiers*, Stone represents southern California as a place filled with random violence, misunderstanding, and betrayal. Having escaped San Francisco with the heroin, Ray Hicks, a Vietnam veteran, and Marge Converse, wife of Hicks's partner in the importation of the drug, stop briefly in an isolated area of the Hollywood hills. During a brief respite from violence, Marge sees people hiding among the trees and asks Hicks what they are seeking. Hicks answers:

> Bodies. . . . Sometimes they find a car off the road with nobody in it. They have to look for the driver. They'll see a drunk run his car into the canyon and they'll creep out at night to take the guy's wallet. They go for the credit cards. . . . The big ones eat the little ones, up here.[172]

Any notion that community is possible is ridiculed in this modern wasteland. Escaping the perversions of the city, Hicks joins Dieter, once the guru of a communal retreat in New Mexico that became corrupted by drugs. Ironically, Dieter seeks to recruit Hicks, still in possession of the heroin, to help him revitalize the retreat. Hicks, however, is unable and unwilling to attempt to resuscitate an ideal that in post–Vietnam America is anachronistic and unworkable. The failure to find or maintain a separate peace is underlined when the commune is shattered by a firefight between Hicks and those seeking to steal the heroin. In this scene the war comes home with all its traumatic force as Hicks is wounded attempting to escape with the heroin.

Hallucinating from the pain of his wounds, Hicks imagines himself accepting and thereby dispelling the pain that existed in Vietnam: "All that cringing, all those crying women, whining kids—I don't want to see that, I don't like it. Give it here. . . . Napalm burns, no problem—just put it here."[173] Hicks's long, painful, and finally fatal retreat from his pursuers focuses his perceptions concerning social conditions within America in the wake of the war in Vietnam:

> [k]now what's out there? Every goddamn race of shit jerking each other off. Mom and Dad and Buddy and Sis, two hundred million rat-hearted cocksuckers in enormous cars. Rabbits and fish. They're mean and stupid and greedy, they'll fuck you for laughs, they want you dead. If you're no better than them you might as well take gas. If you can't get your own on them then don't stand there and let them spit on you, don't give them the satisfaction.[174]

Within this dystopic view of a fraying social fabric is the suggestion that "we" are all victims of the war in Vietnam. This issue and the interrelated notions of (national) identity and pain were subsequently explored in a different way in Larry Heinemann's novel *Paco's Story* (1987).

Pain and suffering, and the memorializing of the effects of war inform Heinemann's novel. One character, Jesse, describes his conception of an official veterans monument planned by "ex-Marine corps heroes . . . and General goddamn William Westmoreland his own self" that mocks Hart's sculpture by representing a "half-hacked Boy Scout lieutenant . . . standing on an effigy of a Purple Heart, with his legs all loosy-goosy, like he's surfing, but holding a corpse of a dead G.I heavenward. . . . " Since "any grunt worth his grit and spit" would disavow such "John Wayne crapola" as contrary to the experience of Vietnam, Jesse proposes a more "fragrant" alternative: a "grassy knoll" of "prime Washington, D.C. property . . . in line with the Reflecting Pool" covered with white marble inscribed with the names of the Vietnam war dead. In the middle of the site he proposes a "big granite bowl . . . about the size of a three-yard dump truck" into which would be laden "every sort of 'egregious' excretion" mixed with thousands of hundred-dollar bills. Jesse suggests that "all comers may fish around in that bowl" for the money.[175]

Such a proposal disputes the idea of national healing, a position that is echoed in other alternative interpretations of the memorial's function. Poet and Vietnam veteran William Ehrhart expresses a radical position that refuses the Wall, or any memorial, as the final arbiter of the national condition when he writes:

> I didn't want a monument
> not even one as sober as that
> vast black wall of broken lives.
> . . . .
> What I wanted
> was an end to monuments.[176]

Another veteran conceived of a memorial as a "one-ton condolence card," and one veteran suggested a searchlight scanning the Washington Mall illuminating a huge crater with the "ashes of 50,000 John Does . . . scattered in the bottom."[177] The issues of identity and anonymity raised in this last suggestion are relevant to Heinemann's novel. As if to parody William Broyles's stereotyping of ethnicity in his interpretation of the names of the war dead, Heinemann's character is named Paco Sullivan, but to those around him he is nameless. Despite his anonymity, Paco has a retrievable identity that is intimated in Jesse's idea for a Vietnam War memorial. Jesse's description implicates pain, or slaughter, on more than one level. The reference to a "grassy knoll" echoes descriptions of the location from which the National Guard shot and killed four students at Kent State University, and also evokes descriptions of the site of a suspected additional gunman in the Kennedy assassination. Such references suggest death and wounding as spectacle, the visible display of a violent culture, and it is within a context of spectacular violence that Paco's identity is defined. During a battle in which everyone else dies, Paco survives—a visibly scarred memorial to the war:

> Our man Paco . . . lies flat on his back and wide to the sky, with slashing lacerations, big watery burn blisters, and broken, splintered, *ruined* legs. . . . [H]e comes to consciousness in the dark of that first long night . . . and he doesn't know what hit him. . . . [H]e imagines looking down at his own body, seeing—vividly—every gaping shrapnel nick, every puckery burn scar, every splintery compound fracture.[178]

Paco *is* pain. Reinforcing the wounding, *carnal*, basis of the war, Heinemann has written elsewhere that the U.S. soldier in Vietnam was "so much meat on the slab to be butchered."[179] As a result of the scarring effects of the war, Heinemann has stated: "I am who I am because of Vietnam . . . —there's no use denying it."[180] Similarly, the experience of war has defined Paco's identity. A glimpse of this experience is revealed in a vivid flashback Paco experiences as a result of listening to his rooming-house neighbor, Cathy, and her boyfriend having sex in the adjoining room. Hearing the sounds through the wall, Paco is confronted by the grisly memory of the platoon's violent rape of a Vietnamese girl that culminated in her murder and scalping. The omniscient narrator comments: "We looked at her and at ourselves, drawing breath again and again, and knew that this was a moment of evil, that we would never live the same."[181] Here, at the end of the scene, the center of attention is the men and the possible effect of this action upon their future lives. As Lorrie Smith has noted, "The sympathetic center of the book is Paco, the ultimate veteran victim. . . . It is *Paco's* pain that matters, not the Vietnamese woman's."[182]

Two days after his voyeuristic eavesdropping, Paco sneaks into Cathy's room and reads the diary in which she has described her fantasies of making love to Paco. Paco reads: "[H]e holds himself up, stiff-armed, and arches his back and reaches up to his forehead and begins by pinching skin there, but he's working the skin loose, and then begins to peel the scars off as if they were a mask." In Cathy's imagination, Paco "lays the scars on [her] chest. It *burns* . . . and I think I hear *screams*."[183] There is no ambiguity in the final words. It is not Cathy who screams—it is Paco, his continued suffering unassuaged by having divested himself of his scars. Women, it seems, are not allowed a voice and must suffer in silence. Although the transference of the scars is meant to suggest the shared burden of pain of war, it is women who are made to pay the price for men's pain. Despite the foregrounding of Paco's anguish and victimization, it is women who are raped, murdered, and inscribed with men's scars. This issue is also evident in the pornographically violent film *Casualties of War* (1989) in scenes depicting the abduction and rape of a Vietnamese woman by a squad of U.S. soldiers. Again it is a (Vietnamese) woman who is made the ultimate victim, even though the title of the film is clearly meant to include (American) male soldiers.

Ironically, then, it is within the privileging of the unhealed, victimized, male veteran that the notion of *universal* suffering is established. Differences and incommensurabilities between the experience of the United States and Vietnam, and between men and women, are subsumed within the image that "we" are all—equally—victims or casualties of the war. This universalizing of victimage is inscribed in a variety of sources, including Herr's coda to *Dispatches*: "Vietnam, Vietnam, Vietnam, we have all been there."[184] The assessment resonates in Stanley Karnow's argument that "the war in Vietnam was a war nobody won—a struggle between victims."[185] Such arguments unwittingly replace the national allegory of healing with a national allegory of wounding.

While both *Paco's Story* and *Dog Soldiers* seek to resist healing through an evocation of the language of the wound, the result is not a coherent and cogent alternative to healing but a return to the problematic dimensions of the wound. Representing cultural division and difference in terms of a wound attaches pejorative connotations to these conditions and, through the irresistible appeal of healing implicit in the metaphor of the wound, undermines attempts to establish the reality of cultural division. Thus, any challenge to the hegemonic project known as healing is severely limited, if not sabotaged, through its reliance on the imbricated language of the wound, which constantly threatens to imply an image of its opposite. The essence of the problem, echoed in a comment by Wittgenstein, is found in the assessment that "[a] picture held us captive. And we could not get outside it, for it lay in our language and language seemed to repeat it to us inexorably."[186]

> The war created an open suppurating wound which has not yet healed, and
> if it does, it may leave a permanent scar on the American body politic.[187]

Within Vietnam, as one survivor of the war has pointed out, many of the
wounds of the war remain open.[188] This situation is in stark contrast to
America, where the wounds of war have been evoked so that the corollary, healing, can be summoned to redress the situation. The outcome of
the healing process implies a consensual and unified culture devoid of disruption, division, and difference. Thus, the main implication of the use of
the seemingly natural language of the wound and healing has been to
offer the opportunity to disavow the reality of division and difference and
to insist upon cultural unity. The inverse of this position is a recognition
of the reality of difference and its positive effects. The existence of cultural constituencies not captivated by the notion of healing as unity produces a contest at the site of representation between difference and unity
in which, to borrow a line from essayist Kobena Mercer, "what matters
most are the moves, strategies, and tactics by which opponents play the
game."[189] In this contest difference has been outmaneuvered by a strategy of unity encoded in the dominant metaphor of healing. The signs of
the effectivity of the moves and tactics of this strategy are inscribed within
culture at the level of the individual, the community, and the nation and
are revealed—at the end of the contest—in the form of a healed scar.

2

The Vietnam Veteran
as Ventriloquist

Who is speaking? . . . Who is qualified to do so?
—Michel Foucault

I am the man, I suffer'd, I was there.   —Walt Whitman

Metaphors and similes related to the act of speaking and to the absence of speech surround the Vietnam veteran. Young men and women were "called" to Vietnam (whether they answered that call was, of course, another matter).[1] Among U.S. troops in Vietnam the collective response to devastating action was the ironic expression "Don't mean nuthin'," suggesting that further comment on violence and its motives was futile. Equally as popular for such circumstances was the laconic "There it is," a line that implies that "nothing more . . . needs to be said, or indeed can be said."[2] The U.S. foot soldier in Vietnam, the GI of earlier wars, became a "grunt," reduced to language's lowest common denominator. In this the veterans all became "quiet Americans." For many years, or so myth would have it, the war in Vietnam was "the War That Dared Not Speak Its Name."[3] This situation was to change during the administration of Ronald Reagan, the "Great Communicator," when the Vietnam veteran was hailed a hero and allowed, even invited, to articulate his/her experience.

The intense concern with giving the veteran a "voice" resulted in the veteran's central positioning within representations of the war and its impact. However, the limitations inherent in this representation are evident in the fact that the far-reaching ramifications of the war for economic, "race," gender, and regional differences are not adequately embodied in or reducible to the figure of the veteran. Rather, an accurate and inclusive portrayal of the impact on U.S. culture of the Vietnam War demanded approaches derived from a variety of subject positions throughout the culture. Despite such provisions, the emphasis on the veteran proved convenient within a culture that has traditionally expressed itself through a virtually exclusive reliance on the (male) individual.

The representational appeal of the veteran also persisted despite the objection that such a focus ignored the Vietnamese people and marginalized the U.S. domestic resistance to the war. Further, within the majority of textual representations the term "Vietnam veteran" has functioned to largely exclude Americans of diverse cultural backgrounds. Contradicting this situation, to a limited degree, are representations of the experiences of ethnic veterans in the novels *China Men* (1981) by Maxine Hong Kingston, *Captain Blackman* (1988) by John Williams, *Coming Home* (1971) by George Davis, and *Love Medicine* by Louise Erdrich (1984), and in the films *Journey through Rosebud* (1972), *Johnny Firecloud* (1975), *Ashes and Embers* (1982), *Latino* (1985) *Powwow Highway* (1989), and the "Billy Jack" cycle of films: *The Born Losers, Billy Jack, The Trial of Billy Jack,* and *Billy Jack Goes to Washington* (1967, 1971, 1974, 1977).[4] Typically, however, these works have not been included in critical discussions of war-related texts. Similarly, women have been almost entirely excluded from representations of the war, or are included to function as the objects of men's aggression. Vietnamese women are especially targeted in this way, often literally—"shooting Vietnamese women" is a popular theme within representations of the war in Vietnam.[5]

A number of texts have, to a limited degree and with varying success, rewritten exclusionary practices and derogatory representations to position women within the definition of "Vietnam veteran." Examples here include the television series *China Beach* (1988) and Lynda Van Devanter's memoir of her time in Vietnam as an army nurse, *Home Before Morning* (1984).[6] Despite the relatively high degree of popular appeal of these examples, texts of the war and its aftermath have traditionally failed to incorporate representations of women in ways that are capable of revising the masculine point of view of the majority of texts concerned with the "Vietnam experience." Attention has been drawn to the elision and derision of women in textual representations of Vietnam through feminist theory's focus "on the appropriation of 'woman' by (masculine) discursive practices that deny women independent speech. The exclusion of these 'other' voices is sustained by a critical enterprise that places its value on the representation of authentic experience."[7] In privileging authentic experience, only those "who were there" (that is, who took part in the war) are legitimated to speak of the experience. As commonly represented, only males existed in Vietnam. Women, therefore, were not allowed to speak since, according to the logic of popular definitions, they were not "there."[8] Van Devanter highlights this problem in her memoir when she refers to the reaction to her presence at a demonstration by Vietnam veterans in Washington, D.C.:

> I took a place near the front. However, one of the leaders approached me.
> "This demonstration is for vets," he said apologetically.
> "I am a vet," I said. "I was in Pleiku and Qui Nhon."
> "Pleiku!" he exclaimed. "No shit! I used to be with the 4th Infantry. You must have been at the 71st Evac."
> "I worked in the OR."
> "You people did a hell of a job," he said. "You folks saved my best friend's life." He smiled at me for a few moments while I shifted awkwardly under his praise.
> "Do you have a sign or something I can hold?" I asked.
> "Well," he said uncomfortably, "I . . . uh . . . don't think you're supposed to march."
> "But you told me it was for vets."
> "It is," he said. "But you're not a vet."[9]

Seeking to contest exclusions and to retrieve marginalized voices, deconstructive critical practices have, together with feminist theory, "added a 'pluralism' to the name of 'Vietnam.'"[10] In this relation, deconstruction, as with feminist theory, becomes a way of understanding what is, and what is not, articulated within representations surrounding the Vietnam War.

Employing ideas since associated almost exclusively with Jaques Derrida, both Catherine Belsey and Pierre Macherey have offered interpretations of deconstruction in terms of presences and absences, silences and articulations. The object of deconstructing a text is, for Belsey, "to examine the process of its production" and "to locate the point at which it is constructed."[11] This point is to be found, as Macherey has argued, within "the tension between the text's *aspiration* to completeness and the *actual* incompleteness which it cannot avoid . . . this is the contradiction which proclaims the position of the text within ideology."[12] According to Macherey, the source of this contradiction can be traced to the language of the text that in its incompleteness can reveal textual "silences."[13] Deconstructive analysis, according to Macherey's method, highlights the absences in texts—that which the text is unable to say.

Deconstruction defined in this way intersects with the popular texts dealing with the war and its impact on the U.S. home front through a consideration that within these works "all except white inarticulate males" remain "missing from the action."[14] A form of analysis that focuses upon the silences inherent in representations is particularly suited, then, to texts in which various languages (literary, cinematic, and scholarly) have together constructed a silent, or silenced, veteran. Working with the direction established by deconstruction as identified here, understanding the privileging of this figure involves locating the point of contradiction within the textual representation of the Vietnam veteran. Such an analysis reveals that the contradiction at the center of the textual construction of the Vietnam veteran centers on "his" ability or inability to articulate his experience.

This contradiction is explicit within a historicization of the cultural and textual trends and assumptions that constructed and reconstructed the veteran in various guises during the twenty-year period from the late sixties to the late eighties. Initially, the veteran was crudely depicted as an inarticulate psychopath, a prejudicial characterization that effectively silenced him within representations. The inarticulate veteran continued as a motif within the dominant representations while at the same time, yet not solely within the same texts, the veteran was being constructed as an authentic spokesperson. The paradox involved in the veteran's speaking role was extended, though not exposed, when the newly constructed veteran-as-spokesperson was permitted to speak only on a limited range of topics, predominantly, if not exclusively, concerned with the common-sense notion of cultural unity. In this way the veteran emerged a hero, valorized, in effect, not for his war experience but for his ability to contribute to the maintenance of cultural homogeneity and holism.

Surrounding the contradiction at the center of the representations of the veteran outlined here is a debate concerning the meaning of the experience known as "Vietnam." The construction of the veteran as psychopath was predicated upon the notion of an unspeakably horrific "Vietnam" that led to psychosis in all those unlucky enough to be sent there. (In this sense the term "Vietnam" is used to evoke both the war and the alien and threatening country in which the war was fought.) Alternatively, yet equally as disturbing in its consequences, the image of the veteran as hero is implicated in the revised view of Vietnam as a "noble cause." A critique of the contradiction that informs the construction of the Vietnam veteran is therefore central to an understanding of the ways in which the experience of the war and its impact were represented in the period under discussion. With this context in mind, the analysis within this part is a form of deconstructive critique focused on the contradictory positions—silence and speaking—centrally implicated within representations of the veteran. The exploration and critique of this contradiction involves seeking answers to certain questions. By refusing to ask questions relating to the veteran's transformation from a silent or silenced figure to a privileged interpreter is to give credence to the spurious assumption that silence continues to surround the war. Certain questions demand to be asked: Why was the veteran silenced? What circumstances allowed him to speak? And, most important, In whose voice did the veteran finally speak?

Comments made by Roland Barthes provide an introduction to an understanding of these questions together with an outline of the conclusion of the deconstructive task undertaken here. Implicit in the way in which the above questions have been posed is the suggestion that there is only one language being spoken in any culture at a given time. However, as Barthes has noted, there are a number of languages within a culture, each stemming from the different positions subjects occupy at various times, or at the same time, within the culture. The result is an "inveterate war of languages."[15] In this way different languages are detrimental to cultural cohesion; they interrupt a shared language and system of meanings, placing the *pax culturalis* in jeopardy.[16] The absence of, or failure to achieve, collective meanings and common discourses thus threatens the maintenance of the cultural and social status quo.

The situation is problematized through the fact that just as there are many languages within a culture, so too there are many competing realities that are defined within and between ideologies that change over time. Complicating these connections is the acknowledgment that truth, like reality, is not a fixed concept. The resolution, then, to the problem of competing languages, realities, and truths resides within the dominant and overriding system of explanation and meanings that Barthes referred to in terms of an absence of language as *"what goes without saying."*[17] An end to the "war of languages" is arrived at through the imposition of the "meta-language of bourgeois mythology,"[18] which answers the question, posed above, "In whose voice did the veteran finally speak?" In the final stage of deconstruction the paradox outlined above dissolves into doxa.

The term "voice" is defined here in a way similar to that used by Bill

Nichols:, "By 'voice' I mean something narrower than style: that which conveys to us a sense of a text's social point of view, of how it is organizing the materials it is presenting to us. In this sense 'voice' is not restricted to any code or feature, such as dialogue or spoken commentary."[19] In one sense, then, "voice" is a metaphor for the ideological effects of the text. Ideology is not only inscribed in the articulations of the veteran, it is etched in the text itself, in the author's language, and the common effects of the cinematic apparatus that permit only certain authorized speakers a certain, limited, speech. To grant sovereignty to the text in this way is to agree with Barthes that *"all speech is on the side of the Law."*[20] Within this conception the veteran's utterances are a sentence—a form of penology, a conformist act. Yet to claim that all speech supports the dominant order is to ignore polysemy, and to deny those texts in which the veteran retrieves a voice from what Pierre Bourdieu calls the "silence of the doxa."[21] "Voice" is thus an ambivalent metaphor—it registers ideological effects and, in a different context, encodes the contestation of ideology.

An understanding of the manner by which what "goes without saying" came to be expressed by the veteran requires an explication and critique of the assumptions implicit in the textual construction of the veteran, and the historical circumstances that attended that construction. Such an analysis is aimed at answering the initial question—"Why was the veteran silenced?"—and begins with one of the earliest representations of the veteran.

Silencing the Messenger

The filmic veteran made his most prominent debut in *The Born Losers* (1967) in the character of Billy Jack (Tom Laughlin), Native American and ex-Green Beret.[22] The film did not augur well for the future of the veteran in mainstream fiction film, in fact it set a B-grade precedent that was to have prominence for the next few years.[23] In *The Born Losers*, the first in a cycle of Billy Jack films, Billy Jack confronts and defeats a gang of renegade motorcyclists that has terrorized the citizens of a small California coastal town. While this sketch suggests the actions of a figure easily appropriated by a law-and-order campaign, Billy Jack's excessive use of violence and the fact that he is, as the introductory voice-over narration informs the spectator, a "trained killer," position him outside acceptable society. When, at the end of the film, he is shot by a policeman, the audience recognizes that legitimate authority has been restored over the potentially wayward and dangerous veteran.

Central to the representation of the veteran in *The Born Losers* is the fact that he is pathetically incapable of speaking for himself. The character of Billy Jack is derived from the traditional cinematic Indian who expresses himself in an absurd pidgin composed of little more than "ugh" and "how." In one scene Billy Jack states: "I'm an Injun, we know how to strike secretly, silently." Silence and violence are the keys to the character of Billy Jack. During a standoff with a member of the motorcycle gang Billy Jack goads his opponent to violence with the words "Are you going to fight or talk me to death?" Billy Jack would rather fight than talk. In *The Trial of Billy Jack* (1974) the character is called upon to express himself in a different way—vocally, in court. And in *Billy Jack Goes to Washington* (1977), the final film in the series, his loquacity is his main weapon against government corruption. However, in *The Born Losers* Billy Jack abrogates the need to express himself verbally, a point that is reinforced early in the film with the opening voice-over being relied upon to inform the spectator of his history. The theme song of the biker/veteran film *Angels from Hell* (1968), "No Communication," ironically summarized the language void that enmeshed the Vietnam veteran. The laconic figure of Travis Bickle (Robert De Niro) in *Taxi Driver* (1976), and the inchoate ramblings of Jack Falen (Dennis Hopper) in *Tracks* (1976), subsequently did little to contest this impression of the veteran as a figure incapable of effective speech.

Silent, or lacking the verbal skills to communicate effectively, the veteran of these films found expression in the only avenue open to him: physical violence. In 1975 Julian Smith commented that the war in Vietnam had failed to inspire films about physically disabled veterans "perhaps because the psychic wounds have been deep enough (and because the returned soldiers have needed all their strength for striking back at a society that is depicted as having betrayed them)."[24] With the eventual change in attitude toward the veteran, the presence of physical disabilities became prominent as a motif for a society seemingly obsessed with the wounds of war. Yet, within its historical context, Smith's comment is accurate. In these early films the veteran's disability is almost exclusively and literally cerebral: an affliction of the cerebrum leading to psychosis and the loss of the ability to formulate language. Smith's observation also highlights another aspect of the early representation of the veteran: the veteran as violent victim. The characteristic is expressed in the veteran's positioning as an outsider in relation to established order—"neither for nor against, he is marked as a classless threat to the dominant values"[25]— who frequently expresses himself through acts of violence against the very order that sent him to Vietnam and ignores him on his return. The veteran-as-victim theme was to prove enduringly popular among the early representations of the Vietnam veteran, continuing until its apotheosis in the film *First Blood* (1982). Smith noted that the "two extremes (violent or victim)" were "so prevalent that Robert Jay Lifton felt the need, apparently, for a disclaimer in the subtitle of his study of the psychological impact of the war: *Home from the War; Vietnam Veterans: Neither Victims nor Executioners.*"[26]

Besides incoherence and inarticulation, the other aspect first associated in *The Born Losers* with the veteran, that of the presence of biker gangs, continued to figure prominently in the early representations of the veteran. The intersection of biker and veteran was exemplified and exploited in films in which the veteran fought against motorcycle gangs (*The Angry Breed*, 1968; *Satan's Sadists*, 1969; *Chrome and Hot Leather* and *The Hard Ride*, both 1971), and in those films featuring a Vietnam veteran as a member of a biker gang (*Motor Psycho*, 1965, *Angels from Hell*, 1968; *The Losers*, 1970). Film historian and Vietnam combat veteran Rick Berg has attributed this association to the position that the motorcycle gangs hold within popular culture. "Since *The Wild One* (1954), [such gangs] have come to signify a marginal and irreconcilable counter-culture, whose members work within the dominant culture but are hardly part of it."[27] Berg's analysis of the experiences of the Vietnam veteran on screen highlights the cultural readiness to represent the veteran as outsider. Berg's observations can be extended by analyzing the reasons behind the demonization and marginalization of the veteran and by examining why, during the early seventies, Vietnam war veterans were linked with bikers and not some other popularly marginalized group, such as the hippies.

Specifically, the equation of the veteran and bikers functioned to ensure that violence, together with marginality, would be associated with the veteran, a prejudicial assessment that increased in currency after the public disclosure of the events at My Lai. That the violence at My Lai was so excessive—so outside acceptable or accepted boundaries (even in war), and was therefore determinately insane—opened the way for a further demonization of the veteran as mentally deranged or psychotic. Indeed, the veteran is literally turned into a fiend in the execrable *Blood of Ghastly Horror* (1971) and *Deathdream* (1972, also known as *The Night Walk* and *Dead of Night*), both of which had release dates corresponding with the revelation of the full extent of the My Lai massacre.[28] This conflation of violence and psychosis proved to be immensely popular in mass-culture representations of the veteran during the early seventies. In a number of films, including *My Old Man's Place* (also known as *Glory Boy*), *The Visitors*, *Welcome Home Soldier Boys*, and *To Kill a Clown* (all 1972), the veteran is marked by the war in his murderous outbursts.

The cliché of the violent veteran reflecting the excessive violence of the war in Vietnam was also carried in various episodes of a number of television series, and can be traced through a variety of novels.[29] In other texts, including the films *The Crazy World of Julius Vrooder* (1974) and *Heroes* (1977), the veteran had overcome senseless violence, to be depicted as merely "senseless" or "crazy." The veteran's derangement was parodied in *The Stunt Man* (1978) in which Pirandelloesque techniques cunningly exposed the veteran's psychosis to be the result of the operation of a cinematic apparatus that ideologizes the everyday conditions of existence. Ironically, beyond the world of film the veteran was chided for having "adjusted too well" to postwar life.[30]

The willingness of the popular media during the late sixties and early seventies to construct and circulate images of demonized veterans is explicable within an historicization of the images. By the early seventies the nightly televised images of body bags and metal coffins signified a failed military venture in which the veteran, albeit the dead veteran, was, in effect, *screaming* to those who would hear of the immorality of the war and of its disastrous human toll. Articulations by veterans provided the potential to further damage the war effort by verbally reinforcing the same issues that the dead exemplified. In this relation, the voices of the Vietnam veterans, informed by the disruptive experience of war, were defined ideologically as a problem in relation to officially sanctioned impressions of the war. While the war was still being fought, the Nixon administration inadvertently conceded the influence of veterans' protest through its anxious yet transparent attempts at delegitimating the actions of antiwar veterans. In 1971, during a weeklong protest against the war organized by Vietnam Veterans Against the War called Operation Dewey Canyon III, named after a series of military operations in Vietnam, "veterans threw their medals at the White House in protest of a war that disgusted and degraded them." In response, "the Nixon administration implied that they weren't really veterans but actors." Similarly, during protests by Vietnam veterans at the Republican National Convention in Miami the following year, "the same administration pointed to [the veterans'] freshly scrubbed, non-veteran peers as a shining hope that would not 'stain America.'"[31]

Evidently, the news media at the time were also unwilling or incapable of accepting the reality of veterans' protest. For example, when veterans gathered in Detroit in February 1971 to publicly confess to having committed crimes related to their service in the war in Vietnam, the so-called Winter Soldier Investigations, CBS refused to screen film of the testimony and generally "[t]elevision barely covered the event. . . . "[32] In a footnote to his study of the media's coverage of the antiwar movement, media sociologist Todd Gitlin suggests that the testimony was not broadcast because, according to the networks, "antiwar veterans were not legitimate sources of jarring news."[33] Alternatively, however, the networks' refusal to screen the sessions points to the veterans' testimony as especially damaging to many of the political positions favored by the networks. Such testimony would have called into question a number of traditional American self-perceptions that were already being tested by the nightly revelations of the incidents at My Lai.

It is significant that during the early seventies, when negative representations of the veteran flourished, veterans' antiwar activity (a phenomenon that is often overlooked in accounts of the antiwar movement) was at its peak. Against this context, the negative media representations can be interpreted as reactions to the rise of veterans' political protest. At issue was the ability of the veteran to continue to protest America's intervention in foreign affairs in ways capable of threatening "not only the specific objectives in Vietnam but the viability—the good sense—of intervention based solely on an overdetermined, hyperpositivist commitment to what (has been called) 'mechanistic anticommunism.'"[34] In another way the veterans' experiences proved a cogent source of criticism of U.S. governmental policy. Contrary to the cliché that the returning veterans were spat upon by antiwar protestors (a view that attempts to deny that many veterans were members of the antiwar movement), the principal agent of mistreatment of the veterans was the U.S. government and its departments and agencies, among them the Veterans Administration, which failed to provide returning Vietnam veterans with adequate benefits and health care. The experience of this maltreatment was the basis of informed criticism by Vietnam veterans of governmental inaction on matters of priority for many veterans.

In effect, the mainstream media, by labeling the veterans as deviant, "damaged the credibility of the veterans as witnesses," as the media analyst Paul Camacho has noted.[35] "That is, regardless of the audience's momentary sympathy for this group, Vietnam veterans still end up victims of the mass produced images—they're crazy, or sick; they are damaged goods. Thus, their testimony about what really happened is nullified."[36] Depicted as mentally deranged, violently emotional, or hysterical, the veteran is forced into silence, the mark of hysteria.[37] The conclusion can, in many respects, be interpreted within the framework proposed by Stanley Cohen in his study of the British urban-youth subculture of the "Mods" and "Rockers" of the early sixties. "A condition, episode, person or group of persons emerges to become defined as a threat to societal values and interests," a threat that Cohen terms a "moral panic." As a result of the perceived threat, the media, functioning in support of the prevailing consensus, resorts to a demonization of those responsible, who thus become, in Cohen's term, "folk devils."[38]

The culture industries, of which the mainstream U.S. commercial cinema known as Hollywood is one, compete with other cultural or economic forces to establish a terrain upon which, and from which, they sell their products. To maximize profits, these industries customize their products to their perceptions and re-creations of the desires of spectators who consume or negotiate industrial cinema's message with every film ticket purchased. The limits on political and experiential horizons referred to as hegemony intervenes by restricting the available ideological space, in effect reinforcing commonsense assumptions by limiting the number of choices open to the audience through the perpetual circulation of clichéd commercially viable genres, formulas, and images. Threats to this status quo in which Hollywood has so much invested are either marginalized or "situat[ed] within the dominant framework of meanings" by a process that involves labeling. To paraphrase British sociologist Dick Hebdige, the veterans as folk devils were "*returned*, as they are represented . . . to the place where common sense would have them fit" as "violent," or "psychotic," or both.[39]

By continuing to circulate derogatory stereotypes, the culture passed judgment on the veterans' wartime experience: it was best forgotten, avoided, negated, or denigrated. This cultural attitude could have been summarized by the Vietnam-era soldier's lament: "Don't mean nuthin'." If the veterans' experience had any utility within the culture, it was restricted to serving as a pretext for psychosis or violence. However, a continuation of this process was, within the terms of common sense, not without its problems. The negative depiction of the veteran ran contrary to the "personalist epistemology" that has a "venerable history" within American representations. Specifically, derogatory images of the veteran contradicted "the American myth that an individual's experience must be significant."[40] The observation is extended through reference to Christopher Lasch's outline of cultural trends within the seventies. The representational privileging of the veteran as psychotic figure contradicted the "therapeutic sensibility" and the cultural need for images of well-being mapped by Lasch.[41] In this way what Lasch called the "culture of narcissism" provided a context for the "redemption" and rehabilitation of the Vietnam veteran leading to his representation in the service of certain cultural dispositions, particularly the need for unity. Through a process of renovation the veteran thus transcended the derogatory associations of the psychotic or sick figure. However, the veteran continued to be plagued by the lingering legacy of inarticulation, examples of which abound within textual representations of the Vietnam veteran.

"If I Only Had the Words"

In *The Deer Hunter* (1978) Cimino's directorial style fails to invest his characters with anything other than a rudimentary level of expression. In one scene Linda (Meryl Streep) asks of Michael (Robert De Niro): "Did you ever think life would turn out like this?" Michael's response is a perfect summation of his communicative abilities: an unelaborated "No." Michael's friends habitually rely on physical gestures such as backslapping or the use of expletives to express themselves—"fucking A" is the response by Axel (Chuck Aspergren) to most situations. Early in the film Steve's mother (Shirley Stoller) had begged of the local priest: "I do not understand, Father. I understand nothing anymore. Can you explain? Can anyone explain?" It is plain that within the film's context the question implies America's failure to understand the essential question "Why are we in Vietnam?" Unfortunately, the question "Can anyone explain?" becomes rhetorical under Cimino's direction. Exemplifying this situation, the prevalence of violence in American culture, elsewhere interpreted as one of the contributing factors for U.S. involvement in the war,[42] is reduced within the film to a puerile piece of sophistry. Preceding a deer hunt Michael holds up a bullet and "explains" to his friends: "This is this." The banal assertion unintentionally informs the spectator that Michael's understanding of violence and the role that it plays in his life is extremely limited. When Michael eventually renounces violence his only comment on this decisive action is, simply, "Okay."

Just as the film fails to present any reasons for U.S. involvement in Vietnam, so too it evades the need to understand the war itself. The old woman's question of the priest is repeated as the group of friends approach a returned Green Beret soldier at the wedding reception for Steve (John Savage) and Angela (Rutanya Alda). Michael's questions "Well, what's it like over there? Can you tell us anything?" are met with a terse "Fuck it!" The response points to "the major ideological problem of the film, Cimino can no more show Vietnam than the Green Beret can speak it."[43] Indeed the in-country segment of the film depicts the Vietnamese people, north and south alike, as devilishly Other, and the war as an inexplicable moral vacuum swallowing young Americans of good intentions.

One of the few references to the nature of the war, besides the implication that the South Vietnamese were not worthy allies, comes in the form of the metaphor of Russian roulette. The crucial scene in which despicably cruel North Vietnamese soldiers force American prisoners to "play" the game replicates, as H. Bruce Franklin points out, the "infamous historical sequence in which General Nguyen Ngoc Loan placed a revolver to the right temple of an NLF prisoner and killed him with a single shot."[44] *The Deer Hunter* manipulates this image to "reverse the roles of victim and victimizer."[45] The spurious nature of the metaphor is reinforced through the fact that the "game" is known as *Russian* roulette, an allusion that implicates broad geopolitical blocs within the Vietnam War in terms consistent with popular Cold War interpretations. As a comment on the war in Vietnam, the metaphor is lamentably inaccurate. The inadequacies of *The Deer Hunter* are further illustrated through reference to Cimino's failure to invest his characters with any opportunity to speak. In the initial roulette scene and in the subsequent scenes of the game being played in Saigon, speaking, other than the hysterical shouts of those betting on the outcomes, is absent. As a result of the violence Nick (Christopher Walken) experiences at the hands of his captors, he is excused from further attempts at speech by retreating into virtual catatonia.

Released the same year as *The Deer Hunter*, the film *Coming Home* explicitly addresses itself to giving the veteran a voice—in fact the film opens with physically disabled veterans speaking of their attempts to come to terms with their situation. Issues that *The Deer Hunter* failed to raise concerning the meaning of the war are here referred to in the course of the veterans' conversation. One paraplegic veteran comments: "You got to justify [the war] to yourself, so that you say it's okay. If you don't do that the whole thing is a waste." Pursuing this notion the film depicts various characters attempting to explain their wartime actions and seeking to address ways in which meaning can be retrieved from the experience of the war. On rest-and-recreation leave in Hong Kong, Bob (Bruce Dern) tells his wife, Sally (Jane Fonda): "I know what [the war is] like. I want to know what it is." Unfortunately, Bob's discoveries, if any, are not revealed. Later, when Sally receives a letter from Bob in Vietnam, Luke (Jon Voight) states: "Whatever he says, it's a hundred times worse." With this comment Luke expresses the position later popularized in representations of the veteran: "You had to be there." "Being there" was, within a variety of textual representations, to become an integrally necessary component for complete understanding of the war. However, Luke's response implies that despite his knowledge of war he is still incapable of communicating his understanding—and with this position the film comes perilously close to validating the suggestion "that the whole thing was a waste."

Devoid of effective communicative skills, Luke would seem an unlikely candidate to teach others of the meaning of the war. Nevertheless, this is exactly what the final scene of the film has him do. Addressing a group of high-school seniors, Luke is reduced to tears as he states: "[War] ain't like it is in the movies." Ironically, in this scene the film exposes its own inability to explain the war or the impact of the war. The result is the inescapable conclusion: it ain't like it is in *Coming Home*. In an overtly visual medium the picture of the weeping wounded veteran is meant to tell a thousand war stories. However, this picture inadvertently tells one story too many. The mise en scène of a weeping veteran in a wheelchair is intended to serve as a statement regarding the wounding impact of the war on U.S. culture. Yet another conclusion is available. The scene suggests that the experience of this particular war defies the veteran's language. Try as he might to express his experience, he is capable only of tears. The veteran is reduced to silence; the war remains unintelligible.

This conclusion is inconsistent with a film that from the beginning seeks to retrieve meaning from the war and to voice certain concerns. At one point in the narrative, at a meeting of the Marine Wives Club, Sally attempts to persuade the group to focus attention on the plight of disabled veterans by including photographs of their circumstances in the base's weekly newspaper. The widespread media denial or "silencing" of the veterans' cause is alluded to here when the group rejects Sally's proposal. Contrary to its own intentions, *Coming Home* contributes to the exclusionary silencing of the veteran that is criticized in this scene.

Like Luke Martin, the Vietnam veteran Emmett Smith in Bobbie Ann Mason's novel *In Country* (1987) is an unlikely teacher. Emmett's enthusiastic seventeen-year-old student Samantha Hughes seeks to uncover information concerning her father, who died in Vietnam, and, by extension, to understand the war. However, Sam's task is complicated by Emmett's reluctance to speak and by his refusal to consider that Sam will understand what he has to say. Emmett's stance is one that Mason criticizes elsewhere in her fiction. In Mason's "Big Bertha Stories" (1990) the strained relationship between Donald, a Vietnam veteran, and his wife, Jeanette, is illustrated by Donald's references to Vietnam, which Jeanette "didn't want to hear about." Pushed to her limit, Jeanette pleads, "[M]aybe I *could* understand if you'd let me." Donald's response, "You could never understand," allows him to retreat once again into silence. Later Jeanette adds: "I think you act superior because you went to Vietnam, like nobody can ever know what you know."[46] The perspicacious comment cuts to the crux of Donald's position and is reconstructed as the basis of Emmett's response to Sam's curiosity.

As with Jeanette, Sam is denied access to knowledge of the war because she is a woman. Emmett reinforces the gendered basis of exclusion when he adds: "Women weren't over there . . . so they can't understand." Emmett summarizes his excommunicatory attitude when he admonishes Sam to "stop thinking about Vietnam. . . . You don't know how it was, and you never will. There is no way you can ever understand. So just forget it. Unless you've been humping the boonies, you don't know." Refused access to the knowledge of the initiated, Sam seeks to recreate the experience of Vietnam by spending a night "in country" alone in a swamp near town. When Emmett finds her there the next morning, he merely repeats his earlier statements and in the process reinforces his own inability to offer Sam any assistance in her quest for understanding: "You think you can go through what we went through out in the jungle, but you can't."[47] Emmett, like the veteran Travis Bickle of *Taxi Driver* (1976), imprisoned in and by his own inability to express himself, is unable to communicate on any level. It is not surprising, then, that Emmett can no longer maintain a relationship with his companion, Anita.

While the characters in *The Deer Hunter* let the words of "God Bless America" speak for them, the words of Bruce Springsteen's ironic anthem "Born in the U.S.A.," a song that provides the novel's inscription and that features throughout the text, speak to Sam of the veterans' predicament. Springsteen's song of the disillusionment and disappointment facing a Vietnam veteran suits Emmett's current situation: "You end up like a dog that's been beat too much / Till you spend half your life just covering up."[48] "Covering up," literally and metaphorically, has become Emmett's chief preoccupation. Emmett spends much of his time digging a hole under the house, like "a foxhole to hide in" according to Sam.[49]

Emmett is not alone in this desire to hide from past experiences. The townspeople of the ironically named Hopewell also refuse to confront the past, and Sam's mother has moved away from town in an attempt to make a new life for herself, leaving behind the clothes and music records of her youth. Sadly, Sam's mother can "hardly even remember" her first husband, Sam's father.[50] Sam's paternal grandparents possess a vague memory of their son, but they fail to confront the person he became in Vietnam. The clues to this identity are contained in his wartime diary, which they refuse to read. To a degree, the silence that surrounds the past is a result of this failure to confront the past. "You get the feeling," comments one reviewer of the novel, that the townspeople would tell Sam "if only they could remember."[51] Alternatively, if they could tell her, they would remember. At fault for these characters is not their memory but their refusal or inability to talk. Memory suffers as speech, through which the collective memory is expressed, atrophies. Mason criticizes this situation by evoking the inane language of mass culture and its invasion of the thought and language of these characters. Language itself is impoverished, replaced by acronyms and brand names: MTV, FM, VA, TV, K-Mart, Dodge Dart, Coke, Burger Boy, Holiday Inn. The market culture is so intrusive that Emmett has named his pet cat after a commercial product: Moon Pie.

However, while Mason may be conscious of the impoverishment of language as a result of the commercialization of culture, her own prose also affects the characters' speech. The prose of the novel is pared to the level of a young adult novel. In one way, this characteristic is a reflection of Mason's ability to capture the language and thought of her young-adult heroine—however, all the characters and actions in this novel, written in the third person, are described in this language. The naiveté of the authorial voice is, for much of the novel, overdetermined; a problem not alleviated by Mason's recourse to the cliché that "veterans don't like to talk up their war experiences."[52] The result is the representation of characters who suffer a triple victimage: they are victims of the war, of their inability to adequately express themselves, and of the novel's inadequate language. In his victimage Emmett reflects the verbal incapacities of Luke Martin (Jon Voight) and presages the experiences of Nick (William Hurt), the veteran character in *The Big Chill* (1983), who is also unable to communicate effectively with those around him.

Like the other veterans described here, Nick is a failed instructor, though he had been an "on-air" radio psychologist, presumably able to communicate in a medium that demands eloquence. His background, however, is inconsistent with his present persona. The character lacks the ability to communicate; he is, in the vernacular, "off the air." Throughout the film Nick is taciturn, alternatively silent, or expressing himself laconically. The friends gathered at the home of Harold and Sarah (Kevin Kline and Glenn Close), ostensibly to mourn the death of a friend, revel in an orgy of conversation. In contrast, Nick retreats to the seclusion of the living room and films a conversation he has *with himself*. Another scene contrasts the group of friends noisily watching a football game on television while, at the same time, Nick is alone at the hosts' cabin listening, in silence, to the sound of bird calls. Elsewhere, Nick's inarticulacy is underscored when, while watching late-night television (ironically, and cruelly, Nick is obsessed, it seems, with the communicative potential of the electronic media), he is interrupted by Sam (Tom Berenger), who asks him what he is watching. Nick answers: "I'm not sure." When Sam asks, "What's it about?" the reply is brief: "I don't know."

In Coppola's film *Apocalypse Now* (1979) a narcotized hippie photojournalist played by Dennis Hopper (of course!) laments his inability to represent "Vietnam" in images or language. "If I only had the words," he rants in one scene. The inarticulacy of the character played by Hopper is emblematic of the veteran's verbal abilities in a range of representations. Nevertheless, despite the prevalence of the practice of silencing the veteran in texts from the seventies and eighties, the simultaneous operation of certain cultural and critical trends indicates that the practice was not universal. In a variety of texts during this time a number of interrelated assumptions concerning representations of the war functioned to reconstruct the veteran, ostensibly, as a spokesperson centrally placed to interpret the war and its impact on the American domestic scene. That this "change" was merely apparent is illustrated by the fact that far from being able to comment on a range of topics, the veteran was restricted to speaking of the culturally necessary topic of union. In this way the construction of the veteran as a "spokesperson" served to overcome the difficulties associated with the earlier representation of the veteran in which he was consistently denigrated and denied a voice. At the same time the veteran's articulacy offered an avenue for the promulgation of the homogenizing notion of unity.

A Unique War

The first step in the process that permitted the emergence of the veteran as a spokesperson or privileged interpreter was the circulation and wide acceptance of a definition of the war in Vietnam as a *unique* conflict. Definitions from a range of sources from the late seventies and early eighties attest to the popularity of this assumption. For example, Myra MacPherson included a chapter in her report *Long Time Passing: Vietnam and the Haunted Generation* (1984) that describes Vietnam as "a different war."[53] In 1981 Lance Morrow, feature writer of *Time* magazine, stated: "Viet Nam was different from other wars. . . . There were no front lines. Reality tended to melt into layers of unknowability. The same person could be a friend and an enemy."[54] Similar comments on recent history came from various quarters. In a typical observation, made in 1980, one commentator preempted *Time* by arguing that the Vietnam War was unique in U.S. military history:

> Soldiers who did enlist or submitted to the draft marched not toward linear objectives ("On to Berlin!") but in circular, inconclusive patrols. Their goal was not the war's end but the duration of three hundred and sixty-five days in the country. . . . Operations were conducted high on grass to the tune of transistorized rock and roll; barracks yielded to apartments or hootches with black light and stereo. Enemies blended with friendlies. There was no front, and no heroes' welcome home for a job well done. Nothing from previous wars seemed to apply.[55]

However, it was Michael Herr's *Dispatches* and the almost universal critical acclaim that the book has received since its publication in 1977 that helped to circulate and make acceptable a definition of the war in Vietnam as unique. Herr's frequent use of hyperbole evokes the impression that this war was unlike any other. In Herr's terms casualties were "unbelievable," and firefights focused "all the dread ever known, *ever* known by *everyone* who *ever* lived."[56] The terrain upon which the war was fought defied typography and normal expectations: the Vietnamese highlands were "spooky, unbelievably spooky, spooky beyond belief."[57] Fredric Jameson argues that the "extraordinary linguistic and representational power" of *Dispatches* exceeds that of previous representations of war. For Jameson, Herr "does not merely *express* the nightmare of the Vietnam War, [he] substitutes a textual equivalent for it."[58] In Herr's interpretation, the war in Vietnam was without precedent in its surreal, unnerving, and finally apocalyptic quality. The quality of uniqueness Herr found in the war was echoed in the Vietnam War novel *No Bugles, No Drums* (1978) by Charles Durden in which the central character, Jamie Hawkins, comments: "Maybe everybody's war is the worst. But I'm here to tell you . . . if the next one is any more fucked up than this one I don't want to know nothin' from nothin'."[59] Walter Capps reiterated the common perception of the war as unique when he wrote that "the Vietnam War did not mean what other wars meant."[60]

It is notable that the assertion of the uniqueness of the war in Vietnam ignores the many parallels that can be drawn between the conflict and earlier wars. The Vietnam author Tim O'Brien elaborated this perception when he commented that "it's very nice and easy to say that Vietnam was special because it was formless and absurd. But certainly World War I must've seemed equally chaotic and absurd to Siegfried Sassoon or Robert Graves or Rupert Brooke or Erich Remarque."[61] O'Brien reinforced this position in his novel *Going After Cacciato* (1980) in which two characters, Doc and Captain Rhallon, discuss whether the war in Vietnam was different from other wars fought by Americans.[62] Although both sides of the argument are presented, O'Brien agrees that he gives Doc's side more credence. Doc's position, O'Brien argues, is that "war kills and maims and rips up the land and makes orphans and widows. These are the things of war. . . . I'm saying that the feel of war is the same in Nam or Okinawa—the emotions are the same, the same fundamental stuff is remembered."[63]

Despite their cogency, comparisons such as O'Brien's, based on the experience of combat, have not dispelled assertions of the singularity of Vietnam. Many claims of the uniqueness of the "Vietnam experience" ignore combat conditions and are based on references to exceptional levels of discrimination faced by soldiers returning to the United States from Vietnam. While simple comparisons demonstrate the sad reality that the veterans of *all* wars are treated badly,[64] the absence of such comparisons favored the continual assertion that the war in Vietnam was unique. Those who sought to define what they saw as the exceptional qualities of the conflict resorted to referring to it as a war to end all modern wars: a postmodern war.

Early in the war Norman Mailer referred (in a statement that has since been commonly cited) to what he perceived as the different—postmodern—basis of the war. "If World War II was like *Catch–22*, this war will be like *Naked Lunch*. Lazy Dogs, and bombing raids from Guam. Marines with flame throwers. Jungle gotch in the gonorrhea and South Vietnamese girls doing the Frug. South Vietnamese fighter pilots 'dressed in black flying suits and lavender scarves' (*The New York Times*)."[65] The experiential uniqueness of the Vietnam War was, for Mailer, summarizable in a shift in literary forms—from *Catch 22* to *Naked Lunch*. Mailer's assumption that this unique war demanded forms of representation capable of depicting its alleged exceptional qualities became widespread in critical and textual circles and is clearly evident within Herr's *Dispatches*.[66] Herr argued that conventional written histories were incapable of adequately representing this war. He decried "traditional historical analysis" as "[s]traight history, auto-revised history, history without handles" in which "something wasn't even answered, it wasn't even asked. . . ." According to Herr, the bankruptcy of "straight history" demanded fictive techniques capable of unlocking the "secret history"[67] to reveal the *truth*.

The encoding of such critical assumptions within *Dispatches* placed it centrally within the field of texts referred to as the "new journalism." Mailer's account of the 1967 March on the Pentagon, *The Armies of the Night* (1968), reproduced the dominant suppositions of this style of journalism. Mailer argued that "an explanation of the mystery of the events at the Pentagon cannot be developed by the methods of history—only by the instincts of the novelist." Therefore, although his "collective novel" is "written in the cloak of an historic style, and . . . scrupulous to the welter of a hundred confusing and opposed facts," it "unashamedly enter[s] that world of strange lights and intuitive speculation which is the novel." According to Mailer, a unique, inherently mysterious event requires a form of representation that mixes the techniques of traditional narrative history with what he calls "interior" history.[68] Only by the fusion of "fact" and "fiction" is it possible to excavate the "truth" of the experience.

In keeping with Mailer's technique, the war in Vietnam—widely considered to be unique—was commonly represented within "stories" that combined fact and fiction to reveal "truth." Graham Greene, for example, opened *The Quiet American* (1955) with the ironic disclaimer that he was not writing "history" but a "story." Lederer and Burdick's *The Ugly American* (1958) closed with a "Factual Epilogue" in which they argued that they had written "not just an angry dream, but rather the rendering of fact into fiction." Robin Moore asserted that his book of nine stories, *The Green Berets* (1965), "blended fact and fiction" to produce "a book of truth."[69] Similarly, during the seventies and eighties "the fictional and quasi-fictional works of Phil Caputo, Tim O'Brien, C. D. B. Bryan, Frederick Downs, James Webb, Mark Baker, Al Santoli, John Del Vecchio, Anthony Grey, and Peter Goldman and Tony Fuller have all been prefaced by the same implicit or explicit rejection of 'formal history.'"[70] In each of these texts a central element reinforces the veracity of the representations. The feature is rarely articulated in criticisms of texts of the war, suggesting that the characteristic is taken for granted as common sense. The implicit element is summarized in the phrase "You had to be there."

You Had to Be There

According to the assumption "You had to be there," only those who experienced the war in Vietnam can legitimately lay claim to the truth of the conflict. This empiricist position is reflected in the fact that texts praised by critics as harboring the "real war" were typically, if not exclusively, written by authors who either participated in the war as soldiers or witnessed it firsthand as journalists. The emphasis on "being there," then, delegitimates nonparticipant accounts of the war, no matter how authentic they may seem. There would be no *Red Badge of Courage* from Vietnam. Indeed the pervasiveness and tenacity of the assumption that "you had to be there" quite likely contributed to the fact that it wasn't until 1989, with the publication of Susan Fromberg Schaeffer's *Buffalo Afternoon*, that a novel dealing with the war by a nonparticipant was published to popular and critical acclaim.[71] In another way the construction of participation as the guarantee of truth ignores and erases the limitations on knowledge encountered in Vietnam. Tim O'Brien has summarized the effect on the troops of these limitations in a passage from his book *Going After Cacciato* (1980) entitled "The Things They Did Not Know":

> They did not have targets. They did not have a cause. They did not know if it was a war of ideology or economics or hegemony or spite. . . . They did not know the names of villages. They did not know which villages were critical. They did not know strategies. They did not know the terms of war,

its architecture, the rules of fair play. When they took prisoners, which was rare, they did not know the questions to ask, whether to release a suspect or beat on him. They did not know how to feel. . . . They did not know good from evil.[72]

"As any Civil War historian will tell us," notes one observer, a claim to comprehensibility and understanding based on personal participation "is not a particularly compelling argument."[73] Despite this admonition, literary texts and documentary films such as CBS's *Christmas in Vietnam* (1965), and the independent productions *The Anderson Platoon* (1967) by Pierre Schoendorffer and *A Face of War* (1968) by Eugene Jones, privileged the "GI's experience of the war . . . as the moment of authenticity and knowledge—of authenticity as knowledge—upon which the war can be evaluated and validated."[74] However, it was not only the GI who had access to this unmediated experience, as memoirs by "in-country" nurses and volunteers suggest. Kathryn Marshall, for example, argues that the stories told by women nurses and volunteers who served in Vietnam produce a sense of "the real."[75]

Similarly, Michael Herr proposes that as a participant journalist he "experienced" the war and witnessed its essential truth. Only by being there, and keeping your eyes open, would the mysteries of the conflict be revealed. Speech was incapable of this task. Herr describes Vietnam as a place where speech was absent, abandoned on entry into the country: "The departing and arriving [troops] passed one another without a single word being spoken."[76] Herr reflects on the poverty of speech when he observes that "sometimes an especially smart grunt or another correspondent would . . . ask me what I was *really* doing there, as though I could say anything honest about it. . . . " He characterizes the talk of reasons for "being there" as "overripe bullshit." His reason for being in Vietnam was simple: he was there "to watch."[77] The emphasis throughout *Dispatches* on eyes and seeing reinforces the notion that the war had to be seen for oneself. Nevertheless, as Herr contends, it was possible to see "far too much." The result, madness, is, ironically, reflected in a person's eyes. As one soldier states, referring to a "crazy" soldier in his squad, "All's you got to do is look in his eyes, that's the whole fucking story right there." Herr notes that the eyes of the marines at Khe Sanh "were always either strained or blazed-out or simply blank, they never had anything to do with what the rest of the face was doing, and it gave everyone the look of extreme fatigue or even a glancing madness."[78] During the battle for the citadel at Hue, "[a] little boy of about ten came up to a bunch of Marines. . . . He was laughing, and moving his head from side to side in a funny way. The fierceness in his eyes should have told everyone what it was, but it had never occurred to most of the grunts that a Vietnamese child could be driven mad too."[79]

The dangers associated with seeing too much leave Herr with an ambivalent attitude: "[Y]ou want to look and you don't want to look." Herr's ambivalence forces him to detail the problems of bearing witness:

> I went [to Vietnam] behind the crude but serious belief that you had to be able to look at anything, serious because I acted on it and went, crude because I didn't know, it took the war to teach it, that you were as responsible for everything you saw as you were for everything you did. The problem was that you didn't always know what you were seeing until later, maybe years later, that a lot of it never made it in at all, it just stayed stored there in your eyes.[80]

For Herr, part of the knowledge derivable from "having been there" is that what is seen can never be articulated—"it just stayed stored there in the eyes," a perception that reinforces the suggestion that only those who participated and witnessed the war can fully understand an experience that is otherwise untranslatable.

The film *The Green Berets* (1968) initiated the basic assumption, raising it to the level of an imperative, that only those who were "there" can hope to understand the truth the war was capable of revealing. Confronted by a journalist (David Janssen) skeptical of the value of American involvement in Vietnam, a Green Beret colonel (John Wayne) asks: "Have you ever been to Southeast Asia?" When the journalist responds that he hasn't, the colonel ends the discussion and walks away in disgust. With this exchange the film unproblematically insists that only those who have experienced the war can judge it or speak of it. The point becomes explicit when the colonel states: "It's pretty hard to talk to anyone about [the war] till they've come over and seen it." The colonel's position returns him, the journalist, and the audience to silence. The problem is reproduced in John Ketwig's memoir . . . *And a Hard Rain Fell* (1985) in the statements "If you were there, you'll know. If you weren't you never will," and "The strangest things happened [in Vietnam], and everybody just sort of shuffled by and accepted it, you can't explain it to someone who wasn't there."[81]

William Broyles, Jr., reinforced this conclusion in his account of a trip to postwar Vietnam. Broyles deduced from his visit "that I had more in common with my old enemies than with anyone except the men who had fought at my side. My enemies and I had something almost beyond words."[82] The function of the exclusion, as Susan Jeffords has observed, "aligns [Broyles] with all men who fought in battle, for whatever side, against all those who took the 'part of staying behind.'"[83] Within this position those who weren't there are the real enemy—they weren't there, they'll never know, and they should thus remain silent. Philip Caputo, author of the Vietnam memoir *A Rumor of War* (1978), upheld this perception when he stated: "I feel . . . the only people who have a *right* to say anything against the war . . . were the ones who were there."[84] The strategy of delegitimating oppositional voices through recourse to "being there" is evident within a number of texts.

In the revisionist film *Hamburger Hill* (1987), for example, the peace movement is consistently criticized for holding what are in the film's terms, ill-informed opinions. However, the strategy of denigration was most clearly enunciated by the character of John Rambo within the film *First Blood* (1982). Rambo's virulent outburst against the demonstrators at the airport on his return to the United States after the war is explicit: "Who are they unless they've been me and been there and know what the hell they're yelling about?" The exclusionary emphasis here would not only deny antiwar opposition; the outcome of the position is to lose "sight of every individual's responsibility to pursue their own, albeit informed, opinion on ethical and moral issues: perplexity and timidity are encouraged."[85] To resist or abandon the emphasis on "being there" is, therefore, the first step in the emergence of an effective, politically astute voice for the veteran. Indeed, the Vietnam Veterans Memorial, a site that "speaks" to many veterans of the experience of the war and that encodes a variety of political perspectives, was designed by a nonparticipant in the war, Maya Lin. The practical outcome of Lin's simple admission—"I don't think you have to live through a trauma to understand it"[86]—effectively subverts and revises the strategy of denigrating antiwar protest implicit within an emphasis on participation in the war as the basis of a right to pass judgment on the conflict.

The critical force of Lin's position is, however, eroded within the continual assertion of variations of the supposition "You had to be there". Throughout the literature of the Vietnam War the narrating of "war stories," the vehicle of truth according to participants in the war and Vietnam authors and their critics, functions to extend the emphasis on being there as an epistemological necessity. Herr recounts a war story he heard in Vietnam that encapsulates a truth that only those who were there can understand:

> "Patrol went up the mountain. One man came back. He died before he could tell us what happened."
>
> I waited for the rest, but it seemed not to be that kind of story; when I asked him what had happened he just looked like he felt sorry for me, fucked if he'd waste time telling stories to anyone as dumb as I was.[87]

The simplicity of the story is repeated in the shortest of all war stories, the line "There it is," which is deemed to contain a truth so patent that explanation is unnecessary. In this case, as Philip Beidler has pointed out in relation to another war story, "A lesson, a message, a truth, in sum, could come off as so simple that it seemed a kind of Orphic movement to the very fulcrum of reality."[88] Stories heard in war and the narrating of war stories in forms that conflate fact and fiction have traditionally informed accounts of war. The process that Vietnam author Stephen Wright describes as the transformation of "crude fact" into an "imaginative truth" is pronounced in narratives of World War I.[89] Robert Graves had summarized this process when he wrote that "the memoirs of a man who went through some of the worst experiences of trench warfare are not truthful if they do not contain a high proportion of falsities."[90]

Obvious traces of this literary tradition are exposed in narratives of the Vietnam War, notably in the nonfiction and fictional work of Tim O'Brien, who cunningly manipulates Walt Whitman's ironic suggestion that the true story of a war is never told by anyone who was there. O'Brien's contradictions of authenticity, inauthenticity, fact and fiction, truth and lies expose the basis of all "war stories." In his memoir *If I Die in a Combat Zone* (1980), O'Brien asks, "Can the foot soldier teach anything important about war, merely by having been there? I think not. He can tell war stories."[91] In *Going After Cacciato*, after listing the things that U.S. soldiers in Vietnam "did not know," O'Brien concludes that these features would not be included in war stories since "uncertainties [were] never articulated in war stories."[92] On one level, O'Brien subverts the notion that participation in the war is a requirement of knowledge (there were many things the soldiers did not know). On another level, participation provides the experiences that form the raw materials that are reconfigured into the essential truths of a war story. O'Brien details the necessity of participation and the transformation of knowledge into truth in the chapter "How To Tell a True War Story" from his book *The Things They Carried* (1991). Throughout the chapter O'Brien states variations of the conclusion that "[i]n war you lose sense of the definite, hence your sense of truth itself, and therefore it's safe to say that in a true war story nothing is ever absolutely true."[93] The point of such assertions resides in Whitman's emphasis on experience as the basis of authenticity and knowledge: "I am the man, I suffer'd, I was there."

William Broyles, Jr., concurs. In an article with the notorious title "Why Men Love War," he argues that the purpose of a war story "is not to enlighten but to put the listener in his place." That the teller of the tale participated in the war and that the listener did not are the only facts that matter. "Everything else is beyond words to tell."[94] Broyles's emphasis on war stories as lies, but lies that "have a moral, even a mythic, truth, rather than a literal one" was disputed by Harry Maurer in the introduction to his book *Strange Ground: An Oral History of Americans in Vietnam, 1945–1975* (1990).[95] Maurer sought to "keep his bullshit detectors out" and to include in his volume only those accounts he perceived as factual. His aim was to "minimize the mythic truth and stay close to what happened."[96] The effect of Maurer's claim that oral testimony would replace the "mythic truth" with fact—the undisputed truth—privileged the large number of oral accounts of the war and formed the basis of the veterans' legitimate right to speak of the reality and, in particular, the truth of the "Vietnam experience."[97]

In his analysis of the "special privilege" accorded the author function within oral histories of the war, John Carlos Rowe comments that "the author's credibility is generally established both by his direct experience of the War *and* his criticism of American conduct in the War. These credentials are generally supported by the popular American mythology of the 'author' as a 'free agent,' who assumes full responsibility for his statements and intentions."[98] The sense of responsibility that Rowe points to is explicit in Maurer's insistence that by asking the contributors to *Strange Ground* "to in effect sign their names to what they said" he would lessen the likelihood of invention and assumption passing as truth.[99] In the preface to *Vietnam: The Heartland Remembers* (1989), an oral history of Oklahomans who served in Vietnam, Stanley Beesley claims the status of a free agent, and accepted the responsibility it involves when he states: "No commission appointed me. No governmental agencies nominated me. No organizations asked me to represent them. No foundations financed the project. No groups bankrolled the book."

Implicit within this statement is the suggestion that editorial decisions were not tainted or influenced by the pressures of partisan sponsorship. Beesley reinforces this position when he asserts: "No single political bent is represented within. I resisted attempts to flavor the book with dogma."[100]

Such assurances function to reinforce the authority of Beesley's text by suggesting that the project provides virtually unmediated access to veracious accounts of the war and the home front scene. Contrary to the implicit assurances of editorial noninterference, however, the four parts to Beesley's work—beginning with the process of volunteering, through descriptions of the war, and impressions of what is defined as an alien and threatening countryside, to the final section, "Getting Home"—reflect a structure common to many oral histories of the war. The pattern of Beesley's text mirrors, for example, Mark Baker's *Nam: The Vietnam War in the Words of the Men and Women Who Fought There* (1982), which, as Rowe notes, "follows precisely the recognizable features of what literary critics term the *Bildungsroman*, or 'novel of education.'" Baker organizes the contents of his work "under the following large headings: INITIATION, OPERATIONS, WAR STORIES, THE WORLD. [The] paradigm is that of mythic heroism, in which the hero undergoes a process of 'initiation' by means of struggle and heroic contest." The result is that the hero "returns from his spiritual and physical ordeal to 'the world' having achieved his identity as hero and subsequently *realizing* that identity more fully in the deeds he performs back in the world: lifting the plague, solving the riddle, restoring social order."[101]

Accompanying the realization of this new identity is the depoliticization of the veteran's voice. For example, despite Beesley's insistence on editorial nonpartisanship, he admits that he had planned "to include a draft dodger [the refusal to specify draft *resistance* is common], but I couldn't find the heart for it. Not in a book from the point of view of those who went."[102] Having "gone" leaves no room, it seems, for oppositional moral or political stances. Al Santoli reinforces this conclusion when, in his editorial preface to *Everything We Had* (1982), a work he claims to be the first oral history of the war in Vietnam, he states: "The American people have never heard in depth from the *soldiers themselves* the complicated psychic and physical realities of what they went through in Vietnam."[103] Santoli's humanism elides the political through an emphasis upon the "psychic and physical." Politics, the expression of power relationships *between* people, is displaced within a focus that presents history at the level of individual actions. This depoliticized voice becomes part of the veteran's new identity, which, as Rowe points out, is achieved through the act of restoring and renovating a social order disrupted and divided by the war. In this way the essential truth alluded to in these texts is beyond politics; it is a transcendental, unifying truth. Specifically, as the following discussion elaborates, it is the truth of *unity*.

Teaching the Truth

The assertion of unity—of the reality and *truth* of unity—was especially pronounced in the early and mid-eighties. The articulation of this truth by the Vietnam veteran positioned him as the bearer of an essential and immutable characteristic of culture. The recuperative power of this message for the veteran was tremendous. Represented as the embodiment of the notion of incorporation, the veteran was no longer an outsider. The veteran had arrived at this position through the operation of a series of interrelated cultural assumptions beginning with the notion that Vietnam was a unique war. These aspects of common sense and, more important, the uses to which they were put are exemplified in Walter Capps's *The Unfinished War* (1982 and 1990). Capps begins from the position that the war was unique,[104] and as a result he considers a focus on the veteran the best way to interpret the exceptional conflict. In chapter 5, "The Combatants," the narrative is donated to lengthy quotations from veterans. Capps believes that it is within "[t]he autobiographical literature" that "the story of the war in Vietnam is being told."[105] He stresses the "disillusionment and ambivalence" felt by the soldiers in Vietnam, which increased on their return to the United States.[106] It is here that Capps's own comments and those of the people he chooses to quote revert to an earlier stereotype: the veteran as victim.

Introducing this theme, Capps asserts that returning veterans met the "spittle of the anti-war protesters lining their pathway,"[107] which is a story found in a number of sources concerned with documenting veterans' experiences. For example, Bob Greene organizes his book *Homecoming: When the Soldiers Returned from Vietnam* (1989) into sections that include the titles: "Yes, it did happen. . . . It happened to me" and "I was never spat upon."[108] The prevalence of references to this experience may prove the validity of the claim. However, the prominence of the assertion also betrays the position of authors who choose to deny veterans any form of agency that would allow them, metaphorically, to "spit" back. In Capps's text there is no mention of antiwar veterans, and antiwar protestors are the rabble that met the returning soldiers with "jeers, taunts, tomatoes, and spittle"[109]—a characterization that comes very close to Rambo's verbal assault on the "maggots at the airport, protesting me, calling me all kinds of vile crap." Capps also avoids any mention of struggle or protest within the army: "fragging," desertion, and acts of disobedience and non-compliance are all absent.

Having defined the veteran as victim, Capps is able to assume that the veteran has firsthand knowledge of anguish and hurt. As a result of this knowledge, the veteran, according to Capps, was uniquely positioned to interpret the postwar confrontation with suffering: the situation referred to as healing. Capps combines the separate experiences of individual veterans into a narrative supportive of the need for healing. Here the figure of the veteran, constructed from many individuals to be a representative of universal human experience, contradicts the historical reality of the veterans' variegated voices. No sooner had the veteran put down one of "the heaviest burdens of the war," in Capps's words, than he was asked to shoulder the weight of leading American society through the task of reunification. Capps's suggestion that "the [national] collective healing process must follow a similar course" to the "acts of confession" that are "taking place daily" in the centers of the national Veterans' Outreach program positions Vietnam veterans as leaders of a form of cultural catharsis leading to national unification. From a battered victim suffering "shock," "disorientation," and especially, "disillusionment," the veteran of the war in Vietnam becomes a model for confessional practices capable of revealing the truth of unity.[110]

The emphasis on the transformation of the veteran into an authentic spokesperson articulating cultural unity is especially pronounced in Oliver Stone's *Platoon* (1986), a film that relies on realistic effects to ensure the experiential truth of the message articulated by the central character, Chris Taylor (Charlie Sheen). The critical reaction to the film supported the perception that, at last, the "real story" of the Vietnam War had been told,[111] and reviewers frequently mentioned Stone's war experience as a crucial element in approving the film's realism. This aspect of Stone's autobiography was exploited in the narrative image of the film—indications of a film's story, its stars, and its director circulated to a potential audience by means of promotional material and reviews[112]—

which included a print advertisement featuring photographs of Stone on duty in Vietnam.

Such extratextual claims to authenticity are supported within the film by the conceit that fiction can be true only if it recreates experience in minute detail. In an attempt to ensure the self-evidentiary aspects of filmic reality, Stone recreates the "things-as-they-really-are" style of documentary films. The audience of documentary film tends to presume "a privileged status for the indexical link between sign and referent" within the documentary text.[113] Documentary claims the status of direct observation; to reproduce, rather than represent, "the facts." The documentary film staple of talking heads, direct address by authoritative figures through interview procedures (or, figures whose authority is validated by the documentary form), supports the notion that documentary films have a pedagogical purpose. Reinforcing this notion, Chris Taylor's voice-over narration, meant to represent the contents of letters he writes to his grandmother, approximates the omniscient instructional voice-of-God narration of many documentary films. Further, the frequent exchanges between Barnes (Tom Berenger) and Elias (Willem Dafoe) equate to the process of interviews in certain documentary films. The replication of documentary interview techniques is, however, most pronounced in a confrontation in a bunker frequented by the platoon's doper "heads" in which Barnes indirectly asks Elias a series of questions focusing on the central issue of "Who do you think you are?"

The camera work of *Platoon* also replicates the methods and techniques of certain forms of documentary film. Use of hand-held cameras in jungle scenes, replete with leaves flapping against the lens on jungle patrols, and a shaking frame following explosions, evokes a style of documentary filmmaking initiated with cinema vérité and direct cinema. However, *Platoon* surpasses the documentary style through the employment of the shot/reverse shot camera technique: a method in which a second shot traces the field from which an establishing shot is assumed to have been taken. The powerful effect of this technique is to present "reality" in an apparently unmediated way. The camera's presence is effaced from the screen as the spectator is presented with a three-hundred-sixty-degree field of vision as opposed to the more common one-hundred-eighty-degree plane of sight. Stone employs the technique on at least one occasion in a scene depicting the platoon's search for enemy bunkers hidden in the jungle.

In an attempt to ensure realism in all aspects of his film, Stone employed Captain Dale Dye, retired, a Vietnam veteran, and the services of his film consultancy company "Warriors Inc." to work in association with his directorial team. In preparation for the film, Dye led the actors through a training course in the jungle of the Philippines. "In Stone," asserted *Time* magazine, "Dye found a kindred spirit who wanted *Platoon*'s actors to experience the fatigue, frayed nerves and fear that preyed on the Viet Nam infantryman and to understand the casual brutality that often emerged." According to *Time*, Dye's consultancy resulted in "the authenticity of every detail, from Barnes' wicked dagger ('Worn upside-down for quicker killing,' Dye explains) to the proper use of white plastic C-ration spoons."[114] During his Oscar-acceptance speech for *Platoon*, Stone stated: "I think that what you're saying [through the presentation of the award] is that for the first time you really understand what happened over there."[115] Only after watching his film could audiences understand what "really" occurred in Vietnam.

The services of Warriors Inc. were also called upon by director Patrick Duncan to aid the production of his film *84 Charlie Mopic* (1989), which, like *Platoon*, seeks to efface its own fictionality by presenting itself as a documentary. The film concerns a U.S. reconnaissance unit in Vietnam on a patrol accompanied by a cameraman who is filming the actions of the unit for an army training film. Notably, Duncan's film erases the distance between spectator and object maintained in Coppola's *Apocalypse Now* and Kubrick's *Full Metal Jacket*. In *Apocalypse Now* a news camera team, which includes Coppola in an acting role, films soldiers during a battle; in *Full Metal Jacket* Kubrick includes a scene in which a film crew interviews his principal characters. The effect of these scenes is to intrude upon the spectator's suspension of disbelief, distancing the spectator from the object and thus relieving the spectator, briefly, from his or her positioning as subject. In this way the acceptance of the world of the film as commonsensical, real, taken for granted is disrupted by self-reflexive moments that function to fullfil the call of the Russian formalist critic Victor Shklovsky in "'making strange' the world."[116] In contrast, *84 Charlie Mopic* returns the spectator to the position of subject of the powerful ideology of realism through the elimination of traces of its own textuality.

One reviewer of *84 Charlie Mopic* asked: "Why did we need a fictional re-creation of a Vietnam documentary? The genuine articles exist."[117] Such a comment overlooks the place of this film, and others like *Platoon*, within the movement toward capturing the "real truth" of the experience of the war in Vietnam. According to the assumptions already outlined, texts that re-create the "secret history" of the war have "more to say," that is, they are supposedly capable of teaching us more, than documentary texts that present "straight" historical accounts. Given this assumption, the conflation of documentary and fictional styles produces texts such as *84 Charlie Mopic* and *Platoon*, which authoritatively and truthfully present the lessons of the war. Duncan, like Stone, sustained this assumption through reference to the fact that he is a Vietnam veteran. "I was in [the war], I felt it from the inside, and I express it from within," Duncan asserted.[118] Duncan's emphasis on factual and truthful instruction (which is supported diagetically—the film being made in *84 Charlie Mopic* is an instructional film) is reinforced in *Platoon*'s presentation of the veteran as a teacher of the lessons of war.

In the introduction to the published film script of *Platoon* Stone underlined the fact that there are many truths of the Vietnam War but maintained the existence of an overriding truth—his own. Stone commented that he wrote the film script "as straight as I could remember it," asserting that, as a result, he had captured the truth of the war.[119] During the filming, he hoped that he would not fail the veterans who had admonished him "not to ruin their dreams that the truth be told."[120] The truth articulated within *Platoon* is summarized in Taylor's final voice-over soliloquy in which he observes that "we did not fight the enemy, we fought ourselves." The comment is repeated in various forms throughout the discourse of "Vietnam," its continual repetition pointing to something that lies deep within the culture beyond the ethnocentrism encoded within the remark. Taylor's statement rewrites the Russian roulette scenes of *The Deer Hunter* in which Americans are depicted as the victims of the North Vietnamese, to suggest self-victimization: the war becomes "something that Americans did to themselves."[121] In *Platoon* the allusion to suicidal tendencies within Taylor's comment intersected with the notion of a fratricidal malaise (Americans fighting one another) to reinforce the conclusion that it was morally wrong for Americans to fight themselves and that such a "civil war" should not recur.

Taylor's most engaging words, however, concern his desire "to teach to others what we know and to try to find a goodness and meaning to this life." Here in a documentary form that the audience expects to be instructive Stone delivers *Platoon*'s ultimate lesson: that it is imperative that the veteran become a teacher and guide to unity on the home front.[122] Chris Taylor must return to impart the knowledge (the truth) that he has learned in Vietnam: that Americans should not fight among themselves, that unity and consensus must be maintained. The veteran had not only found a voice, he was virtually condemned to speak of *unity*.

The Voice of Unity

The construction of the veteran as spokesperson points to the changes that the representation of the veteran had undergone in a relatively short space of time. At the end of *Coming Home* the veteran fails to teach the lesson of "Vietnam." In *Platoon*, released only eight years later, the veteran is clearly defined in a teaching role and is unequivocal in the nature of the lesson to be taught. The end of *Platoon*'s lesson came in Oliver Stone's subsequent representation of the impact of the war, *Born on the Fourth of July* (1989), in which the wounded veteran Ron Kovic (Tom Cruise) is especially vociferous. Kovic's wound needs to be healed and since the VA and medical science cannot help, he turns to frequent tirades against the war and his predicament. In a manner different from, but seeking the same effect as, the psychoanalytic technique by the same name, Kovic's solution is a talking cure. In this way the Kovic character in *Born on the Fourth of July* represents the end of the various maneuvers involved in the construction of the articulate veteran. As a result, it is not surprising to note that earlier attempts to produce the film proved unsuccessful.[123] The construction of the veteran as a vocal figure was a process spanning two decades. By the time *Born on the Fourth of July* was eventually produced, the veteran had already been endowed with a voice that he was able to fully employ in his role of teaching the truth of unity.

The construction of a definition of the Vietnam veteran as one who teaches the lesson of unity was discursively reinforced and expanded within a number of speeches made by President Reagan during the eighties. On Veterans Day 1988 during a ceremony at the Vietnam Veterans Memorial, Reagan spoke of the Vietnam veteran as someone who can offer "a lesson in living love." In this the veteran becomes an exemplar of camaraderie, patriarchy and, finally, patriotism. "Yes, for all of them, those who came back and those who did not, their love for their families lives. Their love for their buddies on the battlefields and friends back home lives. Their love of their country lives." According to Reagan, the veteran was also a figure capable of healing: "Perhaps we are finding . . . new strength today, and if so, much of it comes from the forgiveness and healing love that our Vietnam veterans have shown."[124] Like Capps and Stone, Reagan saw in the "healing" actions of the veteran a prototype for national reconciliation, and it was through this task that he continued to valorize the veteran.

The rhetoric in Reagan's 1988 speech echoed the content of a speech he delivered on October 27, 1983, in which he attempted to defend American foreign policy against criticisms stemming from America's invasion of Grenada and the terrorist bombing of a U.S. Marine barracks in Beirut. Although the 1983 speech makes no reference to Vietnam veterans, and indeed is aimed at veterans of present and future wars, it nevertheless provides a perspective on situations affecting the Vietnam veteran. Speaking of the Marine Corps, Reagan stated that its members "have all been faithful to their ideals. They have given willingly of themselves. . . . They have given every one of us something to live up to." He added that "[t]hey were not afraid to stand up for their country or . . . to give others that last best hope of a better future."[125] Throughout the speech the U.S. soldier is clearly constructed as a role model. Reagan had earlier represented the Vietnam veteran as such a figure when, in August 1980, as a presidential candidate, he first referred to the war in Vietnam as a "noble cause," thereby implying that those who fought for this cause were also valorous.

The valorization of the Vietnam veteran intersected with, and contributed toward, the textual construction of the Vietnam veteran as a privileged spokesperson and was facilitated by a number of planned events, the first of which took place on November 13, 1982, with the dedication of the Vietnam Veterans Memorial in Washington, D.C. The dedication coincided with the National Salute to Vietnam Veterans, which involved a reading of the names of the Vietnam War dead in the National Cathedral and a parade of 150,000 veterans led by none other than William Westmoreland.[126] Additional noteworthy events followed in 1984 when, on Memorial Day, the remains of an unidentified American who died in Vietnam were interred in the Tomb of the Unknowns in Arlington National Cemetery. On Veterans Day of the same year Reagan dedicated the statue of three fighting men that stands near the Vietnam Veterans Memorial. On the same day, in the presence of 150,000 people, he officially accepted the memorial on behalf of the nation, focusing a new round of media attention on what has since become the most visited site in Washington, D.C. The acceptance climaxed a weeklong series of commemorative events called "Salute Two," named after the inaugural "salute" to the Vietnam veteran. In the spring of 1985 a number of "welcome home" parades, beginning with New York City's parade (May 7), were held nationally to coincide with the tenth anniversary of the end of the war. In May 1987 a "Thankyou Vietnam Veterans" parade was held in Los Angeles. In 1989, according to one source, 143 memorials to the war in Vietnam and its veterans had been built or were under construction within the United States.[127]

By themselves such incidents and circumstances would not have fully accomplished the widespread and almost universally accepted valorization of the veteran that contributed to promoting what Reagan called the new morning that had come to America.[128] The growth and spread of a militarized culture created a situation in which the veteran spoke regularly from within mass-media texts of a nation that had strengthened itself militarily and morally. War toys, magazines such as *Soldier of Fortune*, a number of television programs, including *Magnum, P.I.* (which premiered in 1980) and *The A-Team* (1983), together with action-adventure books with militaristic themes contributed to this end. Abetting the (re)militarization of culture, a number of films, including *Private Benjamin* (1980), *Stripes* (1981), *Taps* (1981), *An Officer and a Gentleman* (1982), *Lords of Discipline* (1983), *Heartbreak Ridge* (1986), and *Top Gun* (1986), attempted "to restore the army to its pre-Vietnam credit and, in certain instances, to reintegrate it with a lost patriotic vision of the United States."[129] Indeed, the construction of the veteran as hero involved placing him within this recuperated patriotic vision.

This vision was given impetus with the outpouring of patriotic rhetoric that accompanied Reagan's election to the presidency in 1980 and the return of the hostages from Iran. In his first Inaugural Address (January 20, 1981) the new president summoned Americans to "begin an era of national renewal," which would be accomplished because "after all. . . . [w]e are Americans."[130] A "new national mood" of "We're Number One" prevailed throughout America. The mood continued through 1984 when Reagan's reelection campaign used the theme "America Is Back," and American spectators at the Olympic Games in Los Angeles that year echoed the patriotic enthusiasm of the election slogan in the chant "USA! USA!" in response to the feats of American competitors. The renewed chauvinist spirit was reflected and strengthened in part through the advertising industry. In 1985 the Chrysler Plymouth corporation, for example, employed the slogan "The Pride is Back" (with its echoes of Reagan's "America is Back") and "Born in America" (an appropriation of the title of Springsteen's song "Born in the U.S.A.") to advertise its product. The patriotic vision was further enhanced by the 1986 centennial celebrations for the refurbished Statue of Liberty. The outpouring of patriotism continued in a less hysterical form the following year with the bicentennial celebrations of the U.S. Constitution.

In his sixth State of the Union Address (February 4, 1986), Reagan declared the existence of "a rising America—firm of heart, united in spirit, powerful in pride and patriotism."[131] Within this vision the veteran was once again called into active service and this time, according to the dominant representations, he answered the call willingly committed to patriotic principles. It was through this commitment that the Vietnam veteran emerged a hero and took his place alongside other American heroes. In this relation, Lawrence Grossberg has argued that the essential defining characteristic of a number of contemporary "postmodern Hero[es]"—including Rambo, Oliver North, and Sonny Crockett, all Vietnam veterans—is that the figures are committed. "Apart from the absoluteness of their commitment, they appear to be not very different from the rest of us and more importantly they are no different than the bad guys." What makes them the "good guy[s], what makes [them] better, is, in the end . . . precisely because [their] commitment is absolute and *it is to America*."[132]

Significantly, Reagan frequently apostrophized the "extraordinary 'ordinary Americans'" as America's real heroes, defining them as such through their unswerving patriotism.[133] Reagan pointed to the veterans' patriotism in a speech delivered on Memorial Day 1984 at the Tomb of the Unknowns when he redefined an American hero, the Vietnam veteran, as one who embodies both "courage" and "the spirit, the soul of America."[134] Similarly, his 1984 Veterans Day speech contained as many references to the Vietnam veterans' loyalty as to their courage. Throughout this speech, appropriately delivered at the national Vietnam Veterans Memorial, Reagan made frequent mention of the desire for a healed America, a nation that "in the end [is] stronger than . . . if it had not been broken."[135] According to Reagan, a healed (united) America derived from courage and loyalty. Similarly, the veteran was healed, and heroized, when his voice, body, and actions aligned to articulate loyalty and courage.

The most obvious mass media expression of such a definition is the character of John Rambo (Sylvester Stallone) in *Rambo: First Blood, Part II*. The "spirit, the soul of America" that Reagan spoke of in 1984 became muscle-bound flesh the next year in the form of a character whom the advertisements for the film referred to as a "symbol of the

American spirit."[136] Rambo's patriotism is as well defined as his gleaming deltoid and pectoral muscles. Admonished not to hate his country, Rambo responds: "Hate it! I'd die for it!" In the film's Reaganite rhetoric the patriot is the real hero, and the definition rests as much upon his willingness for self-sacrifice as upon the distinction the film makes between "country" and "government": the hero performs his duty in the name of his country, whereas he may be abused and betrayed by its bureaucratic officials.

The irony of *Rambo* is that it is a film in which the central character reverts to an earlier stereotype—he is virtually inarticulate. However, during a well-timed oration at the end of the film Rambo is permitted to "speak volumes for the Voiceless vet."[137] Having returned with the prisoners of war, having thus contributed to the maintenance of American unity, Rambo's final words concern the veteran: "All they want, and every guy who fought in Vietnam wants, is for our country to love us as much as we love it." Such love would thus seal the patriotic pact, validate the words of the sound track's song, "The strength of our nation belongs to us," bring the veteran home once and for all, and put a seal on the union of American society that had consistently been sought through the figure of the veteran. Officialdom pronounced its desired end on Veterans Day 1988 when Reagan's cloying sentiments praised the Vietnam veterans as "gentle heroes" and concluded that "as a nation, we say we love you."[138]

A measure of the success of the reconstruction of the Vietnam veteran as hero can be found in the number of media accounts that foregrounded experience of the war as a central element in the careers of various politicians, public servants, and business executives. After listing a number of senators and governors who had served in Vietnam John Wheeler, author of *Touched with Fire: The Future of the Vietnam Generation*, emphasized the fact that "[m]any executives in the Reagan Administration are Vietnam veterans, notably Robert McFarlane, the national security adviser," adding that "few people realize that the overnight delivery service, Federal Express, was organized by Vietnam veteran aviator Frederick Smith —using a hub-and-spoke system like the military airnet in Vietnam." Wheeler underlined the redemption of the veteran by noting that "Bruce Caputo's 1982 campaign for the Republican nomination for the U.S. Senate from New York ended when he acknowledged that his campaign literature incorrectly claimed he had served in Vietnam. The fact that the claim was made to begin with is itself instructive."[139] In a different way, Dan Quayle's lack of military service in Vietnam, and the circumstances surrounding his admission to the Indiana National Guard during the war, became a focus for questions concerning his vice-presidential qualities during the 1988 general election campaign. Throughout the Gulf War commentators frequently referred to the leadership qualities, and hinted at the political abilities of both Colin Powell and Norman Schwarzkopf by noting that both men's careers included service in Vietnam.

The irony surrounding the relationship of legitimate leaders and the benefit of service in the Vietnam War is reinforced within a comment made by Samuel Popkin, a political polling consultant, writing in the *Washington Post* on Veterans Day 1984. Within his assessment (one that implies a species of white victimage), Popkin argued that the survival of the Democratic Party rested on the careful selection of presidential nominees:

> Above all, the Democrats will have to nominate a man who, when he says "we," will be able to convince white men that he includes them too. In the context of the 1980s *such a candidate might have to be a Vietnam veteran, or someone too old to have dodged the draft.* Only such a candidate will appeal both to the Democratic Party's new core of blacks and working women and white men who espouse the new patriotism and extol the competitive spirit.[140](italics added)

The Democratic candidates in the 1980s and 1990s did not match either of Popkin's criteria. Nevertheless, Clinton's legitimacy as a presidential leader rested in part on his ability to justify successfully the fact that he had not served in Vietnam.

During the 1980s the patriotic, heroic veteran emerged as the person who spoke of "we." In fact, the Vietnam veteran, represented as hero, was enshrined as *the* voice of a united America—a voice that reached heroic status by speaking only of union. The contradiction at the center of the construction of the Vietnam veteran between a silent, silenced figure on the one hand and an articulate spokesperson and hero on the other was mediated by the intervention of the expression of uniformity and indivisibility. The cultural imperative of indivisibility forced its presence on a range of postwar discourse, but it was through the representational figure of the veteran that this need was most clearly articulated. Unity erased the veteran's silence, lifting him from marginality and reincorporating him into a position where he could speak only of incorporation. The cultural drive to holism therefore constructed a figure who was constrained to speak the truth of unity—and nothing but the truth.

Talking Back

It is possible, however, to resist and revise the above conclusion. A rewriting is available through the fact that the ideology of unity is not total or complete. Within a number of various texts veterans have been denied the opportunity to articulate the meanings of their different experiences. This is not to say that Vietnam veterans as "real concrete individuals," to use Marx's phrase, lacked, or lack, the ability to contest some of the more extravagant demands of a powerful ideology. In select and specific ways Vietnam veterans have drawn upon their experiences within the war and on the home front to inform their criticisms of militarist policies and domestic inequities. Such articulations contradict and contest unity by revealing the inadequacy of a notion that presumes and asserts a basic cultural homogeneity. In this sense the veteran's voice of dissent is a way of "talking back"—an insolent and insubordinate voice that "dare[s] to disagree."[141]

Veterans of the Vietnam War have continued to speak out on issues of U.S. foreign policy and have found a voice for their protests through groups that include Vietnam Veterans Against the War, Vietnam Veterans Against the War—Anti-Imperialist, Vietnam Veterans Foreign Policy Watch, and Veterans for Peace. In the eighties Vietnam veterans contested the Reagan administration's support of the Contras in Nicaragua, and in the nineties veterans of the war in Vietnam were prominent in anti–Gulf War demonstrations. Protest against the lasting effects of Agent Orange and the lamentable level of postwar health services rallied, and continue to rally, Vietnam veterans.

Records of such "insolent" actions and experiences are, typically, located outside the field of recognized textual canons. The role of a core of legitimated and authorized texts is, it has been argued, central to the maintenance of a (unified) culture conceived as a transcendental bearer of civilization.[142] Similarly, the assumptions studied in this part form the basis of a canon of Vietnam War texts in which cultural unity is emphasized.[143] Acknowledgment of the limitations of "central" texts, specifically the impact that canonized texts have on the effectiveness of attempts to articulate experiences that contradict dominant interlocutory positions, informs this archival excavation of the uncanonized voices of veterans speaking on a range of topics beyond "healing" or cultural unity.

An account of veterans "speaking out" discussed in a paper in *Radical History Review* in 1985 raises other issues pertinent to this act of recuperation. Referring to the practice of providing Vietnam veterans as speakers for schools to counteract high school recruitment drives by the armed services, the author commented that "the most effective part of the vets' presentations [in the schools] is their personal testimony about what GIs learned in Vietnam." While evidence could be gathered to support the assertion that "most of the students have never before heard Vietnam discussed in . . . [a] language that facilitates criticism of international aggression," the author's conclusion that "veterans' testimony about the war is a catalyst that can make these debates come alive for Americans too young too remember Vietnam"[144] assumes too much. Those too young to remember Vietnam are not necessarily convinced by the power of veterans' words. The limits of veterans' testimony has been illustrated within a discussion of the reception of the film *Rambo*. Vietnam veterans demonstrating in Boston in February 1986 against the film and Stallone's receipt of an award for the film were "told to 'go home' by a group of teenagers. . . . Stallone, the teenagers screamed, was 'a real veteran.'"[145] The response yet again demonstrates the power of the mass media to submerge popular experiences within and through its recreations. (At the level of the young audience, the most effective critical response to, and delegitimation of, the narrative absurdities of *Rambo* may be the popular parodic critique *Hot Shots II*, [1992].)

The reaction to the veterans in Boston suggests that, by itself, unmediated veterans' testimony is limited in its capacity to produce political or cultural changes. The dismissal of veterans' experience and the revision of the experience within commercialized textual forms have led veterans to explore various forms of representation. Among the projects initiated by veterans are video productions (such as Joseph Gray's *Ambush*, 1992, an exploration of personal motives, memories, and guilt surrounding the war), veterans' poetry (including work published by 1st Casualty Press, a publication house established by poets associated with Vietnam Veterans Against the War), veterans' art works, and theatrical productions (including the works of the Vietnam Veterans Ensemble Theater of New York, and plays workshopped and produced by veterans, such as John DiFusco's *Tracers*).[146] Each of these examples is an attempt by veterans to present viewpoints and voices that contest the dominant representations of a "healed" and "heroic" veteran. However, the examples demonstrate that in order to be heard veterans are required to adopt narrative forms that are readily appropriated or superseded by the mass media. Exemplifying the problem here, John Carlos Rowe mentions the case of a piece of freelance writing submitted in the summer of 1979 to a local newspaper in the southern California area. The piece, "Remembrances of Vietnam," was published as the first of a two-part report. After the publication of the first installment, the newspaper was alerted to the fact that the "report" was in fact a plagiarized extract from Ron Kovic's memoir *Born on the Fourth of July*. Rowe "hesitated long before using this anecdote, because it risks reinforcing that other powerful mythology we use as defense against our responsibility for the War: that is, the 'madness' of the returning veteran." Rowe sees in the incident "that to be *heard at all* [the veteran] had to accommodate himself to the existing channels of communication in this culture: the press, the publishing industry, and the 'readers' whose expectations are shaped by the forms of those media."[147]

Attempts to evade the restrictions of existing forms of mass media have been varied, and include the call by Frankfurt School theorists for the development of forms of "popular media." However, as Robert Ray has argued, "[d]espite the optimism of such media theorists as Walter Benjamin and Hans Enzensberger, the average person in the twentieth century has less access to the means of cultural production than he would have had a hundred years ago."[148] According to cultural historian Jackson Lears, studies of resistant practices—practices that encode the memories of experiences that disrupt traditions of consent—must "distinguish between genuinely popular culture and the corporate-sponsored mass culture that is so often mistaken for it."[149] Unfortunately, Lears does not specify the methodology for such studies. The distinction between "genuinely popular culture" and mass cultural forms is complicated in a number of ways, not the least by the powerful appropriational effects of corporate-sponsored media that can rapidly commercialize new and emerging trends, fashions, genres, and texts.

The naiveté of the Frankfurt School's position, reinforced within countercultural demands to "seize the media," is underlined by the fact that an effective popular political voice in an era of mechanical reproduction is implicated with mass media representations; and the success of alternative or oppositional representations rests, in large part, on the ability to finance and broadcast such representations. Exemplifying this problem, David Rabe's play *Sticks and Bones*, a bitter indictment of the domestic pressures to silence the veteran, was itself silenced on one occasion as a result of a refusal by CBS to screen a production of the play.[150] Similarly, the muddled release of Ivan Passer's film *Cutter's Way*, a film in which a Vietnam veteran attempts to expose and condemn the powerful people and institutions responsible for his being sent to war, did little to ensure that the film's message would be effectively heard by a wide audience.[151]

Such difficulties are further exemplified by the relative obscurity, in relation to a text such as *Rambo*, of films such as *Riders of the Storm* (also known as *The American Way*, 1986) and Haile Gerima's *Ashes and Embers* (1982), both of which effectively encode unusual narratives in forms not commonly manipulated in mass-media texts. *Riders of the Storm* concerns a pirate television station operated by Vietnam veterans from an old B29 bomber circling above the United States. The station is used to interrupt right-wing broadcasts and to subvert the presidential campaign of a candidate seeking to involve the United States in another war. The self-reflexive narrative of the film represents Vietnam veterans contesting the excesses of media and political representations. The film historians David James and Rick Berg have argued that "the worst of *Platoon*'s crimes is that the standard of representation it provided ended a tradition of films that called representation into question (e.g. *The Stunt Man*)."[152] Like *The Stunt Man*, *Riders of the Storm*, released the same year as *Platoon*, continued to self-consciously question the assumptions and representational practices that naturalize the constructions of realistic Vietnam War films.

Ashes and Embers is a nonlinear narrative exploration of the psyche of a black veteran, Nay Charles (John Anderson). The film begins in Los Angeles, where Charles and a friend are stopped by the police, an incident that provokes the first of Charles's violent flashbacks to the war. The frequency and poignancy of the flashbacks foreground "Vietnam" as an additional location within the film as the narrative moves eastward from Los Angeles to the rural South, and then to Washington, D.C., where Charles's strained relationship with his girlfriend (Kathy Flewellen) becomes evident. Increasingly disoriented by the frequent flashbacks, Charles is rescued by his friend Jim (Norman Blalock), who fortifies him with stories of the courage of Paul Robeson and W. E. B. Du Bois. Throughout the film, Nay Charles's flashbacks and deteriorating psychological condition are linked to aspects of experience in the United States, thus implicating racial and economic conditions, together with the war, as the causes of the difficulties faced by black veterans.

Ashes and Embers, then, places the black veteran in historical context. Nay Charles explores features of his personal and ethnic history in his relationships with his friends, his grandmother, and with white figures of authority. In the end, he is depicted moving toward a more informed understanding of black history and experience. With this shift from the personal to the political the film transcends the cliché of the wounded vet and proposes a specific form of resolution for the veteran's adjustment problems—continuing political action—that revises traditional modes of depoliticized healing. *Ashes and Embers* stands apart from the majority of texts dealing with the Vietnam veteran in which a passive form of reintegration is privileged over the need to question the terms of collectivity. Further, in *Ashes and Embers* and *Riders of the Storm*, alternative content is reflected in forms (self-reflexive irony; nonlinear narrative) that interrogate and, to a degree, subvert the content typically conveyed through traditional realist modes of representation.

The issue of the representation of problematic content in realist forms is evident in a number of documentary texts that, ironically, seek to grant the veteran a voice. The documentary films *Interviews with My Lai Veterans* (1972), *Vietnam Requiem: Vets In Prison* (1982), and *Frank: A Vietnam Veteran* (1981), which presents a veteran's admission of atrocities committed in Vietnam and crimes committed on his return to the United States, attempt to represent and analyze aspects of experience not traditionally featured in dominant representations of the veteran. Nevertheless, taken together, or privileged singly, these films reinvoke and reinforce the stereotype of the "sick vet," a dysfunctional or psychotic figure incapable of an informed, or informing, opinion. The continued representation of socially deviant or psychologically troubled veterans functions to displace images of veterans' agency and direct action.

Contrasting with the record of "deviant" images found in a wide variety of sources certain documentary films, while still relying on traditional realist forms, have avoided negative stereotypes in their approaches to a history based on the collective action of veterans. Examples here include *No Vietnamese Ever Called Me Nigger* (1968), *Good Bye and Good Luck* (1969), and *GI José* (1975), in which veterans of color question and protest the war and the postwar treatment of Vietnam veterans, issues explored subsequently in Gerima's *Ashes and Embers*. Other examples include *The Secret Agent* (1983), which examines the lingering effects of exposure to Agent Orange, thus serving as an indictment of the U.S. Air Force, the Veterans Administration, and the Dow Chemical corporation, a maker of the defoliant. *Vietnam Veterans: Dissidents for Peace* (1988) features the continuing political activities of Vietnam veterans, as does *The War in El Cedro* (1988), which focuses on Vietnam veterans who rebuild a clinic in a Nicaraguan village destroyed by Contras. *Going Back: A Return to Vietnam* (1982) follows the journey by the first group of

American combat veterans to return to Vietnam after the war. The return trip leads to a questioning of the justifications for the war and also provides an insight into postwar Vietnamese ways of life.

The representation of Vietnamese experiences found in *Going Back* and other accounts of return journeys to Vietnam provokes, in terms of a thorough archival excavation of the experiences of veterans of the war in Vietnam, the importance of considering veterans of the "other side." The bicultural focus achieved through study of Vietnamese exile narratives is one method of providing insights into the lives of the Vietnamese diaspora in America and, further, offers a way of revising the ethnocentrism of many American studies of the Vietnam War.[153] The project of enhancing cross-cultural understanding implicit in such narratives is extended within the representations of wartime and postwar life in Vietnam found in cultural productions indigenous to Vietnam.[154] The need to circulate Vietnamese representations of the war and its aftermath is underlined by Gayatri Spivak, author of one of the most pressing questions in cultural studies—"Can the subaltern speak?"[155] —who insists that subalterns must speak for themselves. The insistence derives from, but is not dependent upon, the fact that "no amount of raised consciousness field-work can ever approach the painstaking labor to establish ethical singularity with the subaltern."[156] The perspectives of the formerly colonized people of Vietnam, subalterns in this sense, were expressed throughout the war in Vietnamese representations of their (armed) struggle to "find a voice."

One form of cultural production, documentary films, continued throughout the years of the "American war." Such films were made, often under conditions of prolonged aerial bombardment, in the southern zones by the National Liberation Front, and by the state-operated studios in the North, notably the Central Newsreel and Documentary Film Studio. Documentary films of the period include *The Most Dangerous Situation* (1967), *Cu Chi Guerrilla* (1967), *Ngu Thuy Girls* (1969), and *Vinh Linh Fortress* (1970), which depicts the lives of people living underground at this heavily bombed site.[157] The prevailing aesthetic among these films is a starkly realist form of instruction (derisively dismissed in the West as "propaganda") intended to support and extend the "government policy [of] keeping alive the fighting spirit of the people."[158] Vietnamese critics have recognized the aesthetic limitations of these films, while also acknowledging the utility of the films to the war effort.[159]

While documentary film production was maintained throughout the war, the more expensive feature-length fiction filmmaking virtually ceased. Beginning in the late seventies production resumed on fiction films that include a number of works that deal with the war and its aftermath. Notable among an impressive output is Hong Sen's *The Abandoned Field—Free Fire Zone* (1979) in which a family living in a floating house in the Mekong Delta shortly before the 1968 Tet offensive is consistently fired upon by ever-present American helicopters. Dang Nhat Minh's *When the Tenth Month Comes* (1984) concerns a young wife who, after the death of her husband, a soldier at the front, returns to her village burdened with remorse and is subsequently unable to inform her in-laws of their son's death. In 1987 Dang Nhat Minh made *The Girl on the River,* a story of the love between a leader of the Liberation Front and a prostitute from one of the many small boats used as brothels on the Mekong. Le Dan's *Black Cactus* (1991) deals with a different kind of love, that between Lai, a black Amerasian, and a Cham girl, Ma. In Chau Hue's *The Strolling Singers* (1991), Hung, a demobilized soldier suffering eye injuries, attempts a reconciliation with his wife, Tram.[160]

The representation of the painful experiences of veterans of the war found in *The Strolling Singers* is a central theme within postwar Vietnamese film production. The film *Brothers and Relations* (1986), directed by Tran Vu and Nguyen Huu Luyen, both veterans, extends this theme in a story of a Vietnamese veteran who returns from the war to his family who thought him dead. The theme of forgetting the war, and the denial of veterans of the war, is extended when the veteran is sent to recover the remains of a relation killed in the South only to find that the cemetery has been relocated for a housing construction project. The indifference of his family toward the remains of their relative leads the veteran to return the bones to the grave in the South. *Karma* (1986) was the first feature film of postwar Vietnam not financed by the government and is the only Vietnamese film to deal with a veteran of the Army of the Republic of Vietnam. The complicated melodramatic plot involves the return of an ARVN veteran, Binh (Tran Quang), to his wife, Nga (Phuong Dung), during the war. Believing Binh to have been killed in battle, Nga has been working as a bar girl in Saigon. Binh's inability to accept Nga's new occupation drives him back to the front, where after a final attempt at reconciliation in an army hospital, he is killed in battle.

The documentation conducted on film of the experiences of Vietnamese veterans has been extended through the publication of a number of remarkable novels dealing with various aspects of life in Vietnam during the war. Bao Ninh's *The Sorrow of War* (1994) tells the story of Kien, a soldier who returns to the battlefield as part of detachment to bury the dead.[161] Throughout his grim task Kien reflects on his life in Hanoi and grieves for his friends who died in battle, the latter memories inspired by the ghosts of friends that populate the battlefield where he works. Kien's suffering and his intense memories of the war contribute to an identity that is informed by sorrow and loss. In Duong Thu Huong's controversial *Novel Without a Name* (1995) the central character, Quan, journeys to Hanoi after ten years of fighting in the South on a mission to locate his childhood friend.[162] The search becomes a form of personal revelation in which Quan is forced to confront his memories of war, and the consequences of the war for those living in the North. The powerful effect of *Novel Without a Name* owes much to author Duong's own experience, at the age of twenty-one, of leading a communist Youth Brigade on the demilitarized zone. After seven years of fighting, she was one of three survivors of a volunteer group that originally had included forty members.

Drawing on a different set of experiences and employing a divergent aesthetic, Trinh T. Minh-ha's self-reflexive "documentary" *Surname Viet Given Name Nam* (1989) examines the role of women in the war. Trinh's film represents Vietnamese women in America and, purportedly, in Vietnam as they reflect on their lives in the war. The film disrupts audience expectations of the documentary mode through the inclusion of reenactments and the conceit that all the women in the film, even those who supposedly recount their stories from Vietnam, are in the United States. The presence of the fictive mode within a form of representation typically understood to be factual occurs within this "resistant text," one in which understandings are implicated with culturally specific meanings and language that Trinh "translates" to the United States.[163]

The method of translating a plurality of voices reflects on and finally exposes the filmmaker's strategies and the "site from which these voices are brought out and constructed."[164] Trinh's interrogation of the ways in which identities and stories are interwoven raises a number of issues concerning women's identity within and across cultures. In addressing these issues, the film implicitly critiques many of the assumptions common to narratives of "Vietnam": that realist forms are the most appropriate to the task of representing and understanding the "Vietnam experience"; that there is one "truth" to the story of the war (as *Platoon*, for example, proposes); and that this truth is accessible only through males. Trinh's film destabilizes various identities to produce the conclusion that identities, even those as "fixed" as Vietnam veteran, are mutable. In this way,

Trinh's approach to stories and identities becomes a form of "talking back," which is the contestation of the force of the ideology of unity.

In the preface to *Tell Me Lies About Vietnam* (1988), a collection of essays concerned with print and visual representations of the war in Vietnam, the editors state:

> How [the] figure [of the Vietnam veteran] is perceived and constructed is of crucial significance as an index of ideology: narratives of his actions and thoughts are emblematic of meanings, values and attitudes in the wider culture. Indeed, we may claim that the cultural representation of the soldier and particularly the veteran is perhaps the single most influential ideological discourse of the war.[165]

The veteran as a vocal figure was constructed within and through representations, and his ability to speak has been the result of ideological imperatives, while his messages are concerned with unity. The comment quoted above, then, reflects the irony through which the veteran of the war in Vietnam has come to be known: he has been privileged within post–Vietnam cultural discourse because of his ideological importance to unity. Had not the veteran been appropriated ideologically, our perceptions of him would, of course, be entirely different. He has been, as it were, singled out to speak of unity on the basis of his wartime and homefront experiences that authorize his metalinguistic pronouncements.

This observation is not meant to deny or denigrate the veteran's experiences. Rather, it points to the power of the ideology of unity to rewrite experience. Thus, to adopt words Michael Herr used in relation to the representation of the war, something "hasn't been asked"[166] with respect to the veteran: Who *is* this person—an indexical voice of ideology, or a person capable of bringing the experience of the war to bear on the question of unity? The different voices heard talking back speak of a range of experiences beyond the clichéd stories concerning an essential cultural union.

Through a deconstructive and historicized form of critique, the representation of the veteran as a vocal figure and the ideology of unity speaking through this figure have been exposed. The analysis of ideological operations pursued here has involved the paradoxical operation of listening to what is not said within the taken-for-granted assumptions encoded within the narratives of the veteran—those characteristics that, as Stuart Hall puts it, ideology "systematically blips out on."[167] The critique informs communication by assisting in tuning out the ahistorical noise of unity and tuning in to the different messages of diverse voices. This action is capable of revising the impressions of the terrain of post–Vietnam cultural life represented in dominant interlocutory dispositions. It is this terrain—filled with images of resisting and protesting the war, the powerful effects of "race" and class, and the insensitivity of governmental administrations—that is represented in the *voices* of veterans of the war in Vietnam.

However, the efforts to retrieve these voices must contend with a history in which the Vietnam veteran has been characterized and canonized as a heroic figure by the mass media, by commonsense assumptions, and by politicians seeking to appropriate features of the veteran's experience for political gain. In this sense the Vietnam veteran is a figure defined within the specific historical context of post–Vietnam United States culture and the history of the changes undergone by this figure is one of ideological attempts to construct cultural unity from the effects of the Vietnam War.

3

Bringing the War "Home"

America will not be able to rest until all Americans
have returned to the fold.   —John Del Vecchio

America, my home, sweet home.
     —"God Bless America" (As sung by the characters
          in the final scene of *The Deer Hunter*)

"The home front." "The living room war." "The war at
home." Evocations of home resonate in descriptions of the impact upon
American culture of the Vietnam War. In a variety of assessments the connotations of home as the site of the family, community, or the nation, and
descriptions of the effects of the war in terms of trauma to each site intersected to reinforce the notion that the war had "come home." The emphasis in this intersection upon home, singular, is telling. John Fiske has
noted that "those who experience most acutely the crucial contradictions
that we often set up when class, gender, and race intersect, can have multiple 'homes' or habitats, often quite distinct from each other."[1] The foregrounding of a unified whole as home denies the presence of the range of
experiences that Fiske refers to as "homes." Difference, the revelation of
varying conditions, experiences, *homes*, is erased in the essentialist assertion of an homogeneous unity. Given the definition of "home" circulated
within various texts, difference becomes homelessness—a condition that
is outside the boundaries of a convivial collectivity. It is in this contrast
between home and homelessness, between incorporation and exclusion,
that home is exposed as a hegemonic construct. Hegemony is the creation
of "we"; an "adherence to the unifying pronoun" in a variety of contexts.[2] Hegemony attempts to fix meaning, to deny alternatives and differences. Defined as an "articulating principle,"[3] hegemony seeks to link

together different groups and individuals into a unity in which the presence of difference is denied or contained. However, as Fiske argues, the "hegemonic forces of homogeneity" are "always met by the resistances of heterogeneity."[4] The field of this struggle is ideology, "a battlefield where the principal classes" and other groups "struggle for the appropriation of the fundamental ideological elements of their society in order to articulate them to their discourse."[5]

Home is one such fundamental ideological element. Home carries powerful resonances and connotations that position it as the focus of the type of struggle Fiske describes. Aspects of common sense inscribed in language and thought circulate the notion of home as a condition marked by positive qualities. Home is a cheerful, safe haven in a heartless world; it is the intersection of private and public spheres within culture resulting in a collection of members—familial, communal, or national—sharing commonly ascribed characteristics. In this relation, Stuart Hall has suggested that "the people" do not exist as a collectivity, "but ways of representing 'the people' do which seek to . . . constitute them as saying 'yes' to power—[that is] in forms [that are] unified and acquiescent to the present social and political arrangements."[6] Home draws on its commonsensical, ideological associations to naturalize itself as a construct that represents the people as unified and acquiescent, and acquiescent because they are unified. To accept home (unity) is to consent to the maintenance of conditions that reinforce hegemony by banishing or appropriating alternative, different, and thus contestatory, experiences.

Within the analysis in this part of the study, the signs of the common sense that defines "home" as unity are analyzed to expose a number of "home" truths. That is, the various historical manifestations of home in representations of the impact of the war are critiqued to reveal a progression that registers the divisive impact of the war, only to subsume it within a reassertion of unity. The analysis begins in the late sixties with the oppositional position of the antiwar movement, encoded within the slogan "bring the war home," and progresses to the representations of the early to midseventies in which the "war" came "home" with the veteran. Developments during the latter half of the seventies allowed for the reincorporation of the "violent vet" into a reconstructed family unit. The emphasis on home was reinforced by and during the nostalgic mood that accompanied the Reagan administration. In the late eighties home became moveable—achievable by Americans in both the United States and *Vietnam*. Signs of resistance to "home" are noted, although the representation of home in the contemporary, post–Vietnam War world continues to advance the project of unity established in the texts ostensibly concerned with the impact of the war. Finally, and ironically, then, "bringing the war 'home'" is the denial of the effects of the social and cultural divisions—the differences—that the war revealed within American culture.

The Home Front

Toward the end of 1969 the Weathermen, a radical offshoot of Students for a Democratic Society (SDS), called for "National Action" in Chicago on October 11 of that year. Protest was returning to the city a year after the violent events that had accompanied the Democratic National Convention. "This fall, people are coming back to Chicago: more powerful, better organized, more together than we were last August," stated the call to action published in *New Left Notes*, the official weekly newspaper of SDS. The plan of action was "not only to bring 'peace to Vietnam', but [to begin] to establish another front against imperialism right here in America—'to bring the war home.'"[7] In this way, "bringing the war home" involved ending the Vietnam War and "bringing revolution that is already winning in the Third World" back to the United States.[8] Presumably, the rationale behind this call was based on the belief that widespread violent unrest on the "home front" would make the pursuance of the war impossible. According to this logic, the radical interruption of consensus would result in the end of the war and be the means to a new America.

With the call to "bring the war home" the antiwar movement entered a new phase, and the slogan became part of its vocabulary. However, the idea of being separate from, if not radically opposed to, the dominant consensus was one that was already embedded within the movement. Writing of the mass antiwar marches that occurred early in the sixties, Morris Dickstein stated that "[b]y marching we tried to purge ourselves of the least trace of inner complicity with the war; we stepped outside the national consensus and reached out for solidarity with others who shared an alternative idea of America."[9] Walter Capps argues that Dickstein's observation reflects "conflicting or alternative *ideas of America*."[10] What Capps does not add is that these positions were inherently contestatory—that the antiwar protest movement not only sought an alternative to dominant ideas but actively contested those ideas. It was the presence of contestation and struggle throughout the history of the antiwar movement that permitted later chroniclers to use the term "bringing the war home" and permutations such as "the war at home" to refer to protest formations prior to the "national action" in Chicago in late 1969.

The subtlety of distinctions between alternative and contestatory were, however, lost within the mass media's representation of the antiwar movement. Routinely, the news media represented the protest movement, or "framed" it, to use Todd Gitlin's evocatively ambiguous term,[11] in ways that reproduced certain negative assumptions, attitudes, and dispositions. The media's construction and reconstruction of situational definitions of the movement within a process of inclusion, omission, specific amplifications, and focus ultimately contributed to the continuation of the status quo. Gitlin examined this subtle process in his book *The Whole World Is Watching* (1980) in an analysis that featured the decoding of two central methods employed by the mass news media in their coverage of the antiwar movement. These forms of representation began near the middle of the sixties and continued until the movement's demise.

Gitlin summarized the first method employed by the news media as "Certifying Leaders and Converting Leadership to Celebrity."[12] In the initial phase, "certifying leaders," the media focused on members of the movement, thereby legitimating them as spokespersons. In the case of Mark Rudd, for example, Gitlin argues that Rudd did not "directly and formally" represent a majority of students during the occupation and strike at Columbia University in the spring of 1968. Nevertheless, Rudd was visibly involved in the demonstrations in ways that attracted the attention of the media. According to Gitlin, "[T]he media *routinely* present performers who are deviant- that is, unrepresentative of the values, opinions, passions and practices of the larger society. Deviance constitutes their very 'news value'. . . . " As the focus of media attention, Rudd was certified as a leader and subsequently accorded this status by the media.

In contrast, organizers of the 1968 demonstrations in Chicago, including Tom Hayden, Rennie Davis, Dave Dellinger, and with a completely different political style, Jerry Rubin and Abbie Hoffman of the Yippies, all possessed considerable organizational experience in earlier movements. These people were "already *leaders* in some sense . . . ; the media made them *celebrities*." According to Gitlin, "The all-permeating spectacular culture insisted that the movement be identified through its celebrities" and as a result the movement "attracted personalities who enjoyed performance . . . who spoke quotably."[13] Through the media's intervention, then, it was possible for a member of the movement, albeit one who was especially active and vocal, to be elevated to the role of leader and then, as a result of a theatrical or flamboyant style, to have this position transformed into that of celebrity. In this way, the media, in a very real sense, "made" celebrities.

The ability of various news media to construct and reconstruct movement leaders is indicative of the power of the media to decontextualize experience. In the case of the antiwar movement, this decontextualization was reproduced through an emphasis on scenes of violent political protest that ignored the political rationale for violence. Gitlin argues that the movement was "both actor and acted-upon. . . . The media inflated the sense that there was an extremist movement; parts of the movement pursued confrontation for both strategic and expressive reasons; and the State escalated repression."[14] Thus, through its routine codes the mass news media contributed, ultimately, to the "unmaking" of the New Left antiwar movement and to the maintenance of an image of cultural stability and homogeneity.

It is significant that the representational approaches employed by the news media in coverage of the antiwar protest movement are identifiable within a range of fictional and nonfictional texts dealing with the movement. The similarity of approaches between the various narratives indicates the pervasive and persuasive power of the news media. By reproducing the established frames of the mass news media, other textual representations of the antiwar movement contributed to a conservative effect by perpetuating commonsensical interpretations of the movement and of the cultural conditions of the late sixties. Specifically, such representations denigrated, or delegitimated, the antiwar movement and the oppositional forces it embodied. This process contributed toward the continued dominance of one idea of America—the idea of America as one. The strategy of "bringing the war home" was subverted along a broad front of textual representations—including the news media, and the mass-media texts studied here—that reasserted a traditional unified home by denying the recognition of oppositional, or even alternative, ideas of America.

The process of decontextualization examined by Gitlin was particularly evident within a number of commercial fictional films of the early seventies. Within weeks of the shootings at Kent State University on May 4, 1970, and at Jackson State University in Mississippi on May 14, Metro-Goldwyn-Mayer studios released the film *The Strawberry Statement,* and in June of that year Columbia studios released *Getting*

Straight, both of which contained scenes alluding to events on the two campuses. The attempts at exploiting the headlines were misjudged. *The Strawberry Statement* was a financial disaster, and the modest success of *Getting Straight* at the box office can be attributed to the presence of Elliot Gould, already an established commercial star. Historical context reinforced the bathos of the content of these films, further exposing the absurdity of images of motiveless protest and free-floating violence. Any narrative connection between these films and antiwar protest capable of informing the separate plots with a semblance of justifiable relevance is restricted to minor or tangential references.

In *The Strawberry Statement,* for example, students from an unnamed university somewhere in San Francisco have joined with local black residents to protest the university's intention to construct an ROTC building on land used as a playground by neighborhood children. The issues, then, supposedly, revolve around the military and the war in Vietnam, various forms of discrimination, and community access to university property (the latter an oblique and simplified reference to considerations involved in the 1968 Columbia strike and the turmoil of Berkeley's People's Park in 1969).[15] Instead, the justifications for an ensuing strike are contained in the words chanted by the central character, Simon (Bruce Davison): "Strike because you hate cops," "Strike because you hate war," "Strike because there is poverty," "Strike because there's no poetry in your lectures [and] because lectures are a drag."[16] The call falls far short of sustained reference to any of the issues that allegedly motivate the plot. The lack of cogent, or even clear, reasons for protest is paralleled in the final scenes of police violence against students who peacefully await their fate. Protest is spontaneous and aimless; violence is random and unjustified in terms of the plot. *Getting Straight,* in contrast, does contain specific references to the war in Vietnam in the form of a subplot concerning the attempts of one character to avoid the draft, and the central character, Harry Bailey (Elliott Gould), is a veteran of the war. However, these features are not linked to the protest on the campus where Harry is studying to gain his teaching qualifications. The level of political analysis is again summarized by slogans, this time in the form of a placard carried by a protestor that reads "Down with the Establishment!" Unfortunately, this is the closest the film comes to any kind of rationale for the final violent mêlée between students and the National Guard. As in *The Strawberry Statement,* the absence of explanation renders the protest, and the violence, unintelligible.

A similar set of problems besiege Michelangelo Antonioni's *Zabriskie Point* (1970), another film of the era to touch upon antiwar protest. The film begins with an antiwar demonstration during which a policeman is fired upon and killed, although it is not clear whether the central male character, Mark (Mark Frechette), is to blame. It is this tenuous connection to opposition to the war that motivates the ensuing events in which Mark steals an airplane to escape Los Angeles, thereby sealing his fate when he is shot returning the aircraft. Antonioni's dramatic use of color, jump cuts, and slow-motion shots, together with the surreal mise-en-scène that is his vision of Los Angeles, makes the film visually impressive, but therein lies its problem. Form supersedes content, narrative is sublimated to style. In his defense of the film, Antonioni stressed this issue: "You cannot argue that a film is bad but that the color is good, or vice versa. The image is a fact, the colors *are* the story. If a cinematic moment has colors which appear right and good, it means that it has expressed itself. . . . "[17] However, in this case, the privileging of aesthetics is the denial of politics. Scenes of protest mix with scenes of group sex in the desert, which leads to slow motion scenes of a house exploding. Protest, then, has no basis other than its visual impact—the *point* of the protest is irrelevant.

Contrasting with such examples from commercial cinema of the late sixties, a number of independent films of the era employed diverse techniques and various narrative strategies to inform and structure cogent depictions of antiwar protest. In opposition to *Zabriskie Point*, these films linked form and content in an "agitational aesthetic."[18] One example of this work was produced by the interweaving of various styles of a number of independent New York filmmakers in the collaborative film *No Game* (1968), a documentary dealing with the October 1967 March on the Pentagon. *No Game* was the first film released by the Newsreel collective, which went on to produce, among others, the film *Summer of '68* (1968) dealing with the demonstrations at the Democratic National Convention in Chicago. Unlike the popular media's form of representations, *Summer of '68* comments on its own presentation of images, addressing the topic that the networks' exploitation of scenes of violence had displaced the focus of the protest. A narrator to the film states: "The issue of Chicago became police brutality, not the party we'd come to expose, not the war or the racism we'd come to protest. Chicago gave us a success we couldn't use and suggested the limits of any attempt to talk to the media." Implicitly, the film argues for alternative forms of representation to counteract the distortions of the conventional news media.

The protest at the convention was also the subject of Haskell Wexler's film *Medium Cool* (1969). Complementing the approach of the Newsreel films, Wexler was concerned with techniques that would privilege the object of protest. Echoing Godard's *Weekend* (1967), the film opens and concludes with scenes of violent car crashes. Within Wexler's film, images of violence are the correlative of a violent culture, evidence of which appears in scenes of gun practice at suburban rifle ranges and, most specifically, scenes of police rioting during the street demonstrations in Chicago. The film mixes cinema vérité-style documentary filmmaking with a realist fictional mode in such a way that fictional characters appear within scenes of real-life events at Chicago's Grant Park and elsewhere. The aim here is, as David James has pointed out, to "demystify the Hollywood conventions of dramatic action and character ... [and] to force the audience to identify less with the adventure or the hero and to think more about the documentary events."[19] Like the film *Summer of '68*, *Medium Cool* contains a number of aleatory and self-reflexive moments; an example occurs when a tear-gas canister drops in front of a group of demonstrators and a voice on the sound track is heard to shout: "Watch out, Haskell, this is real!" At other times Wexler quite consciously reflects upon the implications and consequences of forms of representation. The opening car-crash scene, for example, questions the ethics of the news media by depicting a news camera team filming the accident before attending to the injuries of the victims. In another way, the mixture of documentary and fictional moments raises the issue of action determined by the presence of the camera. The demonstrators in Chicago knew that "the whole world is watching," chanting the line to draw media attention to the actions of the police in the hope that the presence of television cameras would restrict excessive police violence. Ironically, the implication of the chant evokes the distortion of an historical moment by the intercession of the news media—a distortion critiqued in *Medium Cool* and *Summer of '68*. Further, both films draw attention to the imbrication of power and representational forms. Specifically, the films intimate the ability of the popular media to justify a consensus on the Vietnam War through the delegitimation and marginalization of the voices of antiwar protest.

Contrasting with such depictions, other textual representations advanced an image of consesus by focusing on celebrities within the movement. A small number of people (notably Jane Fonda, Tom Hayden, Abbie Hoffman, and Jerry Rubin) has been privileged in textual accounts of antiwar protest, thereby denying the range of differing opinion embodied within the movement. Charles DeBenedetti and Charles Chatfield indicated the breadth of opposition to the war when they described some of the constituencies involved in the antiwar movement:

> Organized opposition to the war came mainly from middle-class, college-educated whites, materially comfortable and motivated by largely moral considerations. Politically liberal and sympathetic to social justice causes, antiwar activists were also tolerant of changes in popular culture, sexual mores, and race relations. In contrast, the great majority of Americans favoring disengagement from Vietnam ... according to public opinion analysts ... were in the lower economic class, often women and blacks, with grade school educations and low-prestige jobs. Politically inarticulate and generally isolationists, these disaffected citizens opposed the war as a waste of men and money.... Suspicious of most authority, they seemed ambivalent in the face of cultural change, but they made no secret of their dislike for active protestors and street demonstrators.[20]

There is little sense of this diversity in the texts that concentrate on celebrity leaders. Within such texts a range of voices are reduced to the opinions of a few, or those of an individual, as in Godfrey Hodgson's book *America in Our Time* (1978) in which the presence of Tom Hayden dominates the brief chapter dealing with opposition to the war.[21] By relying on impressions gathered from a handful of figures, nearly all from the leadership of the movement, Hodgson fails to evoke any sense that the antiwar movement was largely an oppositional movement composed of rank-and-file members. Another text, fittingly subtitled "A Jaundiced Glance Back at the Movement of the Sixties," opens with a four-page negative characterization of Jerry Rubin. Throughout this bitter text the author continually attacks those he obviously considers to be his opponents.[22] Elsewhere on the right this approach has been honed to the point where aspects of "personality" become the central issue. An example of this approach is the edited collection of essays *Destructive Generation* (1990), a series of sustained ad hominem assaults on the motives and character of individuals associated with the antiwar New Left.[23]

While ostensibly seeking to examine one particular antiwar action—the march on the Pentagon during October 21 and 22, 1967—Norman Mailer's *The Armies of the Night* continued the "star system" by foregrounding Mailer as the center of narrative attention. The spontaneity that Mailer elicited from actors in his films *Beyond the Law* (1967), *Wild 90*, and *Maidstone* (both 1968) is reflected in the style of *The Armies of the Night* "in which there is no script, improvisation is de rigueur, and yet everything seems 'cut' to his 'taste'."[24] Similarly, the fact that Mailer plays the lead role in each of his films is consistent with his foregrounded presence in *The Armies of the Night*. The result of Mailer's narcissistic narrative focus, as with other texts that concentrate on personalities, is a displacement of the presence of opposition to the war. Central to Mailer's narrative attention to the maintenance of personalities or stars is a narrative structure that constructs and privileges the spectacular. Just as the Hollywood star system operated within and through spectacle, so too in Mailer's text the spectacular event narrativized by Mailer presents the opportunity to fulfill his stardom. Guy Debord has indicated that within spectacular contemporary reality, the historical agent becomes the "agent of the spectacle."[25] In *The Armies of the Night*, Mailer enacts his agency in what is, essentially, yet another "advertisement" for himself. He narrates his many personas but fails to describe adequately the participants of the march, who are dismissed as "jargon-mired" and "middle-class cancer-pushers and drug-gutted flower children."[26] His considerable talents of personal description are reserved for fellow personalities such as Robert Lowell. Within *The Armies of the Night* a cult of personality results in the denigration, or displacement, of the antiwar movement and the reaffirmation of an imaginary unity, through a focus on the spectacle of individual ego.

The logic of spectacle structures this text in other ways. The issue of antiwar activity is deflected and displaced by a focus on definitions of "fiction" and "history" that are explored within a context that interprets events of the late twentieth century as spectacle. Supporting Debord's interpretation of contemporary reality, Mailer suggests that spectacle is not inserted into everyday life, it is the everyday. Writing in 1975, Philip Roth echoed Mailer's approach when he suggested that "the American writer in the middle of the twentieth century has his hands full in trying to understand, describe, and then make *credible* much of the American reality." In his frequently quoted conclusion, Roth asserts that "the actuality is continually outdoing our talents, and the culture tosses up figures almost daily that are the envy of any novelist."[27] Within this logic, the spectacular reality exceeds and thus disrupts established categories of understanding—reality outstrips imagination, demanding that imagination evoke new ways to represent history.

Mailer's response to this demand, subsequently adopted within the new journalism as virtually standard practice, was the disruption and redefinition of the categories of "history" and "fiction." Mailer does this not simply by juxtaposing a history of the event with a novelistic narrative but by merging the two forms. In the first half of the text, "History as a Novel," Mailer presents his own experience of the events leading up to the protest and his role in the protest. The second part, "The Novel as History," is a reconstructed version of the event based on a number of different reports. The first half, then, is an autobiographical account; the second half presents an "objective" account using an omniscient narrator. However, the structure does not result in a clear dichotomy between "novel" in the first section, and "history" in the second. In the second section Mailer unexpectedly declares that "the conceit [that] one is writing a history must be relinquished." Thus, the ordering of the categories of "novel" and "history" is reversed, and Mailer's subjective account becomes "to the best of the author's memory scrupulous to facts" and the "history" is represented as a "collective novel."[28]

The narrative function of this inversion and subversion is spectacular: its exposition entrances and entertains the reader with the result that form displaces content. It is, however, an "'entertainment' in its virtually etymological sense—*a holding-in-place, a containment,*" to adopt comments made by film theorist Dana Polan in relation to certain film genres. Polan's remarks intersect with Fredric Jameson's notion of narrative strategies of containment that function to preclude polysemy and impose a specific narrative focus and point of view.[29] The containment operates in *The Armies of the Night* through an absence of "awareness of any realities other than the spectacular." Reality, to continue to quote Polan, "shows forth" but "cannot be told."[30] Its spectacular quality cannot be literalized because it can be described only metaphorically. Having subverted the categories of history and fiction, Mailer employs a web of (spectacular) metaphors to convey (common) sense. The march on the Pentagon cannot adequately be described within the confines of history and fiction; it is both true and false. It is, then, to use one of Mailer's favorite metaphors, schizophrenic.[31]

For Mailer, schizophrenia refers to the degraded—divided—condition of modern America. "Apocalypse" is prominent within this condition.[32] Mailer is not being ironic in his use of metaphors. He does mock himself, although not when it comes to his narrative abilities (he refers to himself as the "best writer in America"),[33] which he employs to provide a rhetorical flourish in a closing that adequately summarizes his feelings and apprehensions for America. Mailer needed to construct an appropriate metaphor—hyperbolic and spectacular—that was capable of providing a satisfactory ending to the pattern of expectation established within the narrative through the frequent use of "schizophrenia" and other metaphors. The conclusion is quoted here at length:

> Brood on that country who expresses our will. She is America, once a beauty of magnificence unparalleled, now a beauty with a leprous skin. She is heavy with child—no one knows if legitimate—and languishes in a dungeon whose walls are never seen. Now the first contractions of her fearsome labor begin—it will go on: no doctor exists to tell the hour. It is only known that false labor is not likely on her now, no, she will probably give birth, and to what?—the most fearsome totalitarianism the world has ever known? or can she, poor giant, tormented lovely girl, deliver a babe of a new world brave and tender, artful and wild? Rush to the locks. God writhes in his bonds. Rush to the locks. Deliver us from our curse. For we must end on the road to that mystery where courage, death, and the dream of love give promise of sleep.[34]

The formation that Mailer hopes will emerge from the apocalypse is a unified place, deducible from the fact that Mailer has derogatorily referred to division as schizophrenia, a condition that brought about the imaginary apocalypse. Schizophrenia is thus overcome through apocalypse leading not to a "fearsome totalitarianism" but to a brave new unified world. Definitions of history and fiction, truth and untruth, are finally resolved through a metaphor that expresses Truth. This Truth, as defined by Hegel, and that Mailer expresses in an entirely different fashion, is the whole.[35]

In Mailer's text, as in a majority of representations from the late sixties, the assertion of unity is implicated with a denigration of the antiwar movement. Indeed, the existence of a mass oppositional social movement is inconsistent with the notion of a unified nation. In the presence of this unpalatable fact the conservative notion of the essential unity of American society is all that is commended. The contention that the war had been, or could have been, imported onto the home front is incompatible with representations that defined "home" as the site of an irreducible unity. Similarly, the decontextualization of protest and the privileging of celebrity leaders evident in Mailer's text, and other texts from the period, functioned to dispel the oppositional presence of antiwar protest capable of subverting the intimation of union. Significantly, the containment of opposition evident in Mailer's text was extended in a number of places throughout post–Vietnam War American culture.

In a specific way, the narrative strategies of various history textbooks contributed to processes operating across a wide cultural terrain that functioned to revise approaches to antiwar resistance and to contain or exclude references to home-front opposition to the war. College textbooks are recognized as central to students' understanding of the past, and as such are situated within the formations involved in the realization of ideological hegemony.[36] Textbooks assist to support this manifestation by contributing to the maintenance of definitional boundaries of legitimate knowledge. The omission of reference to historical events that oppose or contradict the assertion of unity functions to support the reproduction of dominant definitions that contribute in subtle ways to the perpetuation of commonsense assumptions regarding the condition of American culture.

In 1980, Frances FitzGerald expressed fears that representations of the antiwar movement were in danger of being written out of history textbooks. FitzGerald's reference evoked what Pierre Macherey termed a structured absence: the textual omission or repression of aspects of the past in accordance with contemporary ideological imperatives.[37] The texts FitzGerald studied "contain no reference, or almost none, to the peace movement or to any of the political turmoil of the late sixties and early seventies." FitzGerald suggested that "[i]n the future, this slate may be wiped clean. . . . [T]he domestic conflicts may disappear along with the issues that gave rise to them, leaving the impression that Americans in the sixties were always united behind their government, and that the war stopped because President Nixon and Secretary Kissinger decided that it should."[38] FitzGerald's analysis has since been borne out to the degree that various history textbooks have continued to ignore or give only minimal coverage to the role of the antiwar movement of the Vietnam War years.[39] While the strict focus in many textbooks on "the war" may preclude the necessity to study domestic reactions to the conflict, such an approach contributes, nevertheless, to the fear that references to the peace movement are in danger of being erased from the historical record of the conflict in Vietnam.

Just as textbooks may lack reference to the movement opposing the war, so too the courses that presumably employ these textbooks frequently fail to refer to antiwar protest. One list of sources devoted to "teaching the Vietnam war" does not include the role of domestic opposition.[40] Similarly, a proposal for study entitled "Using Literature in a Course on the Vietnam War" makes no mention of texts dealing with antiwar protest.[41] Yet another course, with the broader approach of "The Vietnam Experience," focuses exclusively upon literary texts concerned with combat in Vietnam.[42] The trend is the same where the basis of pedagogy is not literature. Walter Capps's text *The Unfinished War*, for example, rarely mentions antiwar activity or casts it in a negative framework, as when Capps refers to "the jeers, taunts, tomatoes, and spittle of the antiwar protestors."[43] Capps's text illustrates that antiwar protest has not been totally removed from written history narratives. It is present, although depictions such as Capps's seem to outweigh more judicious representations such as Kim McQuaid's *The Anxious Years* (1989).

McQuaid's contribution to the discussion of antiwar opposition is, he argues, a "simple truth." Unlike Godfrey Hodgson in *America in Our Time*, who conflates the antiwar movement and the New Left, McQuaid makes a distinction between the two forms of political expression.[44] He offers a number of reasons that the two terms have typically been indistinguishable and concludes with the assessment that "[t]he result [of the conflation of terms] was that an inaccurate picture of a coherent and well-organized something called 'the movement' was common [in the sixties], and is still common now."[45] To stem such a distortion of history is the motivation behind McQuaid's attention to definitions. In this relation, the distinction made between "antiwar" and "radical" positions is also valuable.[46] McQuaid's contribution includes the fact that he traces the gradual disappearance of mass protest; whereas other texts have suggested that protest, along with the New Left, abruptly culminated at the end of the sixties.[47] In various simple ways, then, McQuaid breaks with common patterns of representing the movement.

The need to stereotype mass protest points to the unease caused by the existence of a movement that not only objected to U.S. foreign policy but also revealed the presence of division within American culture. If the antiwar movement sought to "bring the war home," then derogatory representations of the movement had the effect of reasserting "home" as a place devoid of division. Typical of the form of representation referred to here is William O'Neill's historical study of the war years, *Coming Apart*. Ignoring the distinction McQuaid makes between the antiwar movement and the New Left, the index to *Coming Apart* refers to antiwar action as "Protest—students"—which O'Neill equates to the New Left, which, in turn, he disparages. His unsubstantiated characterization of protestors recycles impressions that were already clichés in 1971, the year of the book's publication. According to O'Neill, "Many protesters, lacking serious reasons for being in college, resented having to study. . . . If one could not expose a discipline for abetting the military-industrial complex, one could damn it as 'elitist,' anti-social, or irrelevant. There were plenty of other rocks lying around for the discontented to throw."[48]

This caricature is extended in the photographs that accompany O'Neill's written text. Photographs are not merely illustrative, they provide important connotative cues to the written text. Roland Barthes informed this point when he argued that the photographic image supersedes the written account, which exists to "sublimate, patheticize or rationalize the image."[49] One image used in O'Neill's book is a photograph of the November 1969 Moratorium in Washington that features a placard depicting the U.S. flag "bleeding" into the flag of the National Liberation Front. The inclusion of this photograph is similar to the news media's coverage of antiwar demonstrators in which NLF flags were often singled out as a way of suggesting the radical or, in these terms, anti-American, stance of the demonstrators. Of the many photographs that could have been chosen to illustrate antiwar demonstrations, the inclusion of this particular image reproduces a particular "framing" tactic of the mass media toward the protest movement.[50]

A further example of dominant attitudes to antiwar protestors encoded within *Coming Apart* is evident in two black-and-white photographs that appear on facing pages in the second half of the book. The first photograph, on the verso, is a close-up of the face of a young white male. Context has been eliminated with the cropping of the photograph, although two other young white males are partially visible in the background. The principal subject is bearded, pimply, with hair covering his ears; and he wears a cap of the type favored by renegade motorcyclists and what appears to be a dirty jacket. On the cap is a badge that reads "Burn pot not people." The words are a dual articulation: they present marijuana use as a viable alternative to the horrors of war and, at the same time, they fix the subject's position on the war. However, his eyes, as much as the words on the badge, are the focus of the frame. His gaze is averted; he doesn't look at the camera. It is the disingenuous look of a recreant. If, according to a widespread masculine ethos, a man is someone who looks you in the eye, then this is not a "man."

The photograph on the opposing page depicts perhaps a dozen U.S. soldiers in Vietnam. The photograph takes in the foreground and stretches to the far distance. The soldiers, both black and white, are sitting slouched in a trench and appear to be exhausted. They smoke cigarettes, one is bare-headed, one wears a bush hat, and the rest wear their helmets. The scene is unmistakably one of war, though not specifically the war in Vietnam—the positioning of these soldiers in a trench evokes a number of earlier wars. The notion of camaraderie, of brothers in arms, is reinforced through the "racial" mix of the group. The attitude of sheer exhaustion that characterizes the scene implies a post-battle stand-down and a respite from the war. The face of the black man in the middle distance and of a white man in the far distance bear the "thousand-yard stare" suggesting that they have paid a high physical price in the performance of their duty. The caption for both photographs reads simply: "Young Americans at home and abroad." The photographs function in a similar way to the popular advertising gimmick of "before" and "after" pictorials. Before Vietnam is the uncouth and craven antiwar demonstrator, juxtaposed to the succeeding phase that depicts "young Americans" who have recently "answered the call" to fight in Vietnam. Although each picture "tells a story," the complete narrative is contained in the contrast of the two: those young male Americans at home are not the men that those abroad have proven themselves to be. In the contrast between the two images, those who opposed the war become suspect. The conclusion, however, does not stem directly from opposition to the war; it derives from a "character flaw" that leads (young male) individuals to oppose war. The decoded narrative of these pictures is a story of war and its opposition told in masculine terms and framed as the rhetorical question Are you man enough to answer the call? Those who fail the test or who refuse to take the test are, by implication, "unmanly."

This conclusion was subsequently reinforced by authors who sought to expunge what was referred to as "Viet guilt," defined as guilt for not having fought in Vietnam.[51] In an article in the *New York Times* in 1981, poet Michael Blumenthal admitted that he felt that veterans of the war "have something that we haven't got":

> It is, to be sure, somewhat vague, but nonetheless real, and can be embraced under several headings: realism, discipline, masculinity (kind of a dirty word these days), resilience, tenacity, resourcefulness. We may have turned out to be better dancers, choreographers, and painters (though not necessarily), but I'm not at all sure that they didn't turn out to be better *men*, in the best sense of the word.[52]

Such statements typically begin with equally guilt-ridden confessions of having avoided the draft. Christopher Buckley, for example, describes his physical examination for induction into the army and his delight at being ruled unfit because of a history of asthma. Buckley adds that at the unveiling of the Vietnam Veterans Memorial he "stood face-to-face" with his own "guilt and shame."[53] It was a particular species of guilt. It was not the guilt that led another observer to confess before the Wall that "although I did oppose the war and all that led to it, I did not do enough and what I did was clearly not effective enough."[54] Buckley's confession does not concern his opposition to the war, which is not mentioned; instead it concerns his "somewhat vague, but nonetheless real" impression that he will never have what the veterans have, and as a result he "will always feel the lack of it and will try to compensate for it, sometimes in good, other times in ludicrous, ways."[55] Guilt, then, is presented as the only response available to those who, as the argument goes, contributed directly to American defeat in Vietnam.

The allusion in this thesis to a link between the antiwar movement and military defeat in Vietnam is manifested and strengthened through the intense concern with defeat evident in the film *First Blood* (1982), the first in the *Rambo* cycle of films. John Rambo (Sylvester Stallone) is invested with aspects of the iconography popularly associated with the antiwar movement and the counterculture—long hair, articles of army surplus clothing, a U.S. flag on his jacket. However, the objectives of the peace movement are perverted and subverted in Rambo's violent actions. In his final speech Rambo implicates the antiwar movement as the cause of all his troubles since his return to the United States, and in this way the film suggests that Rambo's furious spree, the ostensible focus of the film, was a response to the presence of antiwar protestors on the home front:

> I did what I had to do to win, but somebody wouldn't let us win! Then I come back to the world, and see all those maggots at the airport . . . spittin', callin' me baby-killer and all kinds of vile crap! Who are they to protest me? Who are they unless they've been there and know what the hell they're yellin' about?

Rambo's words deny the antiwar position by asserting that only those who experienced the war can legitimately comment on it. This theme, already discussed here in a different context, has certain implications for the representation of the antiwar movement.

In an episode of the television series *Tour of Duty* (1987), a pacifist draftee refuses to fight because "the war is wrong." His sergeant replies:

"Maybe that's not the point." The "point" is illustrated in the revisionist film *Hamburger Hill* (1987) in which another sergeant, referring to draft resisters, insists: "You don't have to like [the war], but you have to show up." The argument refuses to recognize any position other than participation in war. The validity of militarist policy is not disputed in such references to the peace movement, while the implication that certain sectors of society did not "show up" connotes the antiwar movement as morally suspect and treacherous. In other sources opposition to the war was criticized as terroristic. Myra MacPherson's dismissive characterization of the "not-so-nonviolent peace movement" is one type of focus that consistently alludes to certain actions of the Weather Underground, for example, and ignores peaceful mass protest.[56]

Further to images of a peace movement that is abusive and naive, unmanly and treacherous and violent, are representations of the movement as manipulative, particularly of the veteran. Toward the end of the novel *Fields of Fire* (1979) James Webb includes a scene in which his protagonist Goodrich, a one-legged veteran of the Vietnam War, participates in an antiwar rally on the Harvard campus. Though Goodrich queries the motives of the organizers, wary that they want to include him in their protest as an example of an "experiment gone afoul," he nevertheless accepts the invitation to attend the rally. In the middle of what he began as a speech against aspects of the war, Goodrich suddenly turns on the crowd in disgust and accuses them of dishonesty for evading the draft. At the end of the scene Goodrich's feelings of having been manipulated into participating in an event in which he was, as feared, used to promote preconceived ideas on the war manifest themselves as an attack on one of the organizers of the demonstration, whom Goodrich symbolically shoots with his raised crutch.[57] Webb's construction of an unbridgeable gap between victimized veterans and a selfish protest movement denies the fact that many veterans protested the war, and others, rather than feeling betrayed or manipulated by home-front opposition to the war, objected to the violence being used to quell antiwar protests.[58] In the scene from *Fields of Fire*, variations of which are reworked in John Irving's novel *A Prayer for Owen Meany* (1989), the veteran is victimized by an opportunistic and parasitic peace movement.[59] The approach is also evident in the film *Hanoi Hilton* (1987), that features a scene in which members of a delegation from the American antiwar movement attempt to persuade American prisoners in North Vietnam attempt to confess to illegal war-

related actions. McCarthy-era representations are resurrected in this depiction of "communist sympathizers," the antiwar movement, willing to
manipulate fellow countrymen for their cause.

In a different way, the widespread "trashing [of] the 60s"[60] has implications for the social movements of those years, including the antiwar
movement. The "backlash" has taken palpable forms in definitions such
as William O'Neill's trivialization of the decade as "a kind of binge," or
the reference by *Time* magazine to "the long, wild hallucination of the
'60s."[61] The historian Richard Hofstadter called it "The Age of Rubbish." And Allan Bloom, in his controversial book *The Closing of the
American Mind* (1987), criticized the decade for what he perceived as its
multiple failures: "I know of nothing positive coming from that period,"
wrote Bloom.[62] The opinion was repeated by those who had "second
thoughts" about the era.[63] In one of many reassessments during 1988
marking twenty years since the "watershed" year of 1968, *Newsweek*
magazine carried the cover headline: "Will we ever get over the 60s?"
"The implication, of course," noted Jon Wiener, "is that getting over the
sixties is something we ought to do."[64]

In many cases the failure to acknowledge the positive legacies of the
decade rests on a strict periodization that interprets "the sixties" as a dis-
crete entity. While the division between "the 60s" and "the 70s" has
tended to deny the antiwar movement any lasting validity by containing
the movement within the sixties, so too a dichotomization *within* the sixties functions to create the impression that political activity was restricted
to the latter half of the decade. The creation of a "good" early sixties, and
a "bad" late sixties—prominent in books dealing with the New Left[65]—
implies a mythical apolitical period at the beginning of the decade. The
powerful appeal of this early period is demonstrated in films such as
American Graffiti (1973) and *Animal House* (1979), and in television series that include *Happy Days* (1974) *Laverne and Shirley* (1975), and *The
Wonder Years* (1988), all of which refuse to accept the presence of the
war or other cultural or political disruptions during the opening years of
the sixties.[66]

Trashing the sixties has operated along a broad cultural front and has
involved, over the years, Tom Wolfe's criticism that those involved with
progressive causes are merely faddists; George Bush's claim that sixties
welfarism, encoded in references to the Great Society, was responsible for
the Los Angeles uprising of 1992; and Richard Nixon's criticisms of sixties values and ideals in his book *Beyond Peace* (1994).[67] Certain words

that once circulated in media accounts of the sixties—"counterculture," "lifestyle," "permissiveness"—are recycled as the focus of conservative and neoliberal critiques of the decade. The decontextualization of aspects of historical experience enacted in the revision of such keywords is reflected in the common media practice of representing the sixties through collages of images wrenched from the era. Cogent analysis of the meanings of specific representations and the history they denote is forestalled in an approach that reduces cultural and historical events and movements to symbols, or merely reworks known, and in certain cases, hackneyed, images.

One aspect of the approach to the history of the sixties as collage is evident in the sound tracks of various Vietnam War films that pillage rock-music production of the sixties for evocative songs. Newsmagazines also favor collage as a way of representing "the sixties." A typical example of this representational process is found on the cover of a 1988 issue of *Time* magazine depicting "the year that shaped a generation" through photographs of GIs and helicopters in Vietnam, Janis Joplin, Robert Kennedy, and Soviet tanks in Prague.[68] The artist Robert Rauschenberg summarized the sixties through this method in his work *Signs* (1970), a collage of silk-screened images from the decade, including photographs of John and Robert Kennedy, Joplin, a dead Martin Luther King, Jr.; a still from the Zapruder film of the Kennedy assassination; National Guardsmen seated in a Jeep, rifles at the ready; protesting students; wounded GIs in Vietnam; a prostrate and bloody rioter; and "Buzz" Aldrin on the moon.[69] Thus, in representations produced by sources as diverse as corporate publishing and "pop" art, "the sixties" is encoded predominantly as an era of assassinations, rock music, war, riots, and failed political aspirations. In keeping with this approach, one reassessment interpreted 1968 in America in terms of "Music, Politics, Chaos, Counterculture, and the Shaping of a Generation."[70]

Images and icons from the sixties are also routinely dislodged from their original contexts to sell various products to a demographic group supposedly composed of "baby boomers." The history of the period is reified in images, sounds, and impressions that approach a Baudrillardian simulacrum that no longer connotes history but, instead, refers to other decontextualized and recycled representations in a process that validates the observation made by Horkheimer and Adorno that "every reification is a form of forgetting."[71] While certain sources have contributed to amnesia through the "collage effect," other sources have subtly revised aspects of sixties experience in an approach that is more pastiche than collage.

In 1985, Lance Morrow, a feature writer for *Time* magazine who specializes in hyperbolic reports on the Vietnam era, analyzed the war as "a bloody rite of passage" that "cost America its innocence and still haunts its conscience." Morrow claimed that "[t]here is a certain giddy proximity of death in the time—rock stars like Janis Joplin and Jimi Hendrix went tumbling down from drug overdoses, as if to dramatize the war's theme of meaninglessly, profligately blasted youth." According to Morrow, death, the counterculture, and the war were joined: "The war and the counterculture could at certain moments seem part of the same rock 'n' roll, drawing their energy from one dark circuit."[72]

Ten years earlier, in *Dispatches*, Michael Herr observed that during the time he had spent in Vietnam "rock and roll turned more lurid and dangerous than bullfighting, rock stars started falling like second lieutenants," and that once back in America, he "couldn't tell Vietnam veterans from the rock and roll veterans. The Sixties had made so many casualties, its war and its music had run power off the same circuit for so long they didn't even have to fuse."[73] In Herr's account, the sixties influenced both rock music and the war. The conclusion is linked to Herr's emphasis throughout his text on the role of rock in the war, especially the fact that many soldiers relied on rock lyrics to provide interpretative frameworks for their experience in Vietnam. In Morrow's unacknowledged revisions of Herr's text, rock is expelled from the account; replaced by the "blasted youth" of the counterculture. Morrow demonizes the counterculture by linking it, like the war, to a "dark circuit" in a connection that turns the violence of the war into an integral feature of the counterculture. Such a characterization is only a step away from equally outrageous descriptions of the members of the Manson gang as prototype hippies and the Tate-LaBianca murders as the epitome of countercultural beliefs and actions.

Central to each of the various pejorative and stereotypical accounts of the sixties is a form of decontextualization and revision of experience inaugurated in contemporary media reports of the antiwar movement, and in the "youth-against-the-war" films. The perspectives of such texts and the subsequent attacks on aspects of historical experience associated with the sixties "form part of a whole ideological conflict, for which Gramsci's term hegemony remains the most convenient shorthand, a conflict which includes contests over interpretations of history. . . . "[74] This observation is informed through the study of expressions of commonsense assumptions concerning the history and nature of American culture. Implicit within the denigration and revision of the role of the antiwar movement and antiwar protest is an appeal to an essential unity—a whole that will not admit difference, that must deplore, banish, or subsume contradictory voices in order to maintain itself. The contention upheld in the sixties that the antiwar movement was "bringing the war home" questioned and threatened the popular image of home as a place devoid of disruptive presences. The work of the range of texts discussed here is the containment of this suggestion and the attempt to maintain the validity of the notion of unity—the defining characteristic of home.

Repatriation

By the end of the sixties the culture industries had intervened in the struggle for the hearts and minds of the American public, and as a result both the war at home and the one in Vietnam found their way into a number of fictional texts. Despite assertions to the contrary, the film *The Green Berets* (1968) was not the only film to depict the war during the war years.[75] The "Vietnam westerns" of the late sixties alluded to the Vietnam War in representations of nineteenth-century wars against the native inhabitants of North America. The presence of "Vietnam" in representations of the sixties is further suggested in the assessment that "all Hollywood films of the [war] period, from *Bonnie and Clyde* to *The Wild Bunch*, were to some degree oblique metaphors for the war."[76] The production of *metaphorical* interpretations of the war gives a certain credence to the assumption, circulated in many places since the war, that the war was *literally* unrepresentable. The latter assumption was supported by the popular suggestion that the American public was, as a result of nightly wartime news coverage, tired of seeing graphic, "literal," televisual representations of the war. The ability of metaphor to represent one object in terms of another enabled the war to be depicted obliquely, thus overcoming the contradiction involved in the representation of an allegedly unrepresentable war.

The contradictory function of metaphor and its functional ability to overcome contradiction also proved beneficial to certain representations of the impact of the war. The dominant metaphor of the wound, for example, encoded both the deleterious effects of the war and the denial of those effects in healing. Elsewhere in the culture during the seventies issues relating to the war were encoded in visual metaphors that, not being as elaborately specified as the wound metaphor, were open to varying interpretations. For example, critical opinion is divided over the meaning of the so-called disaster films of the early to midseventies, films that include *Airport* (1970), *The Poseidon Adventure* (1972), *Earthquake* (1974), and *The Towering Inferno* (1975). According to certain critics, these films are metaphoric representations of anxieties "brought about by the movements of the 60s," including the movement against the war.[77] This position has been contradicted in the observation that "by asserting that America's enemies remained nature and/or technology, disaster films denied that consensus shattered." In this interpretation, disaster films "were the first wave of reillusionment" after "the apocalyptic breakdowns of the sixties."[78]

A more resolute encoding of a message was achieved at the time within a number of texts that exploited the metaphor of bringing the war home. The project associated with the antiwar movement gained a different resonance within Robert Stone's novel *Dog Soldiers* (1974), and the filmed version, *Who'll Stop the Rain?* (1978), and the films *The Visitors* (1972), *Tracks* (1976), *Taxi Driver* (1976), *Heroes* (1977), and *Rolling Thunder* (1977). The metaphorical associations of each text derived from depictions of the violence of the war enacted on the home front by returned soldiers. The notion inherent in these representations, that the war had been repatriated to the United States with the veteran, became, for a period during the early and midseventies, the standard device employed to evoke the ruinous impact of the war.

Despite its popularity, the metaphor did not escape criticism. The myth of the violent veteran loose on the home front was contested during the late sixties in David Rabe's incisive play *Sticks and Bones* (1969). Rabe's work seeks to confront the violent image of the returned soldier by exploring the basis of the veterans' problems in a scenario that brings a veteran home to a pathetically bewildered family. In the play Harriet, Ozzie, and Ricky await the arrival of David, who is being repatriated by an army sergeant whose job it is to "deliver" the casualties of war. "I've got trucks backed up out there for blocks," says the sergeant.[79] David has been blinded in the war, yet in the first of many bitter ironies it is David's family that fails to see him. Eventually the members of the family choose to recognize David as their son but wish to be rid of this unwelcome intrusion on a domestic scene that is a vicious parody of stereotyped family life represented in the television series *The Adventures of Ozzie and Harriet*. As a result of the disruption of the family's routine, Ozzie is forced at one point to reassure himself of the family's future by asserting: "The air's been cleared ... the wound's acknowledged, the healing begun."[80] However, Ozzie points to his own inability to accept the situation and presages David's disastrous end when he adds: "It's the [wounds] that aren't acknowledged—the ones that aren't talked over—they're the ones that do the deep damage."[81] In a sad reflection of this observation, Ozzie and Harriet are completely incapable of discussing the problems besetting them, and they cannot communicate with David, whose fantasies of a Vietnamese prostitute, Zung, gain substance when Zung appears in the family home. Unable to understand or accept David's bitterness and his vivid hallucinations, David's family encourages him to slit his wrists. "We're all happier," says Ozzie as he watches his son bleed into a vegetative state. "He's not gonna die.... He's only gonna die nearly. Only nearly," are Ozzie's final words as he bleakly reinstates a mandatory "happy ending."[82]

Typically, representations avoided the issues of war-induced family trauma and the postwar problems of assimilation facing the veteran raised by *Sticks and Bones* within a reversion to the formula of exploiting the metaphor of "bringing the war home" by recreating scenes of war within America. In various texts home-front violence was associated with the Vietnam veteran, resulting in the reinforcement of the invidious stereotype of the maladjusted, or sick, veteran. Examples of this depiction include the final scene of the film *Tracks* (1976) in which Jack Falen (Dennis Hopper) jumps into the grave of the soldier he has accompanied home for burial to emerge in military uniform brandishing a rifle, shouting: "You want to know what it's like in Nam!" The war that Falen is about to unleash on the home front also returns to the United States during the traumatic flashbacks experienced by Jack Dunne (Henry Winkler), the emotionally disturbed Vietnam veteran in the film *Heroes* (1977), which turn a quiet California street into a fully realized battlefield.

The linking of the veteran and violence through the metaphor of bringing the war home was further elaborated in bloody detail in Martin Scorsese's *Taxi Driver*, perhaps the most notorious example of the carnage wrought on the home front by a returned soldier. Travis Bickle (Robert De Niro), the Vietnam veteran of *Taxi Driver*, underscores his own marginality and alienation by describing himself as "God's lonely man." Unable to sleep after his long shifts as a cabdriver, he visits sleazy cinemas to watch X-rated films. His frustration is palpable as he becomes increasingly obsessed by what he calls the "filth" on the streets of New York. For Travis, the only pure thing in the city is Betsy (Cybill Shepherd), who works for a liberal presidential candidate, Charles Palantine. As Travis's frustration and anger grows, he writes in his notebook that "something has to change." His first metamorphosis occurs when he buys an arsenal and shaves his head into a "Mohawk" haircut as part of an incoherent plan to assassinate Palantine as a way of impressing Betsy. Paul Schrader, the film's scriptwriter, summarized the plot and Travis's course of action in Oedipal terms when he stated: "[*Taxi Driver* concerns] the girl [Travis] wants but can't have, and the one he can have but doesn't want. He tries to kill the surrogate father of the first and fails, so he kills the surrogate father of the other."[83] The latter surrogate father is Sport (Harvey Keitel), the pimp of the thirteen-year-old prostitute Iris (Jody Foster). The scene Schrader refers to is the violent climax in which Travis murders Sport, wounds the doorman of Iris's apartment building, and kills Iris's client. In this scene, the "body count" clearly testifies to the presence of a war fought on the home front by this psychotic character.

In the script for his subsequent film, *Rolling Thunder* (1977), Schrader transformed the entire male population of America into deranged figures. The issue is highlighted in a scene in which Major Charles Rane (William Devane), having returned home after seven years as a prisoner of war of the North Vietnamese, is told by his wife, Linda (Linda Forchet), that she has been seeing someone else and wants a divorce. Commenting on her relationships, Linda asks, "Why do I always get stuck with crazy men?" Rane replies: "'Cause that's the only kind that's left," thereby establishing the theme of "dementia" that subsequently intersects in the film with a characteristic expression of violence. Soon after this exchange Rane and his family are attacked by a brutal gang of thieves looking for the ten thousand silver dollars he received from the citizens of his home town, San Antonio, as compensation for his imprisonment. The gang murders his wife and son and seriously wounds Rane. With the help of his sergeant from the war, Johnny Vohden (Tommy Lee Brown), Rane follows the gang to a Mexican bordello. In the final scenes the "maddened" Rane unleashes his firepower in a shoot-out that results in a death toll that exceeds that of the climax of *Taxi Driver*. In each of these examples, then, the veteran brings the war home in obvious ways. The metaphor of a "war" on the home front is inescapable in the presence of weapons, violence, blood, and death.

However, there is another side to the metaphor that has not been explored in the various critiques of these texts: in the majority of examples the war returns *home*. The strictures of the metaphorical interpretation of bringing the war "home" demanded that the family—the center of the home—become the dominant site for registering the presence of the war. One example of the linking of the war and the family occurs in Robert Stone's novel *Dog Soldiers*, in which the arrival in the United States of three kilos of heroin smuggled from Vietnam, a symbol of the pernicious effects of the war, signals the beginning of the dissolution of the only family to appear in the book. The husband, John Converse, is separated from his wife, Marge, who flees San Francisco with Converse's friend, Ray Hicks, when both are chased by corrupt narcotic agents in search of the drug. In the wake of their desperation, Hicks and Marge leave Marge's daughter, Janey, with friends. On his return from Vietnam, Converse visits his empty house in Berkeley to find his wife and child missing and notices that "[s]omeone had drawn a devil on the wall above Janey's crib. It had horns and bat wings and a huge erect phallus; there was enough characterization in the details of the face to make it distinctly frightening."[84] It is an augury that the family and the fate of innocence is bedeviled in the wake of the war in Vietnam. Marge and Hicks, having arrived in the hills above Los Angeles to seek refuge in Hicks's cabin, find that the place has been occupied by runaways who have been drugged and held captive by four misfits. Hicks throws them all out. "What happens to those kids?" Marge asks. "You're thinking like a mother," replies Hicks, intimating that in the ruination of post–Vietnam America there is no place for maternal or familial considerations.

The subversion of such considerations was especially marked in *Taxi Driver*. Travis Bickle is a lonely psychotic outsider, yet he is also a family man. For example, during his first conversation with Iris, the child prostitute, Travis attempts to persuade her to return home. Again, before his murderous spree, the good son sends a card to his parents assuring them all is well.[85] Travis's qualities as a family provider are affirmed in a post-battle coda in the form of a letter from "Bert and Ivy Steensma of Pittsburgh," who thank Travis for returning home their daughter, Iris. Travis's elevation to hero and family savior is ironic on a number of levels. During their first conversation, Iris tells Travis: "There ain't nothin' [at home]." However as the letter from her parents states, home is not empty; it is filled with a family attempting to ensure that Iris does not again run away. Schrader's joke is that in the wake of having been a prostitute, and then witness to a harrowing moment of violence as Travis murders everyone around her, Iris can readily return to school and find happiness at home. It is notable that the captivity and search narrative of *Taxi Driver*, like *Rolling Thunder*, and another of Schrader's scripts, *Hardcore* (1978), resemble John Ford's *The Searchers* (1956). Despite the plot resemblances, however, there is no equivalent of *Taxi Driver*'s coda in *The Searchers*.[86] Robin Wood has argued that "the ideological weight of the notion of 'home' [in *The Searchers*] was pretty thoroughly undermined, but it retained sufficient force for the 'happy ending' of Debbie's return . . . to come across as slightly more than a mockery."[87] In contrast, *Taxi Driver* subverts home to such an extent that Iris's fate constitutes a sardonic form of narrative closure.

In the representations referred to here, the fact that the war had come home with the veteran had two obvious effects: the disruption of the home, and the stereotyping of the veteran as psychotic. The persistence of these effects, however, contradicted the basic cultural tenet of unity. Within the stereotype of the "sick vet," the effects of the war were reduced to the pathological. If the veteran could be "cured," then home would be healed of the lingering presence of the war. Reversing the criticisms of the regenerative and recuperative function of the family found in *Taxi Driver* and *Sticks and Bones*, the veteran was cured of the symptoms of war by *returning to the family*. For this situation to occur, the family had to overcome the disruptive presence of the violent veteran. The solution did not depend upon the removal of the veteran from the family—it rested on the healing of the veteran's condition within a reconstructed, therapeutic family. The change in the family signified by these alterations was as remarkable as the transformation undergone by the veteran within its regenerated, regenerative form. Constructed as an essential cultural institution, the family *had* to be salvaged from the inference of division. However, the impetus for this recovery was not the impact of the war. The rehabilitation that occurred during the seventies was precipitated by the well-documented "crisis" of the family. The resolution of the crisis healed the family, overcoming the divisive impact of the war, allowing the veteran to come home. In this way, the achievement of the "therapeutic" family involved some "fantastic" therapy for the family.[88]

The Therapeutic Family

In 1977, Christopher Lasch published a study of the family ominously subtitled "The Family Besieged,"[89] and in May of 1978 a *Newsweek* special report dealt with "Saving the Family."[90] These two examples, indicative of wider perceptions during the late seventies, point to the existence of a condition referred to at the time as the "crisis of the family."[91] Census statistics were rallied as evidence of depressing social trends. The rising divorce rate was a major cause of alarm, as was the decline in the marriage rate, which "began to drop in 1972, reaching a low of ten marriages per thousand people in 1976." Birthrates in the United States "dropped from 18.4 per thousand in 1970 to 14.8 per thousand in 1975." Childlessness increased "dramatically" among married women during the seventies, and the increase in single-person households "seemed to epitomize the collapse of family relations." The "proliferation of couples who lived together without legal sanction" and the increase in the number of working mothers were not overlooked in this relation. "By middecade, the traditional yardstick used by the Department of Labor to define a 'typical' household—a working father, a domesticated mother, and two children—represented a mere 7 percent of all American families."[92] A number of texts of the late seventies reflected and contributed to the perception of familial crisis by representing the traditional family structure in disarray. Using the crisis as the occasion to reassert a strong patriarchal presence, these texts scapegoated women as the destroyers of the family. In *The Champ* (1979), *Kramer vs. Kramer* (1979), *Ordinary People* (1980), *Author! Author!* (1982), and *The World According to Garp* and *Mr. Mom* (both 1983), the father is represented as the strong nurturing presence for his children and the mother is depicted as having selfishly abandoned them.

The combined effect of these films contributed to a well-documented backlash against women and feminism, thus extending a project that was evident, in a different form, in the representations of the impact of the war in Vietnam.[93] Within texts depicting war on the home front, violence is featured as the function and inscription of male action undertaken in relation to the family. The result of this action positions the (male) veteran as *the* causative agent within the family, thus displacing changes to the family resulting from the advances of the second wave of feminism. Of the texts dealing with the veteran's return, only *Coming Home* (1978) attempted to link changes within the family to the agency of women. The displacement of women was advanced in other ways within texts of the Vietnam War.

Susan Jeffords has noted that in many of these texts the male bond is privileged to such a degree that males become, in effect, reproducing fathers who, unencumbered by the mediation of women, give birth to generations of combat soldiers.[94] The foregrounding of male bonds resonates within moves by the men's movement to legitimate the validity of a community of men. According to Robert Bly's influential men's-movement text *Iron John: A Book about Men* (1990), the emotional condition of the family is in danger of being engulfed by the mother. Bly's answer reinvokes the notion of separate gender spheres through its appeal to the construction of a separate male culture. Within their own community men can develop the features of what he calls the "Wild Man." Drawing on a range of mythopoeic sources, Bly argues that the Wild Man archetype represents a basic male condition characterized by fierceness and bold action.[95] The culture of males proposed by Bly leaves little room for women or families. Ironically, problematic considerations of the denial of the family through a privileging of masculine culture dissolved within men's-movement conceptions of the male that implied that a "Wild Man" was capable of protecting a "weaker sex" and an endangered family.

The rewriting of the role of women within the family was not the only consequence of the assertion of familial crisis. Principally, the mythical traditional family unit was resurrected as a panacea to the crisis. The appeal to an essential familial unity implicit in the model of the traditional family was evident in specific ways in the rhetoric of Moral Majority spokesperson Jerry Falwell and moral crusader Anita Bryant. Attempts by such advocates to legitimate the profamily position and to demonize a range of social, sexual, and biological practices exceeded political, moral, or legal arguments through recourse to the necessity of unity. What were conceived as threats to the family were encoded in the rhetoric of the Christian right as unnatural or unlawful because they contradicted a natural law as intrinsic as gravity, namely, that the family is a unit composed of a married heterosexual couple and their children.

The common sense of unity was reinforced in additional ways through images of the traditional family that appeared during the late seventies and early eighties. Coming in the wake of the assertion of familial disarray, the reestablishment of the validity of the assumed basic family unit functioned as a model for the alleviation, or resolution, of the amorphous set of conditions referred to as familial crisis. Among other places in the culture, the traditional family reappeared in the films *The Other Side of Midnight* and *Bobby Deerfield* (both 1977), *Slow Dancing in the Big City* (1978), *Ice Castles* (1979), *Shoot the Moon* (1982), and *Terms of Endearment* (1983). A number of sources beyond film also contributed to the circulation of a renovated model of the traditional family. John Jakes's description of the family in the historical romance series of novels *Kent Family Chronicles* sold, it was claimed, thirty million copies between 1974 and 1980.[96] This emphasis on the family and family history was reinforced with the phenomenal success of Alex Haley's autobiographical family history, *Roots*, which was first published in 1976. The story of black America reached an audience of more than 130 million people when it was broadcast over eight nights on ABC television in January 1977. Other televisual products of the late seventies and early eighties contributed to what Andrew Ross has termed "the reinforced familialism of the 1980s."[97] Notable in this context are the television series *Family Ties* (1982), *The Cosby Show* (1984), *Who's the Boss?* (1984), and *Growing Pains* (1985).

Various signs, then, indicated that by the eighties the family had been healed, and in the process the divisions supposedly created by the war had been overcome. The recuperation of the traditional family after the trauma of Vietnam is an example of the "unique and singular" quality of American ideology and "the speed with which it can incorporate" a variety of positions "in an enveloping rhetorical system designed to maintain traditional order and values."[98] The rewriting of the suggestion of familial crisis through the circulation of images of the traditional family had another significant effect: it denied any notion of familial disruption caused by the war in Vietnam. This is not to say that the Vietnam War was absent from representations of the family after this time. In fact, the "enveloping rhetorical system" that is the ideology of unity negotiated the home-front presence of the war.

Throughout the eighties veterans continued to return home or be associated with Vietnam in ways that tested the strength of family ties. In the made-for-television film *Intimate Strangers* (1986), Sally (Teri Garr), an army nurse who has returned to America after ten years as a prisoner in Vietnam, confronts her husband (Stacy Keach) with the news that the boy who accompanied her home is her son. Sally's homecoming, and the presence of a new member of the family tests, yet finally reinforces, the strengths of spousal and familial bonds.[99] In the film *Welcome Home* (1989) and in the telemovie *The Lady from Yesterday* (1985), the veteran faces a unique problem in the form of two families—the one he began in Southeast Asia and his family in the United States. The overdetermination of familialism in the dual-family device is reinforced when the veteran finally reaffirms his place as the head of his "rightful" (American) family.

While news sources in the mideighties reported on war-related issues—including the problems besieging the postwar Vietnamese economy, the plight of Vietnamese "boat people," and conditions within Vietnamese communities in America—the spate of homecoming films during the period refused to address such issues by remaining fixed at the level of a melodramatic focus on the domestic scene.[100] In *Welcome Home* and *The Lady from Yesterday* the "problems" associated with the war are contained within a domestic sphere that is dominated by the male figure, who, through his actions, institutes what are, in the film's terms, the most lasting "legacies" of the war. Effectively ignoring contemporary political concerns, the intersection of the (re)unified patriarchal family and the impact of the war in these and a number of texts from the eighties focus representation on the incorporation of the veteran into the family. Incorporation cured the veteran's psychosis, erasing or denying the veteran's physical wounds and mental malaise. The sick vet had been returned home a member of the family. Home in these representations was depicted not only as unified and therapeutic but as therapeutic *because it was unified.*

The healing power of the family evident in various texts from the mideighties is further demonstrated in the film *Cease Fire* (1984) through the fate of two troubled veterans, Tim Murphy (Don Johnson) and Luke (Robert Lyons). While Luke seems to be coping with his war-related problems far better than Tim, the reality of Luke's mental health is fully revealed after his estranged wife refuses Luke's offer of a reunion. After a final plea for help in an emotional telephone call to Tim, Luke kills himself. Denied the opportunity to return home, Luke, like Bob Hyde (Bruce Dern) of *Coming Home*, takes the only path available to him. The message is clear: safety and health reside in the family. Closure is attained when Tim, assisted by the patient understanding of his wife, overcomes his wartime flashbacks to be fully reunited with his wife and son. In the film's final scene Tim and his wife hold hands and stare at the Vietnam Veterans Memorial as a passing veteran welcomes them both home. The theme of reunion is reinforced in the words of the sound track song that assert: "We've got each other."

Emmett Walsh of Bobbie Ann Mason's novel *In Country* is another disturbed veteran who is healed in the union that is the family home. Emmett's initial confusion over his role in the family is signified by his transvestism. Emmett's niece Samantha Hughes explains to her boyfriend, Lonnie, that the reason Emmett wears dresses in the house he shares with Sam is that he is imitating the character Klinger of his favorite television series, *M*A*S*H*.[101] The inversion of traditional family roles represented by Emmett's feigned lunacy is extended when Sam adopts the role of head of the household vacated by Emmett. However, the pattern of inversion is repealed when disparate members of the family—Emmett, Sam, and Samantha's paternal grandmother—are united on a trip to Washington to view the Vietnam Veterans Memorial. Motivated by the plan, Emmett sheds his symptoms of psychosis and becomes the true patriarch by adopting the role of leader of the united members of the family, thus redefining familial roles in the wake of the aberrant period of role cross-dressing.

The therapeutic effect of the unified family is especially pronounced in texts dealing with so-called bush vets, or "tripwire" veterans, who retreated into the American wilderness to avoid the unsympathetic gaze of their fellow citizens.[102] The film *Distant Thunder* (1988) portrays a group of Vietnam veterans living in an isolated camp in the Pacific Northwest, and Philip Caputo's novel *Indian Country* (1987) expands on this version of the narrative syndrome of the deranged veteran within a focus on the motives of one veteran's retreat into the enclave of his fortified homestead.[103] Emmett Walsh in Mason's novel *In Country* bears traces of this predilection as he digs a hole under his house "to hide in."[104] In each case the veteran has reduced "home" to "shelter," a word that, as Arthur Danto points out, is related to the Old English root of the word "house": "*hus*." This root was "cognate with huden—to hide, shelter, conceal, cover," thus revealing "the fragile, threatened, exposed side of our self-image as dwellers: beings that need protection, a place to crawl into."[105]

Nevertheless, other resonances of the word "home" have not been lost in these representations. In the English language a house is not a home, but it can be if a family occupies the house. In each of the bush-vet texts referred to here, the availability or proximity of a family demonstrates that the possibility of home is not far away. By coming home and being reunited with family, the veteran is healed of the depression and fear that led to "his" isolation. Coming home, then, means laying down one's arms and accepting the open arms of those who have been awaiting your return all along. Exemplifying this suggestion is the veteran Christian Starkmann of Caputo's *Indian Country*, who accepts the love of his family and removes the barbed wire and mines he had placed around his rural homestead. In *Distant Thunder* the once-troubled veteran, Mark Libby (John Lithgow), is reunited with his son with the help of a friendly woman from the local town. The closure that is reunion is repeated in Mason's novel when Emmett Walsh emerges from the hole he has been digging under his house to be reconciled with his loving family on a trip to the Vietnam Veterans Memorial. In each case the lesson allegedly learned by combat veterans in Vietnam—"you are alone"[106]—is revised. On the home front the veteran realizes that he is not alone and learns the valuable lesson of home: that reconciliation and reunion are palliative and liberating.

Nostalgia

The emphasis in the late seventies and early and mideighties upon the therapeutic family reinforced the familial basis of home. The integral link between the family and home, and the regenerative function of both were firmly reinstalled at this time. The fear during the years of the war that a gap existed between generations and the subsequent anxiety provoked by the signs of a crisis of the family were allayed, if not erased, by the affirmation of a reunited nuclear family. Significantly, the allusion to family life implicit within "home" was manifested and reinforced during the eighties within the Reagan administration's emphasis on the role of the traditional family within the home. The war on drugs, defined as a way of protecting the nation's youth, and Reagan's own mediated persona as a strongly profamily father were two of the obvious signs of a project aimed at instituting a consensual definition of a specific family construct. "Families," Reagan repeated many times, "are the basic unit that hold our society together." According to Reagan, Americans needed "to look to God [and] to the hearthstone, because that's where all hope for America lies."[107] In his second State of the Union Address, those he called "quiet everyday heroes of American life," the "unsung heroes," were "parents who sacrifice long and hard so their children will know a better life."[108] In these ways the individuals he valorized were homespun, local heroes who embodied traditional virtues of home and family.

Coinciding with and informing this affirmation of traditional families was a separate suggestion—encoded in the word "nostalgia"—that functioned to reinforce the notion of home. Signs of a nostalgic resurgence abounded throughout the eighties during a presidency that frequently expressed itself through nostalgic representations. One such image was a mural President Reagan used as a backdrop for selected speeches during the 1984 presidential campaign. The mural depicted an idealized America from a rural past in the form of fields and hills, small farms, a river, and pond. An aspect of pastoral nostalgia exemplified here is that it tells us very little about the past but instead presents a "past which has never existed except as narrative."[109] It is "hostile to history and its invisible signs and yet [it represents a] longing for an impossibly pure context of lived experience."[110] This context was evoked by Reagan's vision of a prelapsarian America devoid of perceived disruptive influences such as war, "racial problems," feminism, and gay rights. The evocation of such influences helped to reinforce the idea that contemporary society was wayward, and dangerous. A return to the past and its attendant "traditional values," coupled with increased military spending, would ensure that the nation was protected from contemporary threats. In this way Reagan's "wilful nostalgia"[111] reclaimed the "sense of wholeness" that the sociologists Stauth and Turner argue motivates the nostalgic mode.[112] Devoid of crises, the idyll proposed by Reagan represents a place to call home. This condition is implicit in the word "nostalgia" which, according to one of its meanings, refers to homesickness, the yearning or longing for home. Nostalgia, then, is not necessarily concerned with the past; rather, it is a reference to the need to return home.

The type of home Reagan had in mind was further suggested in the nostalgic images used in a television commercial for the Republican Party broadcast during the 1984 presidential campaign. Images of the sun rising, the flag being raised, people going to work, and a family moving into its new home were used to construct a narrative that is diegetically referred to as "morning again in America." The voice-over states: "Just about everyone in town is thinking the same thing—now that our country is turning around, why would we ever turn back?"[113] The reference to a "new morning" and the image of a rising sun naturalize the evocation of home and fix the representation as incontestable—"just about everyone" would agree with the commonsense assumptions it contained.

While the articulation of home and family continued throughout Reagan's terms as president, the roots of an appeal to "home" were evident from the first day of the Reagan administration. Coinciding with the return of the Iranian-held U.S. hostages, Reagan's inauguration was thus surrounded by representations of Americans returning home. The ubiquity of the yellow ribbon, a traditional symbol of homecoming, on inauguration day, January 20, 1981, was, in retrospect, an ironic emblem of the new president's nostalgic political agenda. Reflecting and contributing to this agenda were various "Reaganite texts"[114] that affirmed and extended Reagan's nostalgic evocation of the past and reinforced "the *mythification* of 'home' as an almost universal site of utopian (be)longing"[115] capable of providing an alternative to unsatisfactory—and dangerous—contemporary conditions. The central features of this "nostalgic" process were subtly reflected in the popular Reaganite film *The Big Chill* (1983). The past referred to in this film is that of the sixties, a convivial and hospitable time, it seems. The disruptive presence of the war within the era is alluded to in references to antiwar speeches at the University of Michigan and to an antiwar protest march on Washington, and in the form of the emasculating wound Nick (William Hurt) received in Vietnam. Generally, however, these references are subsumed within another perspective on the era evoked by a group of friends united during a weekend who fondly remember a time of camaraderie in which, according to the words of one character, they "were at [their] best." The impression of a stable, beneficent past is reinforced through the film's music sound track, which, although comprising songs of the sixties, fails to include any songs that mention the Vietnam War. The repression of elements of the sixties is objectified through the heavy-handed symbolism involved in the burial of the unseen character Alex. Aspects of the past are literally laid to rest along with the character who typified the divisive features of the sixties.

In keeping with common definitions of nostalgia, this recollection of an idealized past is a reaction to contemporary crises, leading to a reassertion of home. In *The Big Chill* the crisis is ill-defined and is implied largely through reference to the condition of the world outside. Outside is "not home"[116]—it is the cold, cruel world of the film's title. Early in the film Nick (William Hurt) states that "we're all alone out there," and later Meg (Mary Kay Place) repeats that "it's a cold world out there." Harold (Kevin Kline) suggests that when you go into the world you "get your hands dirty," and illustrates this point by taking Nick outside to pass on illegal arbitrage information concerning his shoe company. According to Michael (Jeff Goldblum), the outdoor world is a "giant toilet." Sam (Tom Berenger) stereotypes the outer world when he comments that it is composed of people who are not "like us." "I thought because they looked like us and acted like us they were us," he says, "but they weren't." In turn, Meg redefines these people as *dangerous* when she recounts a story from her law practice of two clients who "broke into a house, tied up the husband, raped the wife, blew the whole place up and ran away." Harold further demonizes the outer world when he says of his home that "this place means something to me, I'm dug in here," suggesting that a bunker is the only way of avoiding the encroachment of the nefarious forces of "outside." Nevertheless, the fortification still needs the security services of the local police, who have "twice kept [his] place from being ripped off." It is little wonder, then, that Michael declares to Harold and Sarah at the end of the film that he and the rest of the group are "not leaving, we're never leaving."

The only alternative to the cold, dangerous, outside world is home. The narrative image created by the film's producers, distributors, and critics established what has been referred to as "the particular sense of home which dominates this film."[117] Richard Corliss for *Time* magazine described *The Big Chill* as "the feel-good movie of '83," thereby providing the distributors of the film with a convenient line of advertising copy and the public with an intimation of the narrative content.[118] The distributors reinforced this impression by commonly advertising the film with a photograph of a number of the smiling characters seated in a row on a comfortable couch in a pleasant, distinctly middle-class, home. The concept of the notion of "home" available through such images is advanced in the film within the fate of the Vietnam veteran, Nick. During the course of the weekend Harold's good-family common sense is primarily directed at Nick, who has been leading an aimless and self-destructive life selling illegal drugs. Nick's new routine of jogging, initiated by a gift from Harold of a pair of his company's jogging shoes, is a sign of Nick's healthy regeneration. The renewal is complete when Nick overcomes the war wound that had previously distanced him from women and announces that he is to move nearby to a cabin with Chloe (Meg Tilly). The difference in age between Nick and Chloe is collapsed as a member of the Vietnam generation and a member of the post–Vietnam generation are joined in their own home. In *The Big Chill* home is the place where everyone is the same. The contrast between inside (home) and outside (not home) reveals that this homogeneity is purchased through the demonization and containment of difference. In this film the safe and secure homogeneous unity that is home is evoked through a nostalgia that is predicated upon paranoia.

Given its emphasis, *The Big Chill* shares, in what at first may appear an odd comparison, a number of features with the texts that constitutes the "POW/MIA" cycle, including *Uncommon Valor* (1983), *Rambo* (1985), and a series of films featuring Chuck Norris, *M.I.A. I, II, III* (1984, 1985, 1988). Critical analyses of Reaganite texts, of which these films can be considered a part, have tended to emphasize the ways in which they position the audience as children, interpellated by a patriarchal ideology that reinforces the "law of the Father."[119] With this emphasis, psychoanalytic critique (and what are, in terms of a discussion of home, its ironic metaphors of the family) has neglected the obvious theme of home in many of these Reaganite texts. For example, the plot of the "Reaganite" film *E.T.* (1982) revolves around an extraterrestrial's departure for "home," and in many cases the focus of the "new cold war films" of the eighties is also a return home.[120] Extending this focus, the POW/MIA narrative is predicated upon the desire, the need, to return home.

Exemplifying this issue, the film *Rambo*, a central text within the genre of POW/MIA narratives, reproduces the emphasis on home in a number of important ways. Early in the film Trautman (Richard Crenna), Rambo's surrogate father, advises another character that "what you call hell, [Rambo] calls home." Thus, logically, what "we" call "home," Rambo calls hell. Home is infernal for Rambo because as a loner and a warrior, he would simply be out of place in such an homogeneous unity. Trautman's final words to Rambo are those of a concerned parent: "How will you live, John?" These words provoke another related question that is unarticulated yet implied in Trautman's query: "How can anyone survive outside the unity that is 'home'?" It is a question that is unstated because it contains a notion of home as unity that is taken for granted as common sense. It also embodies the core of homesickness within which home is expressed as a necessity for personal well-being, without which "we" fall sick.

There's No Place Like It

The intense focus on home in the representations of the POW/MIA cycle was reflected elsewhere in American culture during the early eighties. The New York City welcome home parade of May 7, 1985, foregrounded the veteran in a public expression and celebration of national reunion. Coinciding with the tenth anniversary of the end of the war in Vietnam, this parade became part of a media-generated appeal to reconsider the war in

which, typically, the media displaced or obscured a range of issues associated with the conflict through a focus on the dominant and dominating
metaphor of "healing the wounds" of war. The notion of healing was reinforced in accounts of the New York City parade that foregrounded
human-interest aspects of reconciliation and reintegration associated
with the homecoming. One veteran was quoted as saying: "It was a lousy
war, but a helluva parade," and another said: "Before we felt forgotten.
And now it's time for us to say thank you."[121]

In opposition to such conciliatory views, the veteran and poet W. D.
Ehrhart reacted to the New York City parade by writing that it was "ten,
fifteen, twenty years / too late for kids not twenty / years old and dead in
ricefields." Ehrhart added:

> You'd think that any self-respecting
> vet would give the middle-finger
> to folks who thought of it
> ten years and more too late-
> yet there they were: the sad
> survivors, balding, overweight
> and full of beer, weeping, grateful
> for their hour come round at last.[122]

Ehrhart's anger expresses itself in the voice of political protest. This voice
was partially evident during the parade that preceded the dedication of
the Vietnam Veterans Memorial on November 13, 1982, in which

> men and women marched in and out of uniform, brought along pets, and
> carried either small American flags or placards that criticized political de-
> cisions from the past: "We Killed, We Bled, We Died for Worse than Noth-
> ing"; "No More Wars. No More Lies." This presentation of views in
> opposition to the ideology of national unity and reconciliation and national
> power was another indication that the public discussion over the memory
> of this war involved significant contention and debate. The parade's theme,
> "Marching Along Together Again," actually expressed sentiments of loy-
> alty to a community or brotherhood of soldiers rather than loyalty to a na-
> tion of patriotic citizens.[123]

Surprised by the contrast between this parade and its eloquent opposition to the ideology of national unity, and the 1985 homecoming parade
in New York City, with its "happy mood of reconciliation," essayist
Michael Clark commented in reference to the latter event: "[W]ho *were*

these guys waving flags and choking back grateful tears in response to the cheering crowd in New York? Could they be the same men whose rage and frustration found such an eloquent expression at the time the first memorial was dedicated?"[124] The answer to these questions, the difference between the two events, resides in the object of each parade. The parade held in 1982 marked the dedication of a memorial that foregrounded the dead as the trace of the effects of war. The memory of the war evoked by the memorial was thus a powerful inspiration for the articulation of opinions that contradicted declarations of unity. In contrast, the object of the 1985 New York City parade was home. In this case, the commonsense associations of home as the condition of unity effectively displaced the voice of political opposition. The warm-hearted crowd and the signs of gratitude shown by the veterans combined to express this common sense and to reinforce home as the condition of reconciliation and community.

Ehrhart's observation that the parade held in 1985, ten years after the end of the war, was an anachronism raises another point that can be understood only in terms of the movement toward home. The reason that the parade was, in effect, ten years late can be interpreted as a result of the need to construct and enforce a consensual definition of home, a process that took a number of years. Evidence for this conclusion is found in the tensions surrounding the "Home with Honor" parade for Vietnam veterans held in New York City on April 1, 1973. Although this parade was well attended by onlookers, the notion of "home" was strained. A number of veterans' groups protested the march, and at least one veteran was arrested scuffling with police. In particular, however, "official" reaction to the march was muted—neither New York City's mayor, John Lindsay, nor Governor Nelson Rockefeller attended the event, and although the march was reported on page one of the *New York Times*, it was not mentioned in either of the major weekly newsmagazines, *Time* and *Newsweek*.[125] The lack of a coherent definition of home at this time resulted in a parade in which media and official responses were subdued compared to the popular, political, and media enthusiasm demonstrated for the homecoming parade held in the same city twelve years later. Without the revision of the image of the veteran and without the ideological investment in the construction of a widespread consensus on the condition of home, the concept of a welcome home was premature. Ironically, by the late eighties these ideological efforts had proven so successful that coming home or repatriation was no longer necessary for the evocation or reinforcement of the notion of unity. In a number of representations during this time, home was established among those condemned to (re)fight the war. In these representations the once inexplicable war—"radically ambiguous, undecideable, and indeterminate" in the words of one observer[126]—was rendered intelligible through the structure of the family and home.

The ABC television series *China Beach*, first broadcast in the spring of 1988, depicted the collection of nurses, doctors, and "doughnut dollies" at the China Beach recreation and medical facility near Da Nang as an American family that had found its home. At the end of the two-hour pilot episode for the series, the nurse Colleen McMurphy (Dana Delany) announces that she is going to stay at China Beach. McMurphy recognizes that she cannot return to the United States because, as she says: "I have an even bigger family here. I am home." Although the series attempted to present a form of realism similar to that of the docudrama, it conformed closely to the features of melodrama. Geoffrey Nowell-Smith has argued that "what is at stake [in the melodrama] is the survival of the family unit and the possibility for individuals of acquiring an identity which is also a place within the system, a place in which they can be 'themselves' and 'at home'." He adds that "[i]t is a condition of the [melo]drama that the attainment of such a place is not easy and does not happen without sacrifice. . . . "[127] The idea that characters are willing to endure hardship to attain incorporation into the family unit records the cultural value placed on the need for social unity. Week after week *China Beach* reflected this need in the representation of extreme wartime sacrifices made by its characters to remain part of the "family." Finally, then, "[e]xtending the 'family' to the War involves no irony, but simply the prevailing myth of the organic relation between private and public, between family and society."[128] In this way home can be anywhere. The suggestion that there's no place like home takes on a different meaning in this context. There is no place like it. Home does not refer to a place but to a condition—the ideological, naturalized, construct of unity.

This construct was reproduced in Oliver Stone's commercially successful film *Platoon* (1986), which like *China Beach* after it, appropriated features of home to structure the experience of war. In *Platoon* the (patriarchal) combat unit is a family unit. At the end of the film Chris (Charlie Sheen) exposes this association when, referring to the two squad leaders, Barnes (Tom Berenger) and Elias (Willem Dafoe), he states that at times he felt like "the child born of [these] two fathers." The publicity for *Platoon* reinforces the part played by the family in the restructuring of the experience of Vietnam. An advertisement accompanying the video release of the film features a woman sitting in her kitchen speaking to the camera, informing the spectator that initially she could not understand her husband's refusal to discuss the war. Having seen *Platoon* she now understands not only the experience of the war but also her husband's reluctance to talk. The Vietnam War is here the sign of familial or spousal empathy and reunion.

The family is also a structuring theme in Stone's later film *Born on the Fourth of July* (1989). Before he joins the marines, Ron Kovic (Tom Cruise) lives at home with a domineering mother and ineffectual father. In Vietnam he is involved in an operation in which a Vietnamese family is inadvertently killed. Also during this disastrous event Kovic accidentally shoots a fellow marine. On his return to the United States, Kovic attempts to confront the family of the soldier he killed. Finally, Kovic's rage and guilt are vented against his family. The three families—Vietnamese, the poor southern family of the dead marine, and his own hapless family—are linked through the misfortune of war.

Though linked by war, the differences between each family are maintained. The Vietnamese family and the rural family are given their own specificity, defined not in opposition to but distinct from each other and from Kovic's family. In contrast to the majority of representations discussed in this section, Stone's does not erase the effects of the war on the family, nor does it valorize the family structure as an ameliorative response to the war. However, Stone's refusal to validate a family-mediated form of integration and union is dissipated within the final scenes of the film at the 1976 Democratic National Convention, in which Kovic is heartily and literally welcomed home by well-wishers, and he announces to a reporter, "We're home." There is, behind this welcome, the knowledge of Kovic's paraplegia and impotence, but within the final moment of the film the smiles on Kovic's face and his enthusiasm at receiving the greetings suggest that he is happy to be home. This film, as do other texts dealing with the effects of the war, constructs a dichotomy between the family and home. It is within the family that the impact of the war is registered. Home, in contrast, is the transcendence of that impact in a newfound unity. Stone's film stops short of totally endorsing this home only in the sense that behind the smiles is the knowledge of Kovic's chronic physical condition.

Articulating Difference and Unity

The easy assurances of home as the condition of unity proposed in the majority of texts dealing with the impact of the war are rendered ironic by the presence of the homeless within contemporary America, many of them veterans of the Vietnam War. In the context of the present discussion it can be noted that homelessness does not simply refer to the absence of a dwelling place. Given that the ideological construction referred to as home represents unity and the erasure of difference, homelessness signifies a marginalized and excluded difference.[129] In this way those who are homeless are beyond the boundaries of an assumed unity—they are, by definition, outsiders. This stereotypical construction of difference as otherness is circulated in a culture dominated by images of a convivial community that displace any possible political or textual representation of the homeless.

A politics of difference seeks to redress this situation by retrieving difference from otherness. Such a politics challenges cultural homogeneity through practices that attempt to foreground the experiences and identities of formerly displaced groups. The coalitional politics of the new social movements, and the struggle to textually express and circulate varieties of human experiences are part of the representative practices subsumed under the rubric of the politics of difference. The representation of multiple experiences retrieves difference from polarizing binarisms that turn difference into otherness within a framework that privileges dominant positions.[130] At issue, then, are representational and political practices capable of validating difference, and those that support a variety of discriminatory forms. In regard to the latter, racism, as Stuart Hall has stressed, "operates by structuring impassable symbolic boundaries between racially constituted categories, and its typically binary system of representation constantly marks and attempts to fix and naturalize the difference between belongingness and Otherness."[131] Within this dualism belongingness has typically been represented in terms of order, coherence, and unity (dominant characteristics of home), and "race" has been demonized as "a sign of social disorder and civic decay."[132]

In his book *City of Quartz* (1990), Mike Davis traces this stereotyping of "race" as it is manifested within the specific context of Los Angeles. Davis notes that the contemporary gang scares, "like the Tramp scares in the nineteenth century, or the Red scares in the twentieth," have been used to justify a pattern he calls the "Black-lash." Although legitimated in terms of a "revulsion against youth criminality," the invidious "Black-lash" is, instead, a deeply entrenched reaction by the police and a number of local council members toward the black community. The discriminatory "war at home," which Davis calls "Vietnam Here,"[133] reflects a city deeply divided along "racial" lines, a situation that exposes the multiple assurances of home as unity. One outcome of "racially" focused political and economic repression—the uprising in Los Angeles during late April 1992—further revealed the bankruptcy of home. In these various ways, then, the "racially" structured war zone that is Los Angeles exemplifies in extreme form the changing nature of current urban terrains and the failure to recognize the validity of difference.

Set in contemporary Los Angeles, Lawrence Kasdan's film *Grand Canyon* (1992) seeks to explore the condition of metropolitan life and the place of difference in this experience within a context that is established in the opening scenes to resonate with the Vietnam War. The film begins with a blank screen over which is played the sound track to the cinematic history of the Vietnam War: the pulsating sound of a helicopter's rotating blades.[134] The scene fades in not on the jungles of Southeast Asia but to an inner-city neighborhood of Los Angeles. This neighborhood will be the place in which the resonances of Vietnam intersect with images of "race" to reinforce the validity and value of cultural unity.

Kasdan is concerned to represent the relationship that develops from a fortuitous meeting between Simon (Danny Glover), a black tow-truck driver, and Mack (Kevin Kline), a white-yuppie immigration lawyer. On the way home from watching a basketball game, Mack's car stalls in an unfamiliar black neighborhood. When Mack's cellular telephone ceases to work, he is forced to run to a nearby convenience store to telephone for assistance. Mack finds it impossible to define his location or, in a "military analogy, to give his co-ordinates."[135] Having, finally, completed the telephone call, he waits in his car for help, only to be confronted by a group of black youths. Mack's response to their presence is to utter a line countless war films have attributed to "an American soldier coming down in enemy territory: 'Mayday. Mayday. We're coming down.'"[136] Mack's distress call is answered by the timely arrival of Simon in the tow truck. From this scene, in which the echoes of "Vietnam" play a part in encoding the signs of "race" as a problem for white citizens, the relationship between Mack and Simon is represented sympathetically, suggesting that the "problem" can be transcended in an appeal to an essential commonality between members of various "races" and classes within the community.

This pattern is reproduced throughout the film. Difference is displayed in order for it to be displaced by the assertion of a mystical relationship that supposedly binds all human beings. In part, this relationship is affirmed through chance and coincidence. The meeting of Mack and Simon is not the only case of serendipity in the film. The despair felt by Mack's wife, Claire (Mary MacDonnell), at not being able to have more children is resolved when she finds and keeps an abandoned baby. The randomness of events and the concomitant denial of human agency are further evoked by an earthquake that happily spares the home of Claire and Mack. The suggestion of an essential, inimitable, interconnection between *different* people is reinforced in the final scenes in which the central characters (men, women, and children of different ethnic and class backgrounds) make a trip to view the Grand Canyon. Standing together before this natural divide, the characters overcome their individual differences. Deep down, says this film, "we" are all the same in nature. The conclusion collapses irreducible cultural differences into an appeal to the existence of an immutable, natural, homogeneous unity.

In *Grand Canyon* "we" all come home. The film represents the end of the movement toward unity that has operated through strategic reference to home and family. In this way it is entirely fitting that the film opens with resonances of the war in Vietnam only to dispel them in a focus on family and home. The assertions of home structured in the representations of the impact of the war fulfilled an ideological task by universalizing and normalizing the idea of unity. With the establishment of this notion, the appropriation of the impact of the Vietnam War was complete. In these terms, *Grand Canyon* briefly evokes the Vietnam War within the assertion of the cultural condition of unity in what is, effectively, *post*–Vietnam America.

The recent proliferation across a number of discourses of the prefix "post" suggests a reluctance to accept traditional theoretical interpretations of experience. A post–Vietnam America contradicts this suggestion. It is a conjuncture in which the signs of traditional interpretations thrive. The constant assertion of home evokes a condition that bears the traces of a sedimented common sense that has invested the word "home" with a number of meanings: security, succor, conviviality, and unity. These definitions have circulated within texts representing the impact of the war in Vietnam, and within the majority of these texts the ideology of unity encoded as the common sense of home displaced or revised the divisive effects of the war.

Bringing the war home was a process that began before the end of the conflict and continued throughout the seventies and eighties. It was a movement that infused American culture and that involved at various times and in different ways the opposition to the war; the veteran; the family; and the amorphous concept of the nation. There is, however, another issue involved in this cultural process. It is the inverse of the representation of unity, unacknowledged and excluded and continually denied: the existence of difference. From this perspective, bell hooks has interpreted "[h]ome [as] that place which enables and promotes varied and everchanging perspectives, a place where one discovers new ways of seeing reality, frontiers of difference."[137] In hooks's terms, difference is the voice that questions the assertion of an immutable unity. It is this presence that is finally and disastrously erased in the representation that "we," along with the war, have come home.

Conclusion

The Scar That Binds is a study of contending representations of America at the site commonly referred to as "Vietnam." On the one hand the presence of the impact of the war in Vietnam produced the notion of cultural division; on the other hand it resulted in the assertion of unity. The paradox resulting from the opposing sets of representations has been resolved within American culture through the privileging of certain positions and notions that have reconstructed "Vietnam" as a sign of homogeneity and collectivity. The resolution does not mean that the notion of cultural division has been erased by that of unity. The idea of the divisive impact of the war continues to circulate in various places within American culture. However, the assertion of unity has operated across and through the evocation of rupture and segmentation to result in the foregrounding of union. Barthes has pointed out that in certain situations select and specific words suggest their opposite. He illustrated this point by referring to the slippage that occurs in "bourgeois discourse" between "war" and "peace," specifically the way in which "pacification" frequently implies war.[1] The basic aspect of implication and inevitability expressed in Barthes's observation is applicable to the conditions studied in *The Scar That Binds* in which division *implies* unity. The situation is further exemplified in the fact that U.S. culture in the wake of "Vietnam" circulated two contending concepts while—in the process—it constantly privileged one of them.

The notion of *process* is integral to the outcome of the paradox. Not only has the representation of cultural division and unity involved a process in the sense that representation continually rearranges and reconstructs the reality it purports to depict but historical dispositions and movements have altered the paradox over time. At different moments throughout the period covered by this study (1968–1989) disruption and collectivity were variably emphasized. However, by the mideighties the assertion of cultural holism had resulted in the resolution of the paradox by shifting the grounds of the contradiction toward the idea of union. This study has analyzed the ways in which historical and representational, or ideological, processes (defined here as strategies) operated within the field of culture to achieve this end. Specifically, a wide array of cultural texts dealing with the effects on U.S. culture of the conflict in Vietnam were read or decoded for signs of the common sense of unity. The reading revealed three dominant ideological strategies variously encoded within the majority of these texts. A critical interrogation of each strategy confirmed and further exposed the full extent and complexity of the presence of the strategies within textual representations. The operation of the strategies is briefly reviewed here.

The first strategy, defined as "The Healed Wound," implicated the widespread representational practice of depicting the disruptive effects of the war in terms of the metaphor of a wound. Encoded within the common application of the metaphor was an impression of impotence—a condition that stemmed from the presence of division within U.S. culture. Defined as debilitating and a loss of national power, the wound, as common sense would have it, required healing. The first step in healing the wounds exposed by the war in Vietnam was encoded in the cultural need to forget the war and a range of pernicious, painful, issues associated with the conflict: U.S. defeat, the country of Vietnam, and war-related guilt. The healing that followed involved the individual, the community, and the nation. At each site healing was foregrounded as uniformity and wholeness, thus reproducing and reinforcing the prescriptive formula that a healed nation is a unified place.

Within and through the second strategy the Vietnam veteran spoke the truth of unity on the home front. The operations of a diverse range of cultural processes were responsible for transforming an inarticulate male veteran prone to frequent violent outbursts into an articulate spokesperson. An interrelated set of critical and cultural assumptions functioned, largely on the basis of his "having been there," to privilege the veteran within postwar culture as a hero whose messages were concerned predominantly with the desire for a reunited culture.

The third strategy operated, as did the others summarized here, across a wide cultural terrain throughout the period from the late sixties to the late eighties. The presence of opposition on the home front in response to U.S. intervention in Vietnam signified the beginning of a reconfiguration of cultural and political dispositions summarized within the term "home." In the early to midseventies the culture reworked the slogan associated with the antiwar movement—"bring the war home"—through a series of representations in which the war came home in all its violent and inhospitable force in the form of a manic and deranged veteran. This repatriation of the war was gradually replaced by the reinclusion of the so-called violent or sick veteran within a reconstructed, therapeutic, family unit. The outcome, in effect, healed the veteran and marked the end of the crisis that supposedly had besieged the American family during the seventies. The widespread appeal of nostalgia during the eighties, a condition reinforced by a presidential administration fond of nostalgically evoking the past, consolidated the notion of a consensual, convivial home. Developments in the later eighties indicated the pervasiveness of this definition of home. Representations at this time depicting those condemned to refight the Vietnamese conflict emphasized that home (union) was also achievable within the conditions of war. The movement, then, from battlefront to home front and from home front to battlefront emphasized home not as a place but as a readily available set of homogenizing definitions deeply inscribed throughout the culture.

As indicated in this reconsideration, the operation of each strategy has not been directed by a central power. Rather, the term "strategies" has been used in this study to refer to cultural dispositions and characteristics that have been supported and reinforced by the naturalizing operation of common sense. Common sense reproduces unexamined and obvious assumptions to construct particular worldviews. Each of the specific strategies examined here is encoded in various metaphors—"wound" and "healing," "voice," and "home"—to reproduce certain views of the world. Metaphors effectively convey common sense by encoding what Lévi-Strauss called "the logic of the concrete."[2] He argued that all cultures interpret abstractions (for which can be inserted the example of the impact or effects of the Vietnam War) by summarizing them in terms of daily experience.[3] Lévi-Strauss's observations are informed by noting that the abstractions he referred to are redefined within and through the translation into metaphor. Wounds demand to be healed; to possess a voice is to utter messages that are worth hearing (and that are, on a certain level, truthful); the private sphere of "home" has traditionally been a place or condition marked by familial signs of homogeneity and collectivity. In each case metaphor, and the common sense encoded within it, resulted in a form of closure—unity—that *appeared* to be natural and inevitable.

Inscribed in language in common(sense) metaphors, the ideological strategies of unity contribute to perpetuating and reinforcing the status quo and prevailing cultural arrangements. It is in this function that the nominated commonsense strategies perform a hegemonic function. The ideology of unity asserts a consensual notion not based on readily identifiable political categories such as liberal, left, or nationalist but, rather, on the seemingly apolitical concept of cultural *unity*—an idea that denies and excludes different, or what are from a hegemonic point of view contentious and oppositional elements. The work of the ideology of unity defines, stereotypes, and subsumes "them" in the process of assuming and asserting "us" to be, in the main, white, middle-class, politically conservative, heterosexual males. It is in its performance in support of this "hegemonic order" that the ideology of unity and its strategies have been interpreted within this analysis as a strand of dominant ideology.

The identification of the ways in which ideological strategies have operated within and through the site referred to as Vietnam enables "cultural critiques to evolve into cultural interventions," as critical theorist George Lipsitz has emphasized in another context.[4] Understanding the ways in which ideological strategies operate provides the ability to outflank them in the future. Such a maneuver, then, is the basis of "making a difference" to the study of America. Specifically, the antiessentialist ideological critique developed and applied here has not been followed, to apply the words of Stuart Hall, "to generate another good theory, but to give a better theorized account of concrete historical reality."[5]

History has not been well served by the resolution of the paradox of cultural fragmentation and uniformity, a resolution that reflects a revision of U.S. history since the end of the war in Vietnam. History, according to Fredric Jameson, is what hurts.[6] Jameson's claim is, however, refuted in the history of the impact of the Vietnam War, which is a record of a healed scar that no longer hurts. The logic of this conclusion is underlined in the fact that by the end of the eighties, the history of "the scars" of the war had been revised and translated into the ahistorical construct of cultural unity. Elaine Scarry has noted that wounds—scars—"memorialize [the fact] that [a] war occurred and that the cessation of its occurrence was agreed to."[7] The recognition of a divisive presence within American culture was the scarring effect of the Vietnam War. A brief acknowledgment of the "scars" served as the point of origin of healing the scars in a process of cultural unification that denied the painful divisions and differences exposed by the war. The end of this process was the true "cessation" of the war.

Representations since the eighties confirm the end of the war in this sense, and the end of healing. The history of the decades of the sixties, seventies, and eighties that was revised to achieve unity is repeated (and reworked) in the commercially successful film *Forrest Gump* (1994). The rearticulation of the voice of the veteran in a narrative of coming home is enacted through the characters of Gump (Tom Hanks) and Lieutenant Dan Taylor (Gary Sinise). Gump's experiences of war are melded with events from post–Vietnam War America "in a history that is the concatenated and reified effect of incoherent motives and chance convergences."[8] Though Gump wanders through this history in a Candide-like fashion, there is a trajectory to his actions leading him on a journey to a family and a home he was not aware existed until he meets his son. The theme of "healing," and the postwar condition of the Vietnam veteran, and the notion of coming home are reinforced in the character of Lieutenant Dan, rendered a paraplegic in the war. Lieutenant Dan is healed of his paraplegia, a representational cliché signifying the effects of war, in an amazingly simple way that earlier texts failed to exploit: he is given new legs. Dan's transformation to "wholeness" is finalized through his reconciliation with his war-torn past and marriage to, fittingly, a Vietnamese woman. In achieving closure, *Forrest Gump* works with, and capitalizes upon, the efficacy of the various strategies analyzed in *The Scar That Binds* that have reconfigured and transcended the impact of the Vietnam War.

In other ways, the operations of the strategies analyzed here determined that the war was "over" prior to official claims to that effect in the summer of 1995. The abandonment of the economic embargo against Vietnam in 1994, and U.S. diplomatic recognition of Vietnam on July 11, 1995, depended, in part, on progress on the issue of a "full accounting" of the fate of Americans missing in action since the war.[9] Against this history, the move to confront Vietnam took place at the end of a twenty-year period during which time the ideology of unity functioned to overcome the "scarring" impact of the war that was once the central "tragic legacy" of the war. Legacies dissipated within the condition of a healed—united—America that marked the end of the war, enabling America to confront its old enemy in new ways. In this reassessment, Vietnam's identity is once again reconstructed through American interpretative frameworks. Viet Nam, the "land of the Viet peoples of the south," was Americanized into Vietnam, which, in turn during the late sixties and early seventies, was reworked into the new cartographic and geographic entity of (the) "Nam."

As Michael Herr noted, by 1967 "even the most detailed maps didn't reveal much anymore" about this place.[10] In fact, by this time "Vietnam" had ceased to be a place—it had become, simply, the name of a war. After the war the reconfiguration of national identity continued along different lines: Vietnam, a redoubt of communism surviving even in the presence of multiple claims of the "end of ideology" and the "end of history," was an "outlaw nation" quarantined behind an economic blockade. In its postembargo incarnation Vietnam, no longer the place of a divisive American war, becomes a tourist destination, and the site of a new "Asian (economic) miracle" open to foreign investment. Extending the American peace to Vietnam is, then, the beginning of a new period in which histories and identities, Vietnamese and American, will be reconstructed to produce meanings only dimly related to the war.

Identities—their presence, absence, and revision—and history—its construction, reconstruction, and the structures that set its limits—inform *The Scar That Binds*. Changes to these features have been traced in this study across the healed and united terrain that is post–Vietnam War American culture. This is what it has come to: the reworking of American identity within the history of the operation of ideological strategies of unity is the devastating outcome of American involvement in the Vietnam War.

Notes

NOTES TO INTRODUCTION

1. George Bush, "Inaugural Address: A New Breeze is Blowing" (January 20, 1989), *Vital Speeches of the Day* 40, 9 (February 15, 1989): 259.

2. William J. Clinton, "Remarks at Memorial Day Ceremony at the Vietnam Veterans Memorial, May 31, 1993," *Public Papers of the Presidents of the United States: William J. Clinton, 1993* (Washington, D.C.: Government Printing Office, 1994), 786.

3. Quoted in Ben Franklin, "President Accepts Vietnam Memorial: Crowd of Veterans and Others Hear His Call for Healing," *New York Times* (November 12, 1984): 10.

4. Quoted in "Ronald Reagan Calls Vietnam a Noble and Just Cause, 1988," in M. McMahon (ed.), *Major Problems in the History of the Vietnam War: Documents and Essays* (Lexington, Mass.: Heath, 1990), 606.

5. Bobbie Ann Mason, *In Country* (London: Flamingo, 1987).

6. Philip Caputo, *Indian Country* (London: Century, 1987).

7. Michael Herr, *Dispatches* (London: Picador, 1978), 52, 207.

8. Andrew Martin, *Receptions of War: Vietnam in American Culture* (Norman: University of Oklahoma Press, 1993), xxi.

9. Susan Jeffords, *The Remasculinization of America: Gender and the Vietnam War* (Bloomington: Indiana University Press, 1989).

10. The French semiotician Roland Barthes opened a path for this type of analysis. Barthes studied the common meanings that circulate in everyday life, and in the process exposed "the decorative display of what-goes-without-saying, [to reveal] the ideological abuse which ... is hidden there." Roland Barthes, *Mythologies* (New York: Hill and Wang, 1972), 11.

11. Definitions of "ideology" are problematic—an issue that has been reflected in what, at times, has been intense debate surrounding the word (an example of one such moment was the intervention of Althusserianism within classical Marxist critique). The definition of "ideology" referred to throughout this book is informed by conceptions derived from Gramscian cultural studies, especially the significant work of Raymond Williams and Stuart Hall. See, for example, Williams's *The Long Revolution* (Harmondsworth, Middlesex, U.K.:

Penguin, 1965) and his *Marxism and Literature* (Oxford: Oxford University Press, 1977); Hall's "The Problem of Ideology—Marxism Without Guarantees," *Journal of Communication Inquiry* 10, 2 (1986): 28–44, and "Gramsci and Us," in *The Hard Road to Renewal* (London: Verso, 1988); and Stuart Hall, Bob Lumley, and Gregor McLennan, "Politics and Ideology: Gramsci," in Centre for Contemporary Cultural Studies, *On Ideology* (London: Hutchinson, 1978).

12. Stuart Hall, "Culture, Media and the 'Ideological Effect'," in J. Curran, M. Gurevitch, and J. Woollacott (eds.), *Mass Communication and Society* (London: Edward Arnold, 1977), 325. Gramsci defined "common sense" as "the substratum of ideology," thus placing common sense between "folklore," historically documentable conceptions of ways of life, and "philosophy," defined as a systematic interpretation of the world. Antonio Gramsci, *Selections from the Prison Notebooks* (London: Lawrence and Wishart, 1971), 323, 327.

13. The central feature of the operation of the ideology of unity is the construction of a unity from disparate social elements. What Gramsci called a "historically organic" ideology is one that links a variety of groups into a political and cultural force. Gramsci, *Selections from the Prison Notebooks*, 376–377. Following Gramsci, Stuart Hall argues that "it is not the case that the social forces, classes, groups, political movements, etc. are first constituted in their unity by objective economic conditions and then rise to a unified ideology." The process, he stresses, is the reverse. Groups are unified "by seeing themselves reflected as a unified force in the ideology which constitutes them." As a result, the group becomes a unified force through "forms of intelligibility which explain a shared collective situation." Hall refers to the Rastafarians, the Jamaican religious group, to exemplify this point. The Rastafarians have drawn upon the Old Testament for ideas that they have had to radically alter to fit with their experience. In this way the Rastas have worked to construct a coherent ideology around which they can organize themselves. The result, the attempt to deny contradictions and inconsistencies, is the "unity" of ideology. Stuart Hall, "On Postmodernism and Articulation: An Interview with Stuart Hall," *Journal of Communication Inquiry* 10, 2 (Summer 1986): 55. The ideology identified within this study as ostensibly representing the interests of the majority of Americans is the ideology of "unity." The ideal of unity is that which constitutes the internal coherence of this strand of dominating ideology. Thus, the unity of ideology and the ideology of unity are dialectically related. There could be no unity without ideology and, in this case, there could be no ideology without the notion of unity. The ideology of unity represents the notion of unity. It is an ideology that perpetuates a consensus based upon the object of consensus: unity.

14. The processes of inclusion and exclusion, unity and segmentation, are discussed in the historical context of colonial North America in Philip Morgan (ed.), *Diversity and Unity in Early North America* (London: Routledge, 1993). The "consensus school" of U.S. historiography accepted certain characteristics of American society and culture—notably the immutability of an essentialized

unity—as given. See, for example, Louis Hartz's famous formulation in *The Liberal Tradition: An Interpretation of American Political Thought Since the Revolution* (New York: Harcourt, Brace, 1955). Robert Wiebe's *The Segmented Society* (London: Oxford University Press, 1975) is an insightful essay that argues that U.S. society is segmented along multiple lines of difference (primarily the lines of class, "race," gender, and region), yet historically it has circulated mythical forms of oneness.

15. Strobe Talbott, "The War That Will Not End," *Time* (September 9, 1992): 57.

16. *Difference is who we are*, defined in relation to others. As such, difference is the refusal of a universal and stable identity. Difference is constructed from identities as diverse as those based on "race," class, gender, ethnicity, age, religion, region, occupation, and sexual and political orientation(s). The relationship between difference and identity occurs within a changing field of cultural relations: "[T]he social agent is constituted by an ensemble of subject positions [such as "race", ethnicity, gender, class] that can never be totally fixed in a closed system of difference. . . . The 'identity' of such a multiple and contradictory subject is therefore always contingent and precarious, temporarily fixed at the intersection of those subject positions." Chantal Mouffe, "Citizenship and Political Identity," *October* 61 (Summer 1992): 28. In this way difference is not simply defined through opposition and duality *but through multiple relations*. Thus, difference is endlessly *re*defined in relation to a variety of others whose identity is similarly changing historically and politically. Within this study the approach to difference and identity, and to the refusal of an essential core of characteristics within cultural or political formations is derived in large part from the work of Mouffe and her colleague, Ernesto Laclau. See, in particular, Ernesto Laclau and Chantal Mouffe, *Hegemony and Socialist Strategy: Toward a Radical Democratic Politics* (London: Verso, 1989).

17. The texts are Norman Mailer's *The Armies of the Night: History as a Novel, the Novel as History* (Harmondsworth, Middlesex, U.K.: Penguin, 1968), and Oliver Stone's film *Born on the Fourth of July*, 1989. These central texts mark the limits of the majority of representations concerned with the impact of the Vietnam War upon American culture.

18. Michael Ryan, *Politics and Culture: Working Hypotheses for a Post-Revolutionary Society* (Houndsmill, Basingstoke, U.K.: Macmillan, 1989), 28.

NOTES TO PART 1

1. The on-board cameras and graphic displays of many weapons used in the Gulf War suggested to many journalists the images found in electronic games. This focus is discussed in "The Nintendo Issue," *Washington Post* (February 23, 1991): A16.

2. Margot Norris, "Military Censorship and the Body Count in the Persian Gulf War," *Cultural Critique* 19 (Fall 1991): 224.

3. Alan Sekula, "War Without Bodies," *Artforum* (November 1991): 108.

4. Quoted in Norris, "Military Censorship," 224.

5. Paul Fussell, *Wartime: Understanding and Behavior in the Second World War* (New York: Oxford University Press, 1989), 268, 269–270. On September 20, 1943, *Life* magazine carried the first photographs from World War II of dead and wounded American soldiers. The most famous of these photographs depicts three dead GI's washed up on the beach at Buna in northern New Guinea—all the bodies are intact. One photograph from the same issue *did* feature a soldier missing a limb; it had been recently amputated in a field hospital. Following the U.S. War Department's decision in mid–1943 to allow the publication of photographs of injured American soldiers, the response by newsmagazines and newspapers was "pretty restrained, given what *could* have been pictured." S. Moeller, *Shooting War: Photography and the American Experience of Combat* (New York: Basic Books, 1989), 205. H. Bruce Franklin has noted the ways in which photographs from the Civil War broke with a romantic tradition of war representation. While some of the most famous images from that war, such as Timothy O'Sullivan's photograph "A Harvest of Death, Gettysburg," feature graphic displays of the mortally wounded body, it is apparent that the bodies are intact. H. Bruce Franklin, "From Realism to Virtual Reality: Images of America's Wars," in S. Jeffords and L. Rabinovitz (eds.), *Seeing Through the Media: The Persian Gulf War* (New Brunswick, N.J.: Rutgers University Press, 1994), 25–44.

6. The statistics are from Tim O'Brien, "The Violent Vet," *Esquire* (December 1979): 103. According to John Helmer, the war in Vietnam "produced [*sic*] totally disabled soldiers at three times the rate of World War II, and twice the rate of Korea." *Bringing the War Home: The American Soldier in Vietnam and After* (New York: Free Press, 1974), 226.

7. In contrast, the absence of the injured body in the Gulf War meant that rape, a covert and concealed crime, became the dominant metaphor for interpreting the effects of this particular war. See Susan Jeffords, "Rape and the New World Order," *Cultural Critique* 19 (Fall 1991): 203–216, and Abouali Farmanfarmaian, "Sexuality in the Gulf War: Did You Measure Up?" *Genders* 13 (Spring 1992): 1–29. Wounding, physical and mortal, is a central theme of World War I poetry. See, for example, the description of physical wounds in "Recalling War" by Robert Graves, and the poems of Ivor Gurney in Jon Silkin (ed.), *The Penguin Book of First World War Poetry*, 2nd ed. (Harmondsworth, Middlesex, U.K.: Penguin, 1981). Such poems frequently imply a link between individual wounds and a wounded nation; however, in post–Vietnam War American representations the link is made explicit and is exploited in diverse ways and to degrees unrealized in representations from earlier wars.

8. M. Norton, "Wound That Will Not Heal," *New York Times Magazine*

(November 11, 1979): 134–141; from *Time* magazine see, for example, "Wounds That Will Not Heal," *Time* (July 13, 1981): 22. Not to be outdone, *Newsweek* has also employed the terms: William Broyles, Jr., "Remembering a War We Want to Forget: A Veteran Reflects on Healing the Wounds of War," *Newsweek* (November 22, 1982): 82–83.

9. "Vietnam as Unending Trauma," *Society* 21 (November-December 1983): 4–33; "Vietnam—Will There Be a Collective Healing?" *Center Magazine* 14, 4 (July-August 1981): 14–28; Stewart Powell, "The Healing Nation," *U.S. News and World Report* (April 15, 1985): 35–37.

10. See, for example, William Broyles, Jr., "The Wall That Heals," *Reader's Digest*, 130 (May 1987): 70–76; John Lang, "A Memorial Wall That Healed Our Wounds," *U.S. News and World Report* (November 21, 1983): 68–70; Jan Scruggs and Joel Swerdlow, *To Heal a Nation* (New York: Harper and Row, 1986); Alexander Stanley, "Healing Viet Nam's Wounds," *Time* (November 26, 1984): 44.

11. Johnson spoke of the need "to heal and to build" in a speech to the National Association of Broadcasters, quoted in J. Burns (ed.), *To Heal and to Build: The Programs of President Lyndon B. Johnson* (New York: McGraw-Hill, 1968), 456; Ford's comment on "binding up the nation's wounds" comes from "Excerpts from Ford Address at Tulane," *New York Times* (April 24, 1975): 19; Gerald Ford, *A Time to Heal* (New York: Harper and Row, 1979); Jimmy Carter, "Report on Progress of Veterans of the Vietnam Era," *Congressional Record*, 95th Cong., 2nd sess., October 10, 1978, 34946.

12. William J. Clinton, "Remarks at Memorial Day Ceremony at the Vietnam Veterans Memorial, May 31, 1993," *The Public Papers of the Presidents of the United States: William J. Clinton, 1993* (Washington, D.C.: Government Printing Office, 1994), 786.

13. Originally published in the *New York Review of Books*, reprinted in Sandy Vogelsang, *The Long Dark Night of the Soul: The American Intellectual Left and the Vietnam War* (New York: Harper and Row, 1974), 1.

14. Alexander Kendrick, *The Wound Within: America in the Vietnam Years, 1945–1974* (Boston: Little, Brown, 1974).

15. Walter Capps, *The Unfinished War: Vietnam and the American Conscience*, 2nd ed. (Boston: Beacon Press, 1990), 16.

16. Ibid., 17.

17. Kendrick, *The Wound Within*, 6.

18. David Halberstam, "The Vietnamization of America," in J. Livingstone and R. Thompson (eds.), *The Dissent of the Governed: Readings on the Democratic Process* (New York: Macmillan, 1972), 357–366.

19. Jean Comaroff, "Medicine and Culture: Some Anthropological Perspectives," *Social Science and Medicine* 12B (1978): 253.

20. Mary Douglas, "The Healing Rite," in *Implicit Meanings: Essays in Anthropology* (London: Routledge and Kegan Paul, 1975), 143.

21. George Lakoff and Mark Johnson, *Metaphors We Live By* (Chicago: University of Chicago Press, 1980), 6.

22. A position established by Edward Sapir and Benjamin Whorf, frequently referred to as the Sapir-Whorf hypothesis.

23. The perception informs much of Foucault's work and is elaborated in specific detail in Michel Foucault, *The Archaeology of Knowledge* (New York: Pantheon Books, 1972).

24. Mary Douglas, *Purity and Danger: An Analysis of Concepts of Pollution and Taboo* (Harmondsworth, Middlesex, U.K.: Penguin, 1970), and *Natural Symbols: Explorations in Cosmology* (Harmondsworth, Middlesex, U.K.: Penguin, 1973).

25. The word "race" is placed in quotation marks throughout this study to emphasize the *constructed*, as opposed to natural, features it represents.

26. In *The Birth of the Clinic* (London: Tavistock, 1973) Michel Foucault was concerned with the ways in which medical knowledge and practice manipulate the body to promote and legitimize established power. Similarly, in *Discipline and Punish: The Birth of the Prison* (London: Tavistock, 1977) he examined the effects of penal practices in relation to the construction of a disciplined body.

27. David Cooper, *Metaphor* (Oxford: Basil Blackwell, 1986), 41–42. Cooper's equation of metaphor and myth was prefigured by Paul Ricoeur, who stated that "there is something in the use of metaphor that inclines it toward abuse, and so to myth." Paul Ricoeur, *The Rule of Metaphor* (London: Routledge and Kegan Paul, 1978), 251.

28. Cooper, *Metaphor*, 42.

29. Stuart Hall, "Culture, the Media and the 'Ideological Effect'," in J. Curran, M. Gurevitch, and J. Woollacott (eds.), *Mass Communication and Society* (London: Edward Arnold, 1977), 325.

30. Ibid.

31. Geoffrey Nowell-Smith, "Common Sense," *Radical Philosophy* (Spring 1974): 16–19.

32. John Fiske, *Understanding Popular Culture* (Boston: Unwin Hyman, 1989), 118.

33. Tim O'Sullivan, John Hartley, Danny Saunders, and John Fiske, *Key Concepts in Communication* (London: Routledge, 1989), 217.

34. William J. Searle, "Walking Wounded: Vietnam War Novels of Return," in W. J. Searle (ed.), *Search and Clear: Critical Responses to Selected Literature and Films of the Vietnam War* (Bowling Green, Ohio: Bowling Green State University Popular Press, 1988), 147–159.

35. American Psychiatric Association Staff, *Diagnostic and Statistical Manual of Mental Disorders*, 3rd ed. (New York: American Psychiatric Association, 1980).

36. Albert Auster and Leonard Quart, *How the War Was Remembered: Hollywood and Vietnam* (New York: Praeger, 1988), 23.

37. The quotation is from a brief retelling of the legend in Robert Bly's *Iron John: A Book about Men* (Shaftesbury, U.K.: Element, 1990), chapter 8.

38. Ernest Hemingway, *A Farewell to Arms* (London: Jonathan Cape, 1958). Originally published in 1929.

39. The phrase "historical trauma" is by Kaja Silverman in her paper "Historical Trauma and Male Subjectivity," in E. Kaplan (ed.), *Psychoanalysis and Cinema* (New York: Routledge, 1990), 110–127.

40. Silverman makes this suggestion, ibid.

41. Bobbie Ann Mason, *In Country* (London: Flamingo, 1987), chapter 7.

42. Bobbie Ann Mason, "Big Bertha Stories," *Love Life* (London: Vintage, 1990), 143.

43. Robert Stone, *Dog Soldiers* (London: Wyndham, 1976), 134, 133.

44. Michael Herr, *Dispatches* (London: Picador, 1978), 110.

45. Jonathan Levi, "Norman Podhoretz: Impotence," *Granta* 15 (Spring 1985): 125–128.

46. Quoted in Jeffrey Kimball, "The Stab-in-the-Back Legend and the Vietnam War," *Armed Forces and Society* 14, 3 (Spring 1988): 437.

47. Ibid., 439.

48. Levi, "Norman Podhoretz," 126. The text of this paper is based on an interview.

49. Quoted in Walter LaFeber, "The Last War, the Next War, and the New Revisionists," *Democracy* (January 1981): 93.

50. Susan Jeffords, "Women, Gender, and the War," *Critical Studies in Mass Communication* 6, 1 (1989): 87.

51. Robert Bly, "The Vietnam War and the Erosion of Male Confidence," in W. Capps (ed.), *The Vietnam Reader* (New York: Routledge, 1991), 82.

52. John Wheeler, "Coming to Grips with Vietnam," *Foreign Affairs* 63, 4 (Spring 1985): 753.

53. See Marilyn French, *The War Against Women* (New York: Summit, 1972), and Susan Faludi, *Backlash: The Undeclared War Against American Women* (London: Chatto and Windus, 1991).

54. Christopher Lasch, *The Culture of Narcissism: American Life in an Age of Diminishing Expectations* (New York: Warner Books, 1979), 345.

55. Representations of women on the home front during World War II are discussed in James Deutsch, "Piercing the Penelope Syndrome: The Depiction of World War II Veterans' Wives in 1940s Hollywood Films," *Humboldt Journal of Social Relations*, 16, 1 (1990): 31–42.

56. "Ruby, Don't Take Your Love to Town," written by Mel Tillis, as sung by Kenny Rogers and the First Edition. Tillis's song referred to the experiences of a Korean War veteran; the recycling of the song in the late sixties reinflected the song's message to refer to the experiences of veterans of the Vietnam War. The recording by Kenny Rogers and the First Edition reached number six on the U.S. pop charts in 1969.

57. Susan Jeffords, *The Remasculinization of America: Gender and the Vietnam War* (Bloomington: Indiana University Press, 1989).

58. Reagan, speaking at the Vietnam Veterans Memorial on Veterans Day 1982, quoted in Francis Clines, "Tribute to Vietnam: Words, a Wall," *New York Times* (November 11, 1982): B15.

59. Ernesto Laclau, *Politics and Ideology in Marxist Theory* (London: New Left Books, 1977), chapter 4.

60. Hoggart's perceptions were based on observations of English working-class life. Sennett and Cobb found similar attitudes among the American working class to those illustrated by Hoggart. Richard Sennett and Jonathan Cobb, *The Hidden Injuries of Class* (New York: Vintage, 1973).

61. Richard Hoggart, *The Uses of Literacy: Aspects of Working-Class Life with Special Reference to Publications and Entertainments* (Harmondsworth, Middlesex, U.K.: Penguin, 1977), 73–87. Originally published in 1957.

62. Susan Sontag, *Illness as Metaphor* (Harmondsworth, Middlesex, U.K.: Penguin, 1983), 68.

63. Lasch, *The Culture of Narcissism*, 42, 33.

64. Philip Rieff, *The Triumph of the Therapeutic: Uses of Faith After Freud* (New York: Harper and Row, 1966).

65. T. J. Jackson Lears, *No Place of Grace: Antimodernism and the Transformation of American Culture, 1880–1920* (New York: Pantheon Books, 1981), 56.

66. Robert Bellah et al., *Habits of the Heart: Individualism and Commitment in American Life* (New York: Harper and Row, 1985), 138, 113.

67. Lears, *No Place of Grace,* 56.

68. Lawrence Frank, *Society as the Patient: Essays on Culture and Personality* (Port Washington, N.Y.: Kennikat Press, 1948), 305.

69. Russell Jacoby, *Social Amnesia: A Critique of Conformist Psychology from Adler to Laing* (Boston: Beacon Press, 1975), 1.

70. Michael Rogin, "'Make My Day!': Spectacle as Amnesia in Imperial Politics," *Representations* 29 (Winter 1990): 105.

71. "Excerpts from Ford Address at Tulane," *New York Times* (April 24, 1975): 19.

72. Quoted in Harry Haines, "'What Kind of War?': An Analysis of the Vietnam Veterans Memorial," *Critical Studies in Mass Communication* 3, 1 (March 1986): 2.

73. Quoted in Peter Carroll, *It Seemed Like Nothing Happened: America in the 1970s* (New Brunswick, N.J.: Rutgers University Press, 1990), 166. *Time* magazine supported this view in an essay written to mark the end of the war. The essay concluded: "The U.S. has paid for Viet Nam—many times over. A phase of American history has now finished. It is time to begin anew." "How Should Americans Feel?" *Time* (April 14, 1975): 27.

74. Quoted in Richard Severo and Lewis Milford, *The Wages of War: When*

America's Soldiers Came Home-From Valley Forge to Vietnam (New York: Simon and Schuster, 1990), 419.

75. Bush, "Inaugural Address: A New Breeze is Blowing," 259.

76. Quoted in Carroll, *It Seemed Like Nothing Happened*, 166.

77. Walter Benjamin, "Theories of German Fascism: On the Collection of Essays *War and Warrior*, Edited by Ernst Junger," *New German Critique* 17 (Spring 1979): 120–128. See especially p.123, where Benjamin addresses the question "What does it mean to win or lose a war?"

78. Quoted in Gaines M. Foster, "Coming to Terms with Defeat: Post–Vietnam America and the Post–Civil War South," *Virginia Quarterly Review* 66, 1 (Winter 1990): 31.

79. Melvin Maddocks, quoted in Paul Kattenburg, "Reflections on Vietnam: Of Revisionism and Lessons Yet to Be Learned," *Parameters* 14 (Autumn 1984): 42.

80. See Fox Butterfield, "The New Vietnam Scholarship," *New York Times Magazine* (February 13,1983): 26, 28–35, 45–46, 50–57, 60–61.

81. Within this category Kattenburg, "Reflections on Vietnam," lists W. Scott Thompson and Donald D. Frizzell (eds.), *The Lessons of Vietnam* (New York: Crane, Russak, 1977), Dennis Warner, *Certain Victory* (Mission, Kans.: Sheed, Andrews and McNeel, 1977); and the BDM Corporation study *Strategic Lessons Learned in Vietnam* (Washington, D.C.: BDM Corporation, 1981).

82. Slater, quoted in Kattenburg, "Reflections on Vietnam," 50.

83. Slater, quoted in ibid., 42.

84. Michel Foucault, "Interview," *Edinburgh '77 Magazine* (1977): 24.

85. Harry Summers, *On Strategy: The Vietnam War in Context* (Novato, Calif.: Presidio Press, 1982), 121.

86. Noam Chomsky, "The Remaking of History," in his *Toward a New Cold War: Essays on the Current Crisis and How We Got There* (New York: Pantheon Books, 1982), 138.

87. Aihwa Ong, "Southeast Asian Refugees and Investors in Our Midst," *Positions* 3, 3 (Winter 1995): 807.

88. Alexander Cockburn, *Corruptions of Empire: Life Studies and the Reagan Era* (London: Verso, 1987), 391.

89. James Fallows, "No Hard Feelings," *Atlantic Monthly* 262, 6 (December 1988): 71–78.

90. Chomsky, quoted by the editor of the *Bulletin of Concerned Asian Scholars* as a preface to Noam Chomsky, "The United States and Indochina: Far from an Aberration," *Bulletin of Concerned Asian Scholars* 21, 2–4 (1989): 76.

91. There is a growing number of veterans' autobiographical accounts of return. See, for example: John Balaban, *Remembering Heaven's Face: A Moral Witness in Vietnam* (New York: Poseidon Press, 1991), and his *Vietnam: The Land We Never Knew* (San Francisco: Chronicle Books, 1989); Kevin Bowen, "Seeking Reconciliation in Vietnam," *Christian Science Monitor* (November 10, 1988):

34–35; William Broyles, Jr., *Brothers in Arms* (New York: Knopf, 1986); Frederick Downs, *No Longer Enemies, Not Yet Friends* (New York: Norton, 1991); William D. Ehrhart, *Going Back: An Ex-Marine Returns to Vietnam* (Jefferson, N.C.: McFarland, 1987), and his "A Common Language," *Virginia Quarterly Review* 67, 3 (Summer 1991): 377–396; Rick Graetz, *Vietnam: Opening Doors to the World* (Helena, Mont.: American Geographic Publishing, 1988); Larry Heinemann, "Syndromes," *Harper's* (July 1991): 68–76; Larry Lee Rottmann, "A Hundred Happy Sparrows: An American Veteran Returns to Vietnam," *Vietnam Generation* 1, 1 (1989): 113–139; and "Going Back," the epilogue to Lynda Van Devanter, with Christopher Morgan, *Home Before Morning: The Story of an Army Nurse in Vietnam* (New York: Warner Books, 1984). See also *Going Back: A Return to Vietnam* (1982), a documentary film directed by David Munro.

92. The term is Harry Haines's. See his "The Pride is Back: *Rambo, Magnum, P.I.*, and the Return Trip to Vietnam," in R. Morris and P. Ehrenhaus (eds.), *Cultural Legacies of Vietnam: Uses of the Past in the Present* (Norwood, N.J.: Ablex, 1990), 99–123.

93. Quoted in H. Bruce Franklin, *M.I.A., or Mythmaking in America* (New Brunswick, N.J.: Rutgers University Press, 1993), 156. Franklin's perceptive and important study is supplemented by Elliott Gruner, *Prisoners of Culture: Representing the Vietnam POW* (New Brunswick, N.J.: Rutgers University Press, 1993).

94. Frederick Jackson Turner, "The Significance of the Frontier in American History," in *The Frontier in American History* (New York: Holt, Rinehart, 1958), 13. Originally published in 1893.

95. Norman Mailer, *Why Are We in Vietnam?* (London: Panther, 1970); Herr, *Dispatches*; Arthur Kopit, *Indians* (New York: Bantam, 1971).

96. The term "Vietnam western" was coined by Douglas Pye in a review of the film *Ulzana's Raid* in the British journal *Movie*. Reprinted in Ian Cameron and Douglas Pye (eds.), *The Movie Book of the Western* (London: Studio Vista, 1996).

97. Frances FitzGerald, *Fire in the Lake: The Vietnamese and the Americans in Vietnam* (New York: Vintage, 1972), 492.

98. Richard Slotkin, *Regeneration Through Violence: The Mythology of the American Frontier, 1600–1860* (Middletown, Conn.: Wesleyan University Press, 1973), *The Fatal Environment: The Myth of the Frontier in the Age of Industrialization, 1800–1890* (New York: Atheneum, 1985), and *Gunfighter Nation: The Myth of the Frontier in Twentieth-Century America* (New York: Harper and Row, 1993); John Hellmann, *American Myth and the Legacy of Vietnam* (New York: Columbia University Press, 1986). Milton Bates has informed this discussion in "The Frontier War," a chapter in his book *The Wars We Took to Vietnam: Cultural Conflict and Storytelling* (Berkeley: University of California Press, 1996).

99. Loren Baritz, *Backfire: A History of How American Culture Led Us Into Vietnam and Made Us Fight the Way We Did* (New York: Ballantine, 1985), part 1.

100. William McNeill, "The Care and Repair of Public Myth," *Foreign Affairs*, 61 (Fall 1982): 1–13; James Oliver Robertson, *American Myth, American Reality* (New York: Hill and Wang, 1980).

101. Claude Lévi-Strauss, *Structural Anthropology* (New York: Harper and Row, 1963).

102. Theodor Adorno, "What Does Coming to Terms with the Past Mean?" in G. Hartman (ed.), *Bitburg in Moral and Political Perspective* (Bloomington: Indiana University Press, 1986), 115.

103. Foucault, "Interview," 24.

104. David Thelen, "Memory and American History," *Journal of American History* 75, 4 (March 1989): 1128.

105. Lasch, *The Culture of Narcissism*, 201.

106. Mike Featherstone, "The Body in Consumer Culture," *Theory, Culture and Society*, 1, 1 (Spring 1982): 21–22.

107. Ibid., 28.

108. Naomi Wolf, *The Beauty Myth: How Images of Beauty are Used Against Women* (London: Vintage, 1991).

109. See Martin Norden, *The Cinema of Isolation: A History of Physical Disability in the Movies* (New Brunswick, N.J.: Rutgers University Press, 1994).

110. Quoted in William Mahedy, *Out of the Night: The Spiritual Journey of Vietnam Vets* (New York: Ballantine, 1986), 63.

111. Ibid.

112. Lawrence Suid, "Hollywood and Vietnam," *Journal of American Culture* 4, 2 (Summer 1981): 140.

113. Leonard Quart and Albert Auster, "The Wounded Vet in Postwar Film," *Social Policy* 13, 2 (Fall 1982): 29.

114. Ron Kovic, *Born on the Fourth of July* (New York: Pocket Books, 1977).

115. On the Dow Chemical Company's arguments, see Severo and Milford, *The Wages of War*, 374.

116. The history of the case is briefly reviewed in Institute of Medicine (U.S.), Committee to Review the Health Effects in Vietnam Veterans of Exposure to Herbicides, *Veterans and Agent Orange: Health Effects of Herbicides Used in Vietnam* (Washington, D.C.: National Academy Press, 1994).

117. An extract is reprinted in Joel Brende and Erwin Parson, *Vietnam Veterans: The Road to Recovery* (New York: Signet, 1986), 103–104. However, the definition contained in the third edition of the *Diagnostic and Statistical Manual of Mental Disorders (DSM III)* may not be the final word on classification of the veteran's psychological condition. Controversy continues over many of the definitions in this manual. See S. Garfield, "Problems in Diagnostic Classification," in T. Millon and G. Klerman (eds.), *Contemporary Directions in Psychopathology, Toward the DSM-IV* (New York: Guilford Press, 1986), 99–114.

118. W. Taylor Stevenson, "The Experience of Defilement: A Response to John Wheeler," *Anglican Theological Review* 64, 1 (January 1982): 15.

119. Mahedy, *Out of the Night*, 76.

120. Capps, *The Unfinished War*, 150.

121. Mahedy, *Out of the Night*, 76.

122. Capps, *The Unfinished War*, 149.

123. Mahedy, *Out of the Night*, 64, 63.

124. Ibid., 76, 64.

125. John Wheeler, *Touched with Fire: The Future of the Vietnam Generation* (New York: Avon Books, 1984), chapters 5, 6, 7.

126. See ibid.

127. Michel Foucault, *The History of Sexuality, vol.1* (London: Tavistock, 1977), 61.

128. Capps, *The Unfinished War*, 150.

129. Extracts of which are reproduced in Vietnam Veterans Against the War, *The Winter Soldier Investigation: An Inquiry into American War Crimes* (Boston: Beacon Press, 1972).

130. Capps, *The Unfinished War*, 145.

131. "How Should Americans Feel?" *Time* (April 14, 1975): 27.

132. Quoted in Howard Zinn, *A People's History of the United States* (New York: Harper Perennial, 1990), 555.

133. These figures operate in a post–Vietnam world that values their knowledge of weaponry or their technical expertise (gained in Vietnam) and remembers, or knows, very little else of that period of their lives. Flashback episodes present details of the characters' experiences in Vietnam, but the brief "memory" presented in this way is constrained by the problems I argue in this part: Vietnam (the war and the country) is rewritten through the various strategies that seek to define American unity.

134. C. Vann Woodward, "The Fall of the American Adam: Myths of Innocence and Guilt," *New Republic* (December 2, 1981): 14–15.

135. The representation of the United States as the victim of the war is evident in the title *Charlie Company: What Vietnam Did to Us*, by Peter Goldman and Tony Fuller (New York: Ballantine Books, 1983).

136. Quoted in Foster, "Coming to Terms with Defeat," 28.

137. Bellah et al., *Habits of the Heart*, 251.

138. Scruggs and Swerdlow, *To Heal a Nation*. Most commentaries concerned with the memorial refer at some point to healing. The specific function of healing as unity is stressed by Charles Griswold, who interprets the memorial functioning therapeutically to provide "a sense of wholeness." He explicitly links "wholeness" to national integration and "a reaffirmation of the values for which the nation stands." Charles Griswold, "The Vietnam Veterans Memorial and the Washington Mall: Philosophical Thoughts on Political Iconography," *Critical Inquiry* 12, 4 (Summer 1986): 712.

139. Frederic Henry muses after his war that "[t]he world breaks everyone

and afterward many are strong at the broken places." Hemingway, *A Farewell to Arms*, 216.

140. Quoted in John Wheeler, "The Vietnam Generation," in R. Bremner, G. Reichard, and R. Hopkins (eds.), *American Choices: Social Dilemmas and Public Policy Since 1960* (Columbus: Ohio State University Press, 1986), 259.

141. Quoted in James Mayo, *War Memorials as Political Landscape: The American Experience and Beyond* (New York: Praeger, 1988), 201.

142. For summaries of the clash of interests, see Haines, "'What Kind of War?'," 1–20, and Haines, "Disputing the Wreckage: Ideological Struggle at the Vietnam Veterans Memorial," *Vietnam Generation* 1, 1 (Winter 1989): 141–156. Rick Atkinson's *The Long Gray Line* (New York: Pocket Books, 1991), chapter 17, deals with the contending sides of the debate.

143. Elizabeth Hess, "An Interview with Maya Lin/Frederick Hart," in R. Williams (ed.), *Unwinding from the War: From War into Peace* (Seattle: Real Comet Press, 1987), 272, 273. The realistic statue honoring female veterans of the war (dedicated on Veterans Day, 1993) adds another dimension to the Lin/Hart "debate." The statue, depicting a wounded combat GI attended by three female nurses, foregrounds the injured (male) body in a context of (female) healing. The realistic style and size of the bronze work parallels Hart's conception of an appropriate monument.

144. Elaine Scarry, "Injury and the Structure of War," *Representations* 10 (Spring 1985): 1.

145. Quoted in Charles Gaspar, "Searching for Closure: Vietnam War Literature and the Veterans Memorial," *War, Literature and the Arts* 1, 1 (Spring 1989): 24.

146. Quoted in John Bodnar, *Remaking America: Public Memory, Commemoration, and Patriotism in the Twentieth Century* (Princeton: Princeton University Press, 1992), 4.

147. Quoted by John Lang, "A Memorial Wall That Healed Our Wounds," *U.S. News and World Report* (November 21, 1983): 68.

148. Douglas Crimp, "Mourning and Militancy," *October* 51 (Winter 1989): 3–18. Emphasis added.

149. This is the account presented in Scruggs and Swerdlow, *To Heal a Nation*, 7. For a discussion of alternative versions of this story, see Robin Wagner-Pacifici and Barry Schwartz, "The Vietnam Veterans Memorial: Commemorating a Difficult Past," *American Journal of Sociology* 97, 2 (September 1991): 390.

150. The Wall is represented in this way in the films *Cease Fire* (1984), *To Heal a Nation* (1987), *Hamburger Hill* (1987), *In Country* (1989), and the documentary film *Long Shadows* (1987).

151. Quoted in Lisa Grumwald, "Facing the Wall," *Life* (November 1992): 33.

152. Wheeler, *Touched with Fire*, 112–113.

153. Fredric Jameson, "Third-World Literature in the Era of Multinational Capitalism," *Social Text*, 15 (Fall 1986): 69.

154. Jeffords, *The Remasculinization of America*, 166.

155. Mason, *In Country*, 235–236.

156. David N. Rodowick, *The Difficulty of Difference: Psychoanalysis, Sexual Difference and Film Theory* (New York: Routledge, 1991), 18.

157. Mason, *In Country*, 245.

158. Broyles, Jr., "Remembering a War We Want to Forget," 82.

159. Marita Sturken, "The Wall, the Screen and the Image: The Vietnam Veterans Memorial," *Representations* 35 (Summer 1991): 127. Sturken elaborates her observations on the cultural function of certain forms of memorializing associated with the Vietnam War in *Tangled Memories: The Vietnam War, the AIDS Epidemic, and the Politics of Remembering* (Berkeley: University of California Press, 1997).

160. Sylvia Plath, "Daddy," in *Sylvia Plath's Selected Poems*, selected by T. Hughes (London: Faber and Faber, 1985), 61.

161. Raymond Williams, *Marxism and Literature* (Oxford: Oxford University Press, 1977), 116.

162. Studies of identity politics and new social movements rewrite essentialist conceptions of culture as a unified entity. The antiessentialist emphasis within such studies is informed by a recognition of the existence of cultural difference. Work of this kind includes Stanley Aronowitz, *The Politics of Identity: Class, Culture, Social Movements* (New York: Routledge, 1992); bell hooks, *Yearning: Race, Gender, and Cultural Politics* (Boston: South End Press, 1990); and Shane Phelan, *Identity Politics* (Philadelphia: Temple University Press, 1989).

163. Walter Benjamin, "Theses on the Philosophy of History," in *Illuminations* (New York: Schocken Books, 1969), 255.

164. Charles Maland, "Synthetic Criticism and American Movies," *American Quarterly* 41, 1 (March 1989): 679.

165. In different ways, the films *The Edge* (1967), *Black Sunday* (1976), and *Twilight's Last Gleaming* (1977) deal with veterans taking revenge on the system that sent them to Vietnam.

166. On the class basis of the Vietnam War, see Christian Appy, *Working-Class War: American Combat Soldiers and Vietnam* (Chapel Hill: University of North Carolina Press, 1993).

167. Leonard Quart and Albert Auster, "The Working Class Goes to Hollywood," in P. Davies and B. Neve (eds.), *Cinema, Politics and Society in America* (New York: St. Martin's Press, 1981), 175.

168. Robert Stone, *A Hall of Mirrors* (Harmondsworth, Middlesex, U.K.: Penguin, 1968), 68.

169. Robert Stone, *A Flag for Sunrise* (London: Picador, 1983), 86.

170. Robert Stone, *Children of Light* (London: Andre Deutsch, 1986).

171. Robert Stone, *Outerbridge Reach* (Harmondsworth, Middlesex, U.K.: Penguin, 1992), 44.

172. Robert Stone, *Dog Soldiers* (London: Wyndham, 1976), 164.

173. Ibid., 325–326.

174. Ibid., 323.

175. Larry Heinemann, *Paco's Story* (New York: Penguin, 1987), 157, 158.

176. William D. Ehrhart, "The Invasion of Grenada," *Cultural Critique* 3 (Spring 1980): 91.

177. George Swiers, "'Demented Vets' and Other Myths: The Moral Obligation of Veterans," in H. Salisbury (ed.), *Vietnam Reconsidered: Lessons from a War* (New York: Harper and Row, 1984), 199, and Thomas Roberts, a Vietnam veteran and antiwar activist, quoted in Haines, "Disputing the Wreckage," 143.

178. Heinemann, *Paco's Story*, 18.

179. Larry Heinemann in Bill McCloud (ed.), *What Should We Tell Our Children about Vietnam?* (Norman: University of Oklahoma Press, 1989), 58.

180. Heinemann, "Syndromes," 76.

181. Heinemann, *Paco's Story*, 184.

182. Lorrie Smith, "Back Against the Wall: Anti-Feminist Backlash in Vietnam War Literature," *Vietnam Generation* 1, 3–4 (Summer-Fall 1989): 122.

183. Heinemann, *Paco's Story*, 208.

184. Herr, *Dispatches*, 207.

185. Stanley Karnow, *Vietnam: A History* (New York: Viking Press, 1983), 11.

186. Quoted in Scott Gilbert, "The Metaphorical Structuring of Social Perceptions," *Soundings* 62, 2 (Summer 1979): 184.

187. Kendrick, *The Wound Within*, 4.

188. Le Ly Hayslip, with Jay Wurts, *When Heaven and Earth Changed Places: A Vietnamese Woman's Journey from War to Peace* (New York: Plume, 1990), chapter 3, "Open Wounds."

189. Kobena Mercer, "'1968': Periodizing Politics and Identity," in L. Grossberg, C. Nelson, and P. Treichler (eds.), *Cultural Studies* (New York: Routledge, 1992), 426.

NOTES TO PART 2

1. However, Lee Iacocca, for one, has offered his personal interpretation in a promotional segment accompanying the American video edition of *Platoon* (1986): Such people "knew only one thing, they were called and they went." In Iacocca's interpretation, those who go to war are not only silent (they are called and they go, with no questions asked) but also lacking in intellectual faculties— the only thing they know is to go quietly. Iacocca legitimated this condescension when he elsewhere offered his well-known sales pitch: "I guarantee it."

2. Tania Modleski, "A Father Is Being Beaten: Male Feminism and the War Film," *Discourses: A Journal for Theoretical Studies in Media and Culture* 10, 2 (Spring-Summer 1988): 67.

3. Albert Auster and Leonard Quart, *How the War Was Remembered: Hollywood and Vietnam* (New York: Praeger, 1988), part 2.

4. Maxine Hong Kingston, *China Men* (London: Picador, 1981); John Williams, *Captain Blackman* (New York: Thunder's Mouth Press, 1988); George Davis, *Coming Home* (New York: Random House, 1971); Louise Erdrich, *Love Medicine* (New York: Holt, Rinehart and Winston, 1984). John Rambo is identified in the film *Rambo: First Blood, Part II* (1985) as "half Indian, half German." In contrast to the other works mentioned here, the Rambo character appears in films that have attracted a high degree of popular and critical attention. Little of this attention, however, mentions or analyzes the relevance of the character's ethnicity. The Vietnam veteran of color also features in the films *Some Kind of Hero* (1982) and *Riverbend* (1990), a film concerning three black soldiers on the run from a court-martial who take over a racist southern township. The implausible plot concludes with mawkish scenes of reunion between white and black citizens.

5. See Susan Jeffords, "Point Blank: Shooting Vietnamese Women," *Vietnam Generation* 1, 3–4 (Summer-Fall 1989): 152–167.

6. Lynda Van Devanter, with Christopher Morgan, *Home Before Morning: The Story of an Army Nurse in Vietnam* (New York: Warner Books, 1984). The monument to the women who served in the Vietnam War (unveiled in Washington, D.C., on Veterans Day, 1993) positions women within the definition of "Vietnam veteran."

7. Bette London, *The Appropriated Voice: Narrative Authority in Conrad, Forster, and Woolf* (Ann Arbor: University of Michigan Press, 1990), 4.

8. Throughout this part the Vietnam veteran is referred to by the masculine personal pronoun. The form is used to reflect textual approaches adopted to the veteran and exemplifies the continuing popular representational denial of the role of women in the war.

9. Van Devanter, with Morgan, *Home Before Morning*, 271. Certain projects have addressed the exclusion of women from the field of "Vietnam" by documenting women's memoirs and fictional accounts of service in Vietnam. See, for example, Deborah Butler's *American Women Writers on Vietnam: Unheard Voices: A Selected Annotated Bibliography* (New York: Garland, 1990).

10. John Carlos Rowe, "'Bringing It All Back Home': American Recyclings of the Vietnam War," in N. Armstrong and L. Tennenhouse (eds.), *The Violence of Representation: Literature and the History of Violence* (London: Routledge, 1989), 198.

11. Catherine Belsey, *Critical Practice* (London: Methuen, 1983), 104.

12. In Bob Ashley, *The Study of Popular Fiction: A Source Book* (London: Pinter, 1989), 141.

13. Pierre Macherey, *A Theory of Literary Production* (London: Routledge and Kegan Paul, 1978). Macherey's conceptions of the "absences" that can be located within texts is derived from Althusser's notion of "symptomatic reading." For an interpretation of Althusser's approach, see David N. Rodowick, *The Difficulty of Difference: Psychoanalysis, Sexual Difference and Film Theory* (New York: Routledge, 1991).

14. David James and Rick Berg, "College Course File: Representing the Vietnam War," *Journal of Film and Video* 41, 4 (Winter 1989): 60–71.

15. Roland Barthes, "*Pax Culturalis*," in *The Rustle of Language* (New York: Hill and Wang, 1986), 101.

16. Ibid.

17. Roland Barthes, preface to the first edition of *Mythologies* (1957) (reprint, New York: Hill and Wang, 1987), 7.

18. Dick Hebdige, *Subculture: The Meaning of Style* (London: Methuen, 1979), 97.

19. Bill Nichols, "The Voice of Documentary," in B. Nichols (ed.), *Movies and Methods: An Anthology, vol. 2* (Berkeley: University of California Press, 1985), 260.

20. Roland Barthes, "Writers, Intellectuals, Teachers," in *Image-Music-Text* (New York: Farrar, Straus and Giroux, 1977), 191.

21. Pierre Bourdieu, *Language and Symbolic Power* (Cambridge: Harvard University Press, 1991), 131.

22. According to one filmography, the Vietnam veteran first appeared in fiction films in 1965 in *Bus Riley's Back in Town* and *Motor Psycho*. Mark Walker, *Vietnam Veteran Films* (Metuchen, N.J.: Scarecrow Press, 1991), 159, 179, 183. A number of factors contributed to the prominence of the Billy Jack films: widespread distribution, and a relatively high degree of audience popularity and commercial success. On the success of the films, see Suzanne Donahue, *American Film Distribution: The Changing Marketplace* (Ann Arbor, Mich.: UMI, 1987), 254–262. While most of the early films representing the veteran typically cast the character unsympathetically, *Bus Riley's Back in Town* did depict the veteran in a positive way. For a discussion of this film, see John Baxter, *Hollywood in the Sixties* (New York: Tantivity Press, 1972), 130.

23. "B-grade" films featuring veterans and biker gangs continued to be produced beyond the 1960s. However, more sophisticated representations of the Vietnam veteran subsequently eroded the prominence of the veteran/biker image.

24. Julian Smith, *Looking Away: Hollywood and Vietnam* (New York: Scribners, 1975), 157.

25. Rick Berg, "Losing Vietnam: Covering the War in an Age of Technology," *Cultural Critique*, 3 (Spring 1986): 114.

26. Smith, *Looking Away*, 156.

27. Berg, "Losing Vietnam," 114.

28. Details of the massacre at "Pinkville" on March 16, 1968, had been known publicly since 1969. (For example, Ron Haeberle's photographs of the dead at My Lai appeared in *Life* magazine in November 1969.) The next year a number of publications revealed further details: Seymour Hersh, *My Lai 4: A Report of the Massacre and Its Aftermath* (New York: Random House, 1970), and Richard Hammer, *One Morning in the War: The Tragedy at Son My* (New York: Coward, McCann and Geoghegan, 1970).

29. The episodes of television series that feature the character of a deranged veteran are discussed in Berg, "Losing Vietnam," 95–102. In addition to television series and films, the character can be traced through a number of novels. See, for example, Charles Coleman's *Sergeant Back Again* (New York: Harper and Row, 1980), Robert Bausch's *On the Way Home* (New York: Avon, 1983), and Stephen Wright's *Meditations in Green* (London: Abacus, 1985). Wright's chaotic plot and his emphasis on drugs are features of Jerome Charyn's *War Cries over Avenue C* (New York: Penguin, 1986), another novel to feature the character of a "crazed" Vietnam veteran. The image of a deranged Vietnam veteran is especially pronounced in John Nicholls's graphic descriptions in *American Blood* of the violence wrought by a veteran (London: Grafton Books, 1990). Kurt Vonnegut exposes and ridicules the stereotype in his work *Hocus Pocus* (New York: Berkley Books, 1991). In the year 2001, Eugene Debs Hartke, a Vietnam veteran, encounters a computer simulation package that produces character profiles based on a person's life experiences. Hartke tells the computer "only about [his] life up to the end of the Vietnam War. It knew all about the Vietnam War and the sorts of veterans it had produced. It made me a burned-out case, on the basis of my length of service over there. . . . It had me becoming a wife-beater and an alcoholic, and winding up all alone on Skid Row" (p.103).

30. Tim O'Brien, "We've Adjusted Too Well," in A. D. Horne (ed.), *The Wounded Generation: America After Vietnam* (Englewood Cliffs, N.J.: Prentice-Hall, 1981), 205–207.

31. George Swiers, "'Demented Vets' and Other Myths: The Moral Obligation of Veterans," in H. Salisbury (ed.), *Vietnam Reconsidered: Lessons from a War* (New York: Harper and Row, 1984), 17.

32. The refusal by CBS to screen footage of the testimony is mentioned by Todd Gitlin in *The Whole World Is Watching: Mass Media in the Making and Unmaking of the New Left* (Berkeley: University of California Press, 1980), 192. The quotation comes from John Kerry and Vietnam Veterans Against the War, *The New Soldier*, ed., D. Thorne and G. Butler (New York: Collier Books, 1971), ii.

33. Gitlin, *The Whole World,* 92.

34. Harry Haines, "'They Were Called and They Went': The Political Rehabilitation of the Vietnam Veteran," in L. Dittmar and G. Michaud (eds.), *From Hanoi to Hollywood: The Vietnam War in American Film* (New Brunswick, N.J.: Rutgers University Press, 1990), 84.

35. Paul Camacho, "The Future of Patriotism: The War Film, the Cinema Industry, and the Vietnam Veteran Movement," *New England Journal of History* 47, 1 (1990): 38.

36. Ibid.

37. Hélène Cixous, "Castration or Decapitation?" *Signs* 7, 1 (Autumn 1981): 49.

38. Stanley Cohen, *Folk Devils and Moral Panics: The Creation of Mods and Rockers* (London: MacGibbon and Kee, 1972), 9.

39. Hebdige, *Subculture*, 97.

40. John Carlos Rowe, "Eye-Witness: Documentary Styles in the American Representations of Vietnam," *Cultural Critique* 3 (1986): 129, 137.

41. Christopher Lasch, *The Culture of Narcissism: American Life in an Age of Diminishing Expectations* (New York: Warner Books, 1979).

42. See Norman Mailer, *Why Are We in Vietnam?* (London: Panther, 1970); Philip Slater, *The Pursuit of Loneliness: American Culture at Breaking Point* (Boston: Beacon Press, 1990).

43. Peter Lehman, "'Well, What's It Like Over There? Can You Tell Us Anything?': Looking for Vietnam in *The Deer Hunter*," *North Dakota Quarterly* 5 (Summer 1983): 136.

44. H. Bruce Franklin, "From Realism to Virtual Reality: Images of America's Wars," in S. Jeffords and L. Rabinovitz (eds.), *Seeing Through the Media: The Persian Gulf War* (New Brunswick, N.J.: Rutgers University Press, 1994), 135.

45. Ibid.

46. Bobbie Ann Mason, "Big Bertha Stories," in *Love Life* (London: Vintage, 1990), 134, 137, 143.

47. Bobbie Ann Mason, *In Country* (London: Flamingo, 1987), 107, 136, 220. In the film *Jacknife* (1989), Megs (Robert De Niro) tells his wartime buddy David (Ed Harris) that Martha (Kathy Baker), David's sister, can never understand what they went through in Vietnam. "She doesn't know, she wasn't there," asserts Megs.

48. Bruce Springsteen, "Born in the U.S.A.," from the album *Born in the U.S.A.* (CBS, 1984).

49. Mason, *In Country*, 189.

50. Ibid., 167.

51. Alice Bloom, reprint of review of *In Country*, in D. Marowski and R. Matuz (eds.), *Contemporary Literary Criticism*, vol.43 (Detroit: Gale, 1987), 290.

52. Jonathan Yardley, reprint of review of *In Country*, in D. Marowski, and R. Matuz (eds.), *Contemporary Literary Criticism*, vol. 43 (Detroit: Gale, 1987), 287.

53. Myra MacPherson, *Long Time Passing: Vietnam and the Haunted Generation* (New York: Signet, 1984).

54. Lance Morrow, "The Forgotten Warriors," *Time* (July 13, 1981): 21.

55. Jerome Klinkowitz, *The American 1960s: Imaginative Acts in a Decade of Change* (Ames: Iowa State University Press, 1980), 76.

56. Michael Herr, *Dispatches* (London: Picador, 1978), 160, 111. First published in the United States in 1977.

57. Ibid., 79.

58. Fredric Jameson, *The Geopolitical Aesthetic: Cinema and Space in the World System* (Bloomington: Indiana University Press, and London: BFI Publishing, 1992), 43.

59. Charles Durden, *No Bugles, No Drums* (New York: Charter, 1978), 207.

60. Walter Capps, *The Unfinished War: Vietnam and the American Conscience*, 2nd ed. (Boston: Beacon Press, 1990), 2.

61. Tom LeClair and Larry McCaffery (eds.), *Anything Can Happen: Interviews with Contemporary American Novelists* (Urbana: University of Illinois Press, 1983), 267. Implicit within O'Brien's remark is the suggestion that the literature produced by the novelists and poets of World War I is, on a certain level, comparable with the literature of the war in Vietnam, a suggestion that has been traced in a number of critical sources. See, for example, John Hellmann, *Fables of Fact: The New Journalism as New Fiction* (Urbana: University of Illinois Press, 1981), chapter 6.

62. Tim O'Brien, *Going After Cacciato* (London: Triad/Granada, 1980), 189–197.

63. O'Brien, in Leclair and McCaffery, *Anything Can Happen*, 266. In *Acts of Battle: The Behavior of Men in Battle* (New York: Free Press, 1985), Richard Holmes asserts that the experience of war is essentially the same regardless of the technology involved. The many descriptions of the Vietnam War as "discontinuous" and "unreal" resonate in Eric Leed's description of the experience of World War I: "It was nothing if not an experience of radical discontinuity on every level of consciousness." Eric Leed, *No Man's Land: Combat and Identity in World War I* (Cambridge, U.K.: Cambridge University Press, 1979), 3. Assertions of the uniqueness of the Vietnam War have been especially pronounced in manuals designed to help veterans recover from the adverse effects of the war. Examples here include Dolores Kuenning, *Life After Vietnam: How Veterans and Their Loved Ones Can Heal the Psychic Wounds of War* (New York: Paragon House, 1991), chapter 2, "Why Vietnam Was a Different War," and Patience Mason, *Recovering from the War: A Woman's Guide to Helping Your Vietnam Veteran, Your Family, and Yourself* (New York: Penguin, 1990), chapter 7, "So What's Different about Vietnam?" Such assertions of the unique nature of the Vietnam conflict function to focus governmental and familial resources on the needs of veterans who suffered most acutely the effects of what is in terms of these studies an exceptionally devastating war.

64. See Richard Severo and Lewis Milford, *The Wages of War: When Amer-

ica's Soldiers Came Home—From Valley Forge to Vietnam (New York: Simon and Schuster, 1989).

65. Norman Mailer, "Mailer's Reply," in *Cannibals and Christians* (New York: Delta, 1966), 85–86.

66. The assumptions that the Vietnam War was a unique conflict and that as such it required an innovative form of representation have, through repetition, acquired their own common sense within critical analyses of the literature of the war. The assumptions have been circulated in a wide array of sources, including among others Philip Beidler, *American Literature and the Vietnam Experience* (Athens: University of Georgia Press, 1982); Tobey Herzog, *Vietnam War Stories: Innocence Lost* (New York: Routledge, 1992); Lloyd Lewis, *The Tainted War: Culture and Identity in Vietnam War Narratives* (Westport, Conn.: Greenwood Press, 1985); Philip Melling, *Vietnam in American Literature* (Boston: Twayne, 1990); Thomas Myers, *Walking Point: American Narratives of Vietnam* (New York: Oxford University Press, 1988); and Donald Ringnalda, *Fighting and Writing the Vietnam War* (Jackson: University Press of Mississippi, 1994).

67. Herr, *Dispatches*, 46.

68. Norman Mailer, *The Armies of the Night: History as a Novel, the Novel as History* (Harmondsworth, Middlesex, U.K.: Penguin, 1968), 268.

69. Graham Greene, *The Quiet American* (London: Reprint Society, 1955), ii; Walter Lederer and Eugene Burdick, *The Ugly American* (New York: Norton, 1958), "Authors' Note"; Robin Moore, *The Green Berets* (New York: Crown, 1965).

70. Robert Wright, "'History's Heavy Attrition': Literature, Historical Consciousness and the Impact of Vietnam," *Canadian Review of American Studies* 17, 3 (Fall 1986): 308. The books by the authors Wright refers to are Philip Caputo, *A Rumor of War* (London: Arrow Books, 1978); Tim O'Brien, *If I Die in a Combat Zone* (London: Granada, 1980); C. D. B. Bryan, *Friendly Fire* (New York: Putnam, 1976); Frederick Downs, *The Killing Zone: My Life in Vietnam* (New York: Berkley Books, 1983); James Webb, *Fields of Fire* (New York: Bantam, 1972); Mark Baker, *Nam: The Vietnam War in the Words of the Men and Women Who Fought There* (London: Abacus, 1982); Al Santoli, *Everything We Had: An Oral History of the Vietnam War by Thirty-three American Soldiers Who Fought It* (New York: Ballantine, 1982); Anthony Grey, *Saigon* (Boston: Little, Brown, 1982); Peter Goldman and Tony Fuller, *Charlie Company: What Vietnam Did to Us* (New York: Ballantine, 1983).

71. Susan Fromberg Schaeffer, *Buffalo Afternoon* (New York: Knopf, 1989). Trends in the publication of Vietnam War novels prior to the release of Schaeffer's novel are discussed in William J. Searle, "The Vietnam War Novel and the Reviewers," *Journal of American Culture* 42, 2 (Summer 1981): 83–94.

72. O'Brien, *Going After Cacciato*, 257.

73. Kali Tal, "When History Talks Back: The Voice of the Veteran," in M. J.

Gilbert (ed.), *The Vietnam War: Teaching Approaches and Resources* (New York: Greenwood Press, 1991), 166.

74. David James, "Presence of Discourse/Discourse of Presence: Representing Vietnam," *Wide Angle* 7, 4 (1985): 42.

75. Quoted in the introduction to Kathryn Marshall, *In the Combat Zone: An Oral History of American Women in Vietnam, 1966–1975* (Boston: Little, Brown, 1987), 14.

76. Herr, *Dispatches*, 129.

77. Ibid., 24.

78. Ibid., 21, 13, 75.

79. Ibid., 68.

80. Ibid., 23–24.

81. John Ketwig, . . . *And a Hard Rain Fell* (New York: Pocket Books, 1985), 4, 6.

82. William Broyles, Jr., *Brothers in Arms: A Journey from War to Peace* (New York: Knopf, 1986), 275.

83. Susan Jeffords, *The Remasculinization of America: Gender and the Vietnam War* (Bloomington: Indiana University Press, 1989), 26.

84. Philip Caputo, quoted in a symposium in A. D. Horne (ed.), *The Wounded Generation: America After Vietnam* (Englewood Cliffs, N.J.: Prentice-Hall, 1981), 116.

85. Claudia Springer, "*Vietnam: A Television History* and the Equivocal Nature of Objectivity," *Wide Angle* 7, 4 (1985): 58.

86. Quoted in "Monumental Talent," *U.S. News and World Report* (November 6, 1989): 18.

87. Herr, *Dispatches*, 14.

88. Philip Beidler, *American Literature and the Vietnam Experience* (Athens: University of Georgia Press, 1982), 176.

89. Stephen Wright, quoted in Timothy Lomperis, *Reading the Wind: The Literature of the Vietnam War—An Interpretative Critique* (Durham, N.C.: Duke University Press, 1987), 51.

90. Robert Graves, quoted in Donald Ringnalda, "Unlearning to Remember," in O. Gilman, Jr., and L. Smith (eds.), *America Rediscovered: Critical Essays on Literature and Film of the Vietnam War* (New York: Garland, 1990), 65.

91. O'Brien, *If I Die In a Combat Zone*, 29.

92. O'Brien, *Going After Cacciato*, 257.

93. Tim O'Brien, *The Things They Carried* (New York: Penguin, 1991), 88.

94. William Broyles, Jr., "Why Men Love War," *Esquire* (November 1984): 61.

95. Ibid.

96. Harry Maurer, *Strange Ground: An Oral History of Americans in Vietnam, 1945–1975* (New York: Avon, 1990), 5.

97. In "Vietnam Remembered," *Journal of American History* 73, 1 (June 1986): 152, George Herring states that "[o]ral history gained respectability dur-

ing the Vietnam era and proved particularly suitable for Vietnam-related subjects," although he doesn't say why this should have been the case. The rise and
respectability of oral accounts of the war in Vietnam was directly related to the
series of interrelated assumptions that have been established here—beginning
with the definition of Vietnam as a unique war. Oral historical accounts of the
Vietnam War include Mark Baker, *Nam: The Vietnam War in the Words of the
Men and Women Who Fought There* (London: Sphere, 1982); Stanley Beesley,
Vietnam: The Heartland Remembers (New York: Berkley Books, 1989); Matthew
Brennan, *Headhunters: Stories from the 1st Squadron, 9th Cavalry in Vietnam,
1965–1971* (Novato, Calif.: Presidio Press, 1987); Larry Engelmann, *Tears Be-
fore the Rain: An Oral History of the Fall of South Vietnam* (New York: Oxford
University Press, 1990); Dan Freeman and Jacqueline Rhoads, *Nurses in Vietnam:
The Forgotten Veterans* (Austin: Texas Monthly Press, 1989); Stanley Goff,
Robert Sanders, and Clark Smith, *Brothers: Black Soldiers in the Nam* (Novato,
Calif.: Presidio Press/Arms and Armour Press, 1982); Goldman and Fuller, *Char-
lie Company*; Martha Hess, *Then the Americans Came: Voices from Vietnam*
(New York: Four Walls/Eight Windows, 1993); Marshall, *In the Combat Zone*;
Maurer, *Strange Ground*; Elizabeth Norman, *Women at War: The Story of Fifty
Military Nurses Who Served in Vietnam* (Philadelphia: University of Pennsylva-
nia Press, 1990); John Clark Pratt, *Vietnam Voices: Perspectives on the War
Years, 1941–1982* (New York: Viking, 1984); Al Santoli, *Everything We Had*;
and his *To Bear Any Burden: The Vietnam War and Its Aftermath in the Words
of Americans and Southeast Asians* (London: Sphere, 1986); Wallace Terry,
Bloods: An Oral History of the Vietnam War by Black Veterans (New York: Ran-
dom House, 1984); Keith Walker, *A Piece of My Heart: The Stories of Twenty-six
American Women Who Served in Vietnam* (Novato, Calif.: Presidio Press, 1985);
Kim Willenson, with the correspondents of *Newsweek*, *The Bad War: An Oral
History of the Vietnam War* (New York: New American Library, 1987); and
James Wilson, *Landing Zones: Southern Veterans Remember Vietnam* (Durham,
N.C.: Duke University Press, 1990).

98. Rowe, "Eye-Witness," 135.

99. Maurer, *Strange Ground*, 5.

100. Beesley, xix, xv.

101. Rowe, "Eye-Witness, 136. The bildungsroman structure also informs
numerous novels of the war. Indeed, so pervasive is the structure that its essential
features of innocence, initiation, disillusionment, and return form the basis of
what C. D. B. Bryan refers to as a "Generic Vietnam War Narrative." C. D. B.
Bryan, "Barely Suppressed Screams," *Harper's* (June 1984): 68.

102. Beesley, xv.

103. Santoli, *Everything We Had*.

104. Capps, *The Unfinished War*, 2.

105. Ibid., 86.

106. Ibid., 97.

107. Ibid., 94.

108. Bob Greene, *Homecoming: When the Soldiers Returned from Vietnam* (New York: Ballantine, 1989).

109. Capps, *The Unfinished War*, 94.

110. Ibid., 149, 150, 9, 92–93.

111. *Time* magazine exemplified a trend in critical reaction to Stone's film. Its cover proclaimed that Stone had represented "Viet Nam As It Really Was." *Time* (January 26, 1987).

112. John Ellis, *Visible Fictions: Cinema, Television, Radio* (London: Routledge, 1982), 31.

113. Bill Nichols, "Questions of Magnitude," in J. Corner (ed.), *Documentary and the Mass Media* (London: Edward Arnold, 1986), 107.

114. Dan Goodgame, "How the War Was Won," *Time* (January 26, 1987): 56. Among his other ventures, Dye has been executive editor of the mercenary soldier's companion, *Soldier of Fortune* magazine, and the author of a number of action adventure novels with war themes.

115. Quoted in Judy Lee Kinney, "*Gardens of Stone, Platoon,* and *Hamburger Hill*: Ritual and Remembrance," in M. Anderegg (ed.), *Inventing Vietnam: The War in Film and Television* (Philadelphia: Temple University Press, 1991), 157.

116. Victor Shklovsky, "Art as Technique," in L. Leman and M. Reis (eds.), *Russian Formalist Criticism: Four Essays* (Lincoln: University of Nebraska Press, 1965), 12.

117. Stanley Kauffmann, "Fact-facing," *New Republic* (April 24, 1989): 24.

118. Quoted in Karen Jaehne, "Company Man," *Film Comment* 25, 2 (March-April 1985): 15.

119. Stone's filmic interpretation of the truth behind the assassination of John Kennedy raised a storm of debate. Historians censured the historical accuracy of Stone's interpretation and in doing so rendered themselves incapable of addressing, or answering, Stone's argument that he had captured the "cultural myth" at the center of the event. For Stone, "[M]yths are dynamic. They reinterpret history to create lasting, universal truths." Oliver Stone, "The Killing of JFK: A Very American Coup," *Weekend Australian* (December 28–29, 1991), Review, 3.

120. Oliver Stone, "One from the Heart," *Platoon/Salvador: The Screenplays* (London: Ebury Press, 1987), 5, 6.

121. Scenes in *The Deer Hunter* of Americans with guns to their heads resonate in a scene in *Platoon* in which Chris sucks dope smoke Elias blows through a rifle barrel. Mixed with the homoerotic allusions implicit within the act is the image of Chris holding a shotgun to his head.

122. Critics assuming the authenticity of *Platoon* have deferred to Stone's tour of duty in Vietnam in support of their assumption. Further investigation of Stone's autobiography would have revealed that he first went to Vietnam in 1965 as a teacher, a point that the critical deference to Stone's life history would, no

doubt, interpret as the basis of Chris Taylor's desire to impart the lessons he has learned in Vietnam.

123. See Christian Appy, "Vietnam According to Oliver Stone: John Wayne Rides Again," *Commonweal* (March 23, 1990): 187–188.

124. Ronald Reagan, "Veterans Day Ceremony: Vietnam Veterans Memorial, November 11, 1988," in *Speaking My Mind: Selected Speeches* (London: Hutchinson, 1990), 367–368.

125. Quoted in Tod Lindberg, "Of Arms, Men and Monuments," *Commentary* 68, 4 (October 1984): 56.

126. These details come from Harry Haines, "Disputing the Wreckage: Ideological Struggle at the Vietnam Veterans Memorial," *Vietnam Generation* 1, 1 (Winter 1989): 48, and Tom Morganthau and Mary Lord, "Honoring Vietnam Veterans—At Last," *Newsweek* (November 22, 1982): 32–33, 36.

127. Peter Ehrenhaus, "Commemorating the Unwon War: On *Not* Remembering Vietnam," *Journal of Communication* 39, 1 (Winter 1989): 106.

128. The image of a new day in America is from a Reagan campaign commercial. See Sidney Blumenthal, *The Rise of the Counter Establishment: From Conservative Ideology to Political Power* (New York: Times Books, 1986), 279.

129. Michael Ryan and Douglas Kellner, *Camera Politica: The Politics and Ideology of Contemporary Hollywood Film* (Bloomington: Indiana University Press, 1988), 207.

130. Irving Sloan (ed.), *Ronald Reagan, 1911– : Chronology–Documents– Bibliographical Aids* (Dobbs Ferry, N.Y.: Oceana, 1990), 107.

131. Ibid., 221.

132. Lawrence Grossberg, "It's a Sin: Politics, Post-Modernity and the Popular," in L. Grossberg, T. Fry, A. Curthoys, and P. Patton, *It's a Sin: Essays on Post-modernism, Politics and Culture* (Sydney: Power Publications, 1988), 60.

133. See Sloan, *Ronald Reagan*, 104, 140, 185, 188, 197, 228.

134. Quoted in Paul D. Erickson, *Reagan Speaks: The Making of an American Myth* (New York: New York University Press, 1985), 57.

135. The speech is quoted in part in John Wheeler, "The Vietnam Generation," in R. Bremmer, G. Reichard, and R. Hopkins (eds.), *American Choices: Social Dilemmas and Public Policy Since 1960* (Columbus: Ohio State University Press, 1986), 259.

136. Quoted by Stanley Kauffmann, "Now About Rambo . . . ," *New Republic* (July 1, 1985): 16.

137. Thomas Doherty, "Rambo: First Blood Part II," *Film Quarterly*, 39, 3 (Spring 1986): 54.

138. Reagan, "Veterans Day Ceremony," 368.

139. John Wheeler, "Coming to Grips with Vietnam," *Foreign Affairs* 63, 4 (Spring 1985): 755. *National Lampoon* magazine commented on the trend toward claiming veteran status when it produced a "Vietnam Combat Veterans Simulator Kit," a humorous guide to the successful impersonation of a Vietnam

combat veteran. Tod Carroll and P. J. O'Rourke, "Born Again on the Fourth of July," *National Lampoon* (July 1978): 65–70, 96.

140. Wheeler, "Coming to Grips with Vietnam," 755.

141. bell hooks, "Talking Back," in R. Ferguson, M. Gever, Trinh T. Minh-ha, and C. West (eds.), *Out There: Marginalization and Contemporary Culture* (New York: New Museum of Art, 1990), 337.

142. See, for example, E. D. Hirsch, Jr., *Cultural Literacy: What Every American Needs to Know* (New York: Bantam/Schwartz, 1989).

143. The issue of a canon of Vietnam War texts was discussed during three sessions at the twentieth annual meeting of the Popular Culture Association in Toronto, March 7–10, 1990; see program of meeting (Bowling Green, Ohio: Bowling Green State University, 1990). In the preface to *America Rediscovered: Critical Essays on Literature and Film of the Vietnam War* (New York: Garland, 1990) the editors, Owen Gilman, Jr., and Lorrie Smith, accept the notion, "only partially in jest," that they "are engaged in building a new canon" (p. ix).

144. Priscilla Murolo, "Remembering Vietnam," *Radical History Review* 33 (1985): 184.

145. Kevin Bowen, "'Strange Hells': Hollywood in Search of America's Lost War," in L. Dittmar and G. Michaud (eds.), *From Hanoi to Hollywood: The Vietnam War in American Film* (New Brunswick, N.J.: Rutgers University Press, 1990), 229.

146. Veterans' poetry from the 1st Casualty Press is published as Larry Lee Rottmann, Jan Barry, and Basil Parquet (eds.), *Winning Hearts and Minds: War Poems by Vietnam Veterans* (Brooklyn: 1st Casualty Press, 1972), also issued by McGraw-Hill in 1972. William Ehrhart has edited two excellent collections of Vietnam veteran poetry: *Unaccustomed Mercy: Soldier-Poets of the Vietnam War* (Lubbock: Texas Tech University Press, 1988) and *Carrying the Darkness: The Poetry of the Vietnam War* (Lubbock: Texas Tech University Press). For a perceptive discussion of Ehrhart's own poetry, see Kali Tal, *Worlds of Hurt: Reading the Literature of Trauma* (New York: Cambridge University Press, 1996). The 1st Casualty Press has also published a volume of short fiction: Wayne Karlin, Basil Parquet, and Larry Lee Rottmann (eds.), *Free Fire Zone: Short Stories by Vietnam Veterans* (Brooklyn: 1st Casualty Press, 1973), reprinted by McGraw-Hill in 1973. Veterans' art works were displayed in the major exhibition "War and Memory: In the Aftermath of Vietnam," Washington, D.C., September 15–December 19, 1987. See, for details, the catalog: Washington Project for the Arts, *War and Memory: In the Aftermath of Vietnam* (Washington, D.C.: The Project, 1987). John DiFusco collaborated with other Vietnam veterans to produce the play *Tracers* (New York: Hill and Wang, 1986).

147. John Carlos Rowe, "Vietnam and American Literary Historiography," in D. Nye and C. Thomsen (eds.), *American Studies in Transition* (Odense, Denmark: Odense University Press, 1985), 280.

148. Robert Ray, *A Certain Tendency of the Hollywood Cinema, 1930–1980* (Princeton, N.J.: Princeton University Press, 1985), 364.

149. T. J. Jackson Lears, "Power, Culture, and Memory," *Journal of American History* 75, 1 (June 1988): 140.

150. In early 1973, William Paley, chairperson of CBS, refused to screen an adaptation of *Sticks and Bones*. According to Paley, the play was too "'abrasive' [at a time] when Americans were rejoicing in the return of prisoners of war." Albin Krebs, "Paley, C.B.S Chairman, Personally Vetoed Showing 'Sticks and Bones,'" *New York Times* (March 20, 1973): 76.

151. The film, based on Newton Thorburg's novel *Cutter and Bone* (London: William Heinemann, 1978), was originally released by United Artists in New York in March 1981 under the name of the novel. An adversely critical review by Vincent Canby of the *New York Times* seems to have been the reason that United Artists, jittery in the wake of the financial disaster accompanying the film *Heaven's Gate* (1980), withdrew *Cutter and Bone* from distribution. The film was passed to United Artists' "Classics" division, which rereleased it as *Cutter's Way* in June 1981. It became a modest commercial success and received generally favorable reviews. See "Ivan Passer," *American Film* 14, 2 (November 1988): 14, and Richard Jameson, "Passer's Way," *Film Comment* (July/August 1981): 18.

152. David James and Rick Berg, "College Course File: Representing the Vietnam War," *Journal of Film and Video* 41, 4 (Winter 1989): 72.

153. One study in this area is Renny Christopher, *The Viet Nam War/The American War: Images and Representations in Euro-American and Vietnamese Exile Narratives* (Amherst: University of Massachusetts Press, 1995).

154. The Hawai'i International Film Festival presented itself as an American venue for the screening of Vietnamese films. The first Vietnamese film to be shown in America, *When the Tenth Month Comes* (1984), was screened at the 1985 festival. Many of the films that premiered in America at the 1988 festival subsequently toured mainland America as "The Vietnam Film Project." See John Charlot, "Vietnam, the Strangers Meet: The Vietnam Film Project," in The East-West Center, *The 8th Hawai'i International Film Festival, 1988* (Honolulu, 1988), 44–49; and Geoffrey Dunn, "Vietnam: The Strangers Meet," a review of the project, in the *San Francisco Review of Books* 14, 1 (Summer 1989): 29–31. The William Joiner Center for the Study of War and Social Consequences of the University of Massachusetts at Boston frequently invites Vietnamese authors and poets to its conferences. The center is actively engaged in translating Vietnamese poetry into English, and poetry by American veterans into Vietnamese. Beyond such ventures, access in the United States to Vietnamese cultural production has continued to prove problematic. See the account of the exhibition "As Seen By Both Sides," which featured both American and (North) Vietnamese art of the Vietnam War, in Robin Cembalest, "Sensitivity or Censorship?" *Artforum* 92 (November 1993): 49.

155. Gayatri Spivak, "Can the Subaltern Speak?" in C. Nelson and L. Grossberg (eds.), *Marxism and the Interpretation of Culture* (Urbana: University of Illinois Press, 1988), 271–313.

156. Mashasweta Devi, *Imaginary Maps*, translated and introduced by G. Spivak (New York: Routledge, 1994).

157. These and other films produced during the war are discussed in Bui Phu, "The Seventh Goddess," *Framework* 25 (1984): 71–93, and Ngo Phong Lan, "Vietnam: Witness to History," *Cinemaya* 28–29 (Summer 1995): 4–7. Certain films produced in South Vietnam by the National Liberation Front are described in "Propaganda Films about the War in Vietnam," *Film Comment* 4, 1 (Fall 1966): 4–13.

158. Ngo Phong Lan, "Vietnam: Witness to History," *Cinemaya* 28–29 (Summer 1995): 5.

159. Phu, "The Seventh Goddess," 71–93.

160. Accounts of Vietnamese film production since the end of the war include John Charlot, "Vietnamese Cinema: The Power of the Past," *Journal of American Folklore* 102 (October-December 1989): 442–452, and "Vietnamese Cinema: First Views," *Journal of Southeast Asian Studies* (March 1991): 33–62; Karen Jaehne, "Cinema in Vietnam: When the Shooting Stopped," *Cineaste* (February 17, 1989): 32–37; Gina Marchetti, "Excess and Understatement: War, Romance, and the Melodrama in Contemporary Vietnamese Cinema," *Genders* 10 (Spring 1991): 47–74; and the special issue of the journal *Cinemaya* edited by Tadao Sato, "Voice of Vietnam," *Cinemaya* 16 (1992): 46–67.

161. Bao Ninh, *The Sorrow of War* (London: Minerva, 1994). First published in Vietnam in 1991.

162. Duong Thu Huong, *Novel Without a Name* (New York: Morrow, 1995). The author was imprisoned without trial for seven months in 1991 on charges of "anti-socialist propaganda and the illegal transfer of documents abroad." The documents were in fact the manuscript of *Novel Without A Name*. The incident is mentioned in Suzanne Charlé, "Good Morning Vietnam," *Harper's Bazaar* (May 1993): 60–61, 182.

163. Dorris Sommer, "Cortez in the Courts: The Traps of Translation from Newsprint to Film," in M. Garber, J. Matlock, and R. Walkowitz (eds.), *Media Spectacles* (New York: Routledge, 1993), 109.

164. Trinh T. Minh-ha, "Why a Fish Pond? Fiction at the Heart of Documentation," an interview conducted by L. Jayamanne and A. Rutherford, *Filmnews* [Sydney](November 1990): 12.

165. Alf Louvre and Jeffrey Walsh (eds.), *Tell Me Lies about Vietnam: Cultural Battles for the Meaning of the War* (Milton Keynes, U.K.: Open University Press, 1988), 5.

166. *Dispatches*, 46.

167. Quoted in John O'Hara, "The Narrative Construction of Reality: An Interview with Stuart Hall," *Southern Review* [Australia] 17, 1 (March 1984): 11.

NOTES TO PART 3

1. John Fiske, "Cultural Studies and the Culture of Everyday Life," in L. Grossberg, C. Nelson, and P. Treichler (eds.), *Cultural Studies* (New York: Routledge, 1992), 164.

2. Tony Crowley, "Language and Hegemony: Principles, Morals and Pronunciation," *Textual Practice* 1, 3 (Winter 1982): 278.

3. See Ernesto Laclau and Chantal Mouffe, *Hegemony and Socialist Strategy: Toward a Radical Democratic Politics* (London: Verso, 1989), 93–148.

4. John Fiske, *Reading the Popular* (Boston: Unwin Hyman, 1989), 8.

5. Chantal Mouffe, "Hegemony and the Integral State in Gramsci: Toward a New Concept of Politics," in G. Bridges and R. Brunt (eds.), *Silver Linings: Some Strategies for the Eighties* (London: Lawrence and Wishart, 1981), 173.

6. The paraphrase is by Leslie Johnson in "The Study of Popular Culture: The Need for a Clear Agenda," *Australian Journal of Cultural Studies* 4, 1 (June 1986): 4.

7. Students for a Democratic Society, "Bringing the War Home," reprinted in J. Alpert and S. Alpert (eds.), *The Sixties Papers: Documents of a Rebellious Decade* (New York: Praeger, 1984), 247, 250.

8. Shin'ya Ono, "You Do Need a Weatherman," originally published in *Leviathan*, December 1969, reprinted in J. Alpert and S. Alpert (eds.), *The Sixties Papers: Documents of a Rebellious Decade* (New York: Praeger, 1984), 257.

9. Morris Dickstein, *Gates of Eden: American Culture in the Sixties* (New York: Penguin, 1989), 261.

10. Walter Capps, *The Unfinished War: Vietnam and the American Conscience*, 2nd ed. (Boston: Beacon Press, 1990), 15.

11. Todd Gitlin, *The Whole World Is Watching: Mass Media in the Making and Unmaking of the New Left* (Berkeley: University of California Press, 1980), chapter 2.

12. Ibid., chapter 5.

13. Ibid., 152–153.

14. Ibid., 203.

15. *The Strawberry Statement* is based in part on James Simon Kunen's memoir *The Strawberry Statement: Notes of a College Age Revolutionary* (New York: Avon 1970). The book narrates Kunen's impressions of the 1968 strike at Columbia University. The issue of the university's appropriation of a section of Morningside Park to build an eleven-story building containing a gymnasium and its decision to restrict community access to the new gymnasium were factors that precipitated the strike.

16. The lines come verbatim from a poster printed by students during the 1969 Harvard University student strike. Those responsible for the film *The Strawberry Statement* obviously looked to various contemporary sources in an attempt to provide the film with "relevance." The poster is reprinted in Alexander

Bloom and Winifred Brienes (eds.), *"Takin' It To The Streets": A Sixties Reader* (New York: Oxford University Press, 1995), 400.

17. Quoted in Seth Cagin and Philip Dray, *Hollywood Films of the Seventies* (New York: Harper and Row, 1984), 125.

18. David James, *To Take the Glamour out of War: American Film Against the War in Vietnam* (New York: Whitney Museum of Modern Art, 1990), iii.

19. Michael Ryan and Douglas Kellner, *Camera Politica: The Politics and Ideology of Contemporary Hollywood Film* (Bloomington: Indiana University Press, 1988), 33.

20. Charles Chatfield, "The Antiwar Movement and America," an appendix to C. DeBenedetti and C. Chatfield, *An American Ordeal: The Antiwar Movement of the Vietnam Era* (Syracuse, N.Y.: Syracuse University Press, 1990), 393–394.

21. Godfrey Hodgson, *America in Our Time* (New York: Vintage, 1978), chapter 14.

22. Joseph Conlin, *The Troubles: A Jaundiced Glance Back at the Movement of the Sixties* (New York: Franklin Watts, 1982).

23. Peter Collier and David Horowitz (eds.), *Destructive Generation: Second Thoughts about the Sixties* (New York: Summit Books, 1990).

24. Carl Rollyson, *The Lives of Norman Mailer: A Biography* (New York: Paragon House, 1991), 203.

25. Guy Debord, *Society of the Spectacle* (Detroit: Black and Red, 1983), paragraph 61.

26. Norman Mailer, *The Armies of the Night: History as a Novel, the Novel as History* (Harmondsworth, Middlesex, U.K.: Penguin, 1968), 292, 45.

27. Philip Roth, "Writing American Fiction," in M. Bradbury (ed.), *The Novel Today: Contemporary Writers on Modern Fiction* (London: Fontana, 1977), 34. Roth's essay originally appeared in the United States in 1975.

28. Mailer, *The Armies of the Night*, 283, 267, 268.

29. Fredric Jameson, *The Political Unconscious: Narrative as a Socially Symbolic Act* (New York: Routledge, 1989).

30. Dana Polan, "'Above All Else to Make You See': Cinema and the Ideology of Spectacle," in J. Arac (ed.), *Postmodernism and Politics* (Manchester, U.K.: Manchester University Press, 1986), 56.

31. Writing of the 1964 Republican National Convention, Mailer stated: "There had been an undeclared full-scale struggle going on in America for twenty years—it was whether the country would go mad or not." "In the Red Light: A History of the Republican Convention in 1964," in *Cannibals and Christians* (New York: Delta, 1966), 6. In *Advertisements for Myself* (New York: Putnam, 1959), 20, he describes his own nature as "divided." In *The Armies of the Night*, 200, Mailer states that "the center of America might be insane. The country had been living with a controlled, even fiercely controlled, schizophrenia. . . . "

32. Mailer frequently uses the term in *The Armies of the Night*; see, for example, 15, 45, 46, 235, 280.

33. Ibid., 32.

34. Ibid., 300. Mailer's metaphor draws on Yeats's "The Second Coming" and bears a striking resemblance to Lyndon Johnson's account of the "growth" of the "Great Society": "I figured her growth and development would be as natural and inevitable as any small child's. . . . In the first year, as we got the laws on the books, she began to crawl. Then in the second year, as we got more laws on the books, she began to walk, and the year after that she would be off and running, all the time bigger and healthier and fatter. And when she grew up, I figured she would be so big and beautiful that the American people couldn't help but fall in love with her." Quoted in William Chafe, *The Unfinished Journey: America Since World War II* (New York: Oxford University Press, 1986), 341. The similarity between Mailer's and Johnson's descriptions is Mailer's way of ironically indicating the death of the Great Society in the birth of a new social formation.

35. John Findlay, *Hegel: A Re-examination* (London: Allen and Unwin, 1958), 36.

36. The representation of the past in college textbooks is discussed in the forum "Textbooks and Teaching" introduced by Sara Evans and Roy Rosenzweig in *Journal of American History* 78, 4 (March 1992): 1377–1379. The contribution of textbooks to ideological hegemony is studied in Jean Anyon, "Ideology and United States History Textbooks," *Harvard Educational Review* 49, 3 (August 1979): 361–386. See also the conclusion to William Griffen and John Marciano, *Teaching the Vietnam War: A Critical Examination of School Texts and an Interpretative History Utilizing the Pentagon Papers and Other Documents* (Montclair, N.J.: Allenheld, Osmun, 1979).

37. Pierre Macherey, *A Theory of Literary Production* (London: Routledge and Kegan Paul, 1978).

38. Frances FitzGerald, *America Revised: History Schoolbooks in the Twentieth Century* (New York: Vintage, 1980), 127.

39. William Chafe has commented, "The literature on the anti-war movement, student protest, the New Left, and the counterculture is voluminous." Chafe, *The Unfinished Journey*, 498. However, if the antiwar movement is removed from this list, the result is a minimal number of texts in which the movement is represented as a broad-based coalition of protest against the war. Chafe's own bibliographic essay suggests this—the only text included that refers to antiwar protest is Gitlin's analysis of New Left protest, *The Whole World Is Watching*. The publication of a number of books during or near 1988 that reflect on the history of the war years (presumably a marketing ploy to exploit the anniversary of twenty years since the "watershed" year of 1968), only partially informed existing analyses of U.S. domestic resistance to the war. The focus in the majority of these texts on the actions of Students for a Democratic Society displaces a wide range of antiwar activity.

40. The list referred to here is contained in Joe Dunn, "Texts and Auxiliary Resources," in M. J. Gilbert (ed.), *The Vietnam War: Teaching Approaches and Resources* (New York: Greenwood Press, 1991), 223–225.

41. Jonathan Goldstein, "Using Literature in a Course on the Vietnam War," *College Teaching* 37, 3 (Summer 1989): 91–95.

42. The course was run by Kali Tal and is outlined in her paper "When History Talks Back: The Voice of the Veteran," in M. J. Gilbert,(ed.) *The Vietnam War: Teaching Approaches and Resources* (New York: Greenwood Press, 1991), 161–169.

43. Capps, *The Unfinished War*, 94. Of the courses that were surveyed for this part, only one includes substantial reference to the antiwar movement, integrally incorporating it into the syllabus—see David James and Rick Berg, "College Course File: Representing the Vietnam War," *Journal of Film and Video* 41, 4 (Winter 1989): 60–74.

44. Hodgson, *America in Our Time*; Kim McQuaid, *The Anxious Years: America in the Vietnam-Watergate Era* (New York: Basic Books, 1989).

45. Ibid., 144.

46. Ibid., 146.

47. See, for example, William O'Neill's *Coming Apart: An Informal History of America in the 1960's* (New York: Times Books, 1971), 303.

48. Ibid., 301.

49. Roland Barthes, "The Photographic Message," in *A Barthes Reader*, ed. S. Sontag (New York: Hill and Wang, 1982), 204.

50. O'Neill, *Coming Apart*. The photographs in O'Neill's text can be contrasted to those used in Morris Dickstein's *Gates of Eden*. The three photographs used in Dickstein's text depict a cross-section of the antiwar movement. The photographs are captioned "Playful and solemn scenes of antiwar protest" and include a demonstrator playing a flute to National Guardsmen at the Democratic National Convention in Chicago in 1968, "guerrilla theater" demonstrators in New York City, and orderly picketers in Washington, D.C.

51. Christopher Buckley, "Viet Guilt," *Esquire* (September 1983): 68–72.

52. Michael Blumenthal, "Of Arms and Men," *New York Times* (January 11, 1981): section 4, 23.

53. Buckley, "Viet Guilt," 70.

54. Gordon Zahn, "Memories in Stone," *America* 149, 11 (October 15, 1983): 213.

55. Buckley, "Viet Guilt," 72. Buckley's reference to "lack" alludes to a form of masculine impotence that is implicated in many assertions of "Viet guilt." Psychologist and Vietnam veteran Arthur Egendorf has written that those who voiced the slogan "Hell no! I won't go" "identified themselves by negativism.... They are resigned to impotence." Quoted in Lynne Hanley, *Writing War: Fiction, Gender, and Memory* (Amherst: University of Massachusetts Press, 1991), 104. Susan Jacoby "wondered whether the millions of men my age who avoided the

draft may feel 'unmanned' in a way that no woman can truly understand." Susan Jacoby, "Women and the War," in A. D. Horne (ed.), *The Wounded Generation: America After Vietnam* (Englewood Cliffs, N.J.: Prentice-Hall, 1981), 199.

56. Myra MacPherson, *Long Time Passing: Vietnam and the Haunted Generation* (New York: Signet, 1984), 106.

57. James Webb, *Fields of Fire* (New York: Bantam, 1979), 406, 410.

58. Harry Haines quotes the reaction expressed by an army combat medic at Cam Ranh Bay after reading a *Newsweek* report of the killings of war protestors at Kent State University, 1970: "Now the sons-of-bitches are killing us back at home." Harry Haines, "Hegemony and the GI Resistance: Introductory Notes," *Vietnam Generation* 2, 1 (1990): 3.

59. John Irving, *A Prayer for Owen Meany* (London: Corgi, 1989).

60. Sonya Sayres, Anders Stephanson, Stanley Aronowitz, and Fredric Jameson (eds.), *The 60s Without Apology* (Minneapolis: University of Minnesota Press, 1984), 8.

61. O'Neill, *Coming Apart*, 426; Lance Morrow, "An Elegy for the New Left," *Time* (August 15, 1977): 43.

62. Richard Hofstadter, "The Age of Rubbish," *Newsweek* (July 6, 1970): 15; Allan Bloom, *The Closing of the American Mind* (New York: Simon and Schuster, 1987), 320.

63. Collier and Horowitz, *Destructive Generation*.

64. Jon Wiener, "The Sixties and Popular Memory," *Radical America* 21, 6 (November-December 1987): 24.

65. Todd Gitlin summarized the dichotomy in the subtitle of his book *The Sixties: Years of Hope, Days of Rage* (New York: Bantam, 1989). Wini Brienes discusses the dichotomy of "good" and "bad" sixties in "Whose New Left?" *Journal of American History* 75, 2 (September 1988): 1071–1082.

66. George Lucas's *American Graffiti* does allude to the existence of the Vietnam War, notably in Toad's fate. At the end of the film Toad (Charles Martin Smith) is registered as missing in action near An Loc. Such references can only be cursory, however, because, as Colin McCabe has argued, the external world cannot be allowed to impinge on the homogeneous and contained society of small-town California without creating unresolvable narrative contradictions. The repression of Vietnam also functions in relation to Curt Henderson (Richard Dreyfuss), who, at the end of the film, is a writer living in Canada. The suggestion that he has gone to Canada to evade the draft remains unspoken. Colin McCabe, "Theory and Film: Principles of Realism and Pleasure," in his *Theoretical Essays: Film, Linguistics, Literature* (Manchester, U.K.: Manchester University Press, 1985), 73–74.

67. Tom Wolfe describes what he sees as the fashionable games of certain wealthy patrons of progressive causes in *Radical Chic,* published as part of *Radical Chic,* and *Mau-Mauing the Flak Catchers* (New York: Bantam, 1971). Richard Nixon, *Beyond Peace* (New York: Random House, 1994).

68. "1968: The Year That Shaped a Generation," *Time* (January 11, 1988).

69. Rauschenberg's *Signs* is reproduced on the cover of Chafe, *The Unfinished Journey*.

70. Charles Kaiser, *1968 in America: Music, Politics, Chaos, Counterculture, and the Shaping of a Generation* (New York: Weidenfeld and Nicolson, 1988).

71. Max Horkheimer and Theodor Adorno from *The Dialectic of Enlightenment*, quoted in Martin Jay, "Anamnestic Totalization: Reflections on Marcuse's Theory of Remembrance," *Theory and Society* 11, 1 (January 1982): 5.

72. Lance Morrow, "A Bloody Rite of Passage," *Time* (April 15, 1985): 22, 23.

73. Michael Herr, *Dispatches* (London: Picador, 1978), 206.

74. Sonya Sayres, Anders Stephanson, Stanley Aronowitz, and Fredric Jameson, introduction to *The 60s Without Apology*, 8.

75. Auster and Quart, and Christensen refer to *The Green Berets* as the only film about the war made during the war years. Albert Auster and Leonard Quart, "Hollywood and Vietnam: The Triumph of the Will," *Cineaste* 9, 3 (Spring 1979): 4; Terry Christensen, *Reel Politics: American Political Movies from Birth of a Nation to Platoon* (New York: Blackwell, 1987), 147.

76. A Auster and Quart, "Hollywood and Vietnam," 4.

77. Michael Ryan and Douglas Kellner, *Camera Politica: The Politics and Ideology of Contemporary Hollywood Film* (Bloomington: Indiana University Press, 1990), 51.

78. John Hoberman, "Vietnam: The Remake," in B. Kruger and P. Mariani (eds.), *Remaking History* (Seattle: Bay Press, 1989), 181.

79. *Sticks and Bones* (1969) is reprinted in David Rabe, *The Vietnam Plays, vol. 1, "The Basic Training of Pavlo Hummel" and "Sticks and Bones"* (New York: Grove Press, 1993), 104.

80. Ibid., 122.

81. Ibid., 122.

82. Ibid., 175.

83. Quoted in Mary Pat Kelly, *Martin Scorsese: A Journey* (London: Secker and Warburg, 1992), 89.

84. Robert Stone, *Dog Soldiers* (London: Wyndham, 1976), 116.

85. In the card that he writes to his parents, Travis adds: "One day there'll be a knock at the door and it'll be me." Given Travis's predilection for unleashing violence on the home front, the line takes on a sinister resonance.

86. For the influence of *The Searchers* on new Hollywood filmmakers, including Scorsese, see Stuart Byron, "*The Searchers*: Cult Movie of the New Hollywood," *New York Magazine* (March 5, 1979): 45–48. David Boyd elaborates the relationship between *The Searchers* and *Taxi Driver* in "Prisoner of the Night," *Film Heritage* 12, 2 (Winter 1976–1977): 24–30.

87. Robin Wood, *Hollywood from Vietnam to Reagan* (New York: Columbia University Press, 1986), 53.

88. Rick Berg and John Carlos Rowe, "The Vietnam War and American Memory," introduction to J. C. Rowe and R. Berg (eds.), *The Vietnam War and American Culture* (New York: Columbia University Press, 1991), 6.

89. Christopher Lasch, *Haven in a Heartless World: The Family Besieged* (New York: Basic Books, 1977).

90. K. Woodward et al., "Saving the Family," *Newsweek* (May 15, 1978): 49–54.

91. Arlene Skolnick, *Embattled Paradise: The American Family in an Age of Uncertainty* (New York: Basic Books, 1991), 104–105.

92. Peter Carroll, *It Seemed Like Nothing Happened: America in the 1970s* (New Brunswick, N.J.: Rutgers University Press, 1990), 279.

93. In *Backlash: The Undeclared War Against Women* (London: Chatto and Windus, 1991), Susan Faludi analyzes adverse reactions to the second wave of feminism. Faludi charts the backlash at various sites, including its manifestation in popular culture (in the representations of print news media, film, television, fashion, and the beauty industry), and its inscription in the writings of neoconservative and "neofeminist" authors. Other studies of the backlash against women and feminism include Marilyn French, *The War Against Women* (New York: Summit, 1992), and Naomi Wolf, *The Beauty Myth: How Images of Beauty Are Used Against Women* (London: Vintage, 1991). Susan Jeffords considers an aspect of the backlash as it operates within representations of the Vietnam War in *The Remasculinization of America: Gender and the Vietnam War* (Bloomington: Indiana University Press, 1989).

94. Susan Jeffords, "Reproducing Fathers: Gender and the Vietnam War in American Culture," in R. Morris and P. Ehrenhaus (eds.), *Cultural Legacies of Vietnam: Uses of the Past in the Present* (Norwood, N.J.: Ablex, 1990), 124–144.

95. Robert Bly, *Iron John: A Book about Men* (Shaftesbury, U.K.: Element, 1990). The characterization of the figure of the mother and descriptions of the features of the "Wild Man" are located throughout the text, see particularly chapter 8.

96. Quoted in Carroll, *It Seemed Like Nothing Happened*, 297.

97. Andrew Ross, "Cowboys, Cadillacs and Cosmonauts: Families, Film Genres, and Technocultures," in J. Boone and M. Cadden (eds.), *Engendering Men: The Question of Male Feminist Criticism* (New York: Routledge, 1990), 9.

98. John Carlos Rowe, "'Bringing It All Back Home': American Recyclings of the Vietnam War," in N. Armstrong and L. Tennenhouse (eds.), *The Violence of Representation: Literature and the History of Violence* (London: Routledge, 1989), 200.

99. Darrell Hamamoto has noted a number of television reports from the eighties that concentrate on the theme of "Amerasian love children." See *Monitored Peril: Asian Americans and the Politics of TV Representation* (Minneapolis: University of Minnesota, 1994), 150–152.

100. Louis Malle's *Alamo Bay* (1985) is one of the few films of the period to represent a Vietnamese community in America. Malle's film deals with life in a fishing town on the Texas Gulf Coast and the prejudice faced by Vietnamese members of the community in their attempts to earn a living from the sea.

101. Bobbie Ann Mason, *In Country* (London: Flamingo, 1986), 27.

102. Reports dealing with "tripwire" veterans include Joanne Davidson and John Lang, "Vietnam's Sad Legacy: Vets Living in the Wild," *U.S. News and World Report* (March 12, 1984): 38–39, and Larry Heinemann, "'Just Don't Fit': Stalking the Elusive 'Tripwire' Veteran," *Harper's* (April 1985): 55–63.

103. Philip Caputo, *Indian Country* (London: Century, 1987).

104. Mason, *In Country*, 189.

105. Arthur Danto, quoted in Lori Askeland, "Remaking the Model Home in *Uncle Tom's Cabin* and *Beloved*," *American Literature* 64, 4 (December 1992): 786.

106. William Broyles, Jr., "Remembering a War We Want to Forget," *Newsweek* (November 22, 1982): 82.

107. Quoted in Paul D. Erickson, *Reagan Speaks: The Making of American Myth* (New York: New York University Press, 1985), 54.

108. Quoted in Irving Sloan (ed.), *Ronald Reagan, 1911– : Chronology–Documents–Bibliographical Aids* (Dobbs Ferry, N.Y.: Oceana, 1980), 140.

109. Catherine Stewart, *On Longing: Narratives of the Miniature, the Gigantic, the Souvenir, the Collection* (Baltimore: Johns Hopkins University Press, 1984), 23.

110. Ibid.

111. Roland Robertson, "After Nostalgia? Wilful Nostalgia and the Phases of Globalization," in B. Turner (ed.), *Theories of Modernity and Postmodernity* (London: Sage, 1990), 45–61.

112. Quoted, ibid., 53.

113. The description of the commercial is based on details given in Sidney Blumenthal, *The Rise of the Counter-Establishment: From Conservative Ideology to Political Power* (New York: Times Books, 1986), 279. The images that were used in the commercial were selected from an eighteen-minute film first broadcast at the 1984 Dallas Republican National Convention. Details of the film are provided in Tim Luke, *Screens of Power: Ideology, Domination, and Resistance in Informational Society* (Urbana: University of Illinois Press, 1989), 147–148.

114. Andrew Britton, "Blissing Out: The Politics of Reaganite Entertainment," *Movie* 31–32 (Winter 1986): 9, 10.

115. Angelika Bammer, editorial ("The Question of 'Home'"), *New Formations* 17 (Summer 1992): vii.

116. The term "not home" is Carlos Baker's; he used it in a discussion of Hemingway's *A Farewell to Arms*. According to Baker, Hemingway constructed a dichotomy between the safe and satisfying world of "home" and the dangerous,

different world of "not home." Carlos Baker, *Hemingway: The Writer as Artist* (Princeton, N.J.: Princeton University Press, 1956), 94–116.

117. John Higgins, "The Big Chill," in M. Davis, F. Pfeil, and M. Sprinker (eds.), *The Year Left: An American Socialist Yearbook* (London: Verso, 1985), 307.

118. Richard Corliss, "You Get What You Need," *Time* (September 12, 1983): 72.

119. See, especially, Britton, "Blissing Out," 24–42, and Robin Wood, "80s Hollywood: Dominant Tendencies," *CineAction!* (Spring 1985): 2–5.

120. Robert Phillip Kolker, *A Cinema of Loneliness: Penn, Kubrick, Scorsese, Spielberg, Altman*, 2nd ed. (New York: Oxford University Press, 1988), chapter 4.

121. Quoted in Michael Clark, "Remembering Vietnam," *Cultural Critique* 3 (Spring 1986): 47.

122. Quoted in Harry Haines, "The Pride Is Back: *Rambo, Magnum, P.I.*, and the Return Trip to Vietnam," in R. Morris and P. Ehrenhaus (eds.), *Cultural Legacies of Vietnam: Uses of the Past in the Present* (Norwood, N.J.: Ablex, 1990), 107.

123. John Bodnar, *Remaking America: Public Memory, Commemoration, and Patriotism in the Twentieth Century* (Princeton, N.J.: Princeton University Press, 1992), 7.

124. Clark, "Remembering Vietnam," 48.

125. Robert McFadden, "Thousands Here Honor Vietnam Veterans," *New York Times* (April 1, 1973): 1, 76.

126. Rowe, "'Bringing It All Back Home,'" 197.

127. Geoffrey Nowell-Smith, "Minnelli and Melodrama," in C. Gledhill (ed.), *Home Is Where the Heart Is: Studies in Melodrama and the Women's Film* (London: BFI Publishing, 1987), 73. Andrew Martin has written of the connections between melodrama and Vietnam War texts in *Receptions of War: Vietnam in American Culture* (Norman: University of Oklahoma Press, 1993). I am indebted to certain of Martin's observations concerning the function of melodrama.

128. John Carlos Rowe, "From Documentary to Docudrama: Vietnam on Television in the 1980's," *Genre* 21, 4 (Winter 1988): 473.

129. Homi Bhabha has used the word "unhomely" to refer to the "shock of recognition of the world-in-the home." The perception of difference that Bhabha identifies by this word is similar to the condition I refer to as "homelessness." Homi Bhabha, "The World and the Home," *Social Text* 31–32 (1992): 141.

130. See Homi Bhabha, "The Other Question . . . ," *Screen* 24, 6 (November-December 1983): 18–36.

131. Stuart Hall, "New Ethnicities," in *Black Film, British Cinema*, ICA Documents 7 (London: Institute of Contemporary Art, 1988), 28.

132. Stuart Clarke, "Fear of a Black Planet," *Socialist Review* 21, 3–4 (1991): 37.

133. Mike Davis, *City of Quartz: Excavating the Future in Los Angeles* (London: Vintage, 1990), 270, 289, 292, 267.

134. The use of helicopters to signify U.S. military endeavor in Vietnam is parodied in Tony Scott's *True Romance* (1993) during a scene in which a director plays rushes of his new film, "Coming Home in a Body Bag"—the images consist entirely of helicopters flying across the screen.

135. Hazel Carby, "Genealogies of Race and Nation: *Grand Canyon*, a Narrative for Our Times," in D. Bennett (ed.), *Cultural Studies: Pluralism and Theory* (Melbourne: University of Melbourne, 1993), 80.

136. Ibid.

137. bell hooks, quoted in Doreen Massey, "A Place Called Home?" *New Formations* 17 (Summer 1992): 15.

NOTES TO CONCLUSION

1. Roland Barthes, "African Grammar," in *The Eiffel Tower: And Other Mythologies* (New York: Hill and Wang, 1979), 105.

2. Claude Lévi-Strauss, *The Raw and the Cooked: Introduction to a Science of Mythology* (New York: Harper and Row, 1969), 9.

3. Ibid.

4. George Lipsitz, "Listening to Learn and Learning to Listen: Popular Culture, Cultural Theory, and American Studies," *American Quarterly* 42, 4 (December 1990): 621.

5. Stuart Hall, "The Toad in the Garden: Thatcherism Among the Theorists," in C. Nelson and L. Grossberg (eds.), *Marxism and the Interpretation of Culture* (London: Macmillan, 1988), 69–70.

6. Fredric Jameson, *The Political Unconscious: Narrative as a Socially Symbolic Act* (Ithaca, N.Y.: Cornell University Press, 1981), 102.

7. Elaine Scarry, *The Body in Pain: The Making and Unmaking of the World* (New York: Oxford University Press, 1995), 114.

8. Vivian Sobchack, "History Happens," introduction to V. Sobchack (ed.), *The Persistence of History: Cinema, Television, and the Modern Event* (New York: Routledge, 1996), 2.

9. H. Bruce Franklin has provided a masterful interpretation of the role of MIA's in U.S. relations with Vietnam in *M.I.A., or Mythmaking in America* (New Brunswick, N.J.: Rutgers University Press, 1993).

10. Michael Herr, *Dispatches* (London: Picador, 1978), 11.

Bibliography

Adorno, Theodor. "What Does Coming to Terms with the Past Mean?" in G. Hartman (ed.), *Bitburg in Moral and Political Perspective*. Bloomington: Indiana University Press, 1986.

American Psychiatric Association Staff. *Diagnostic and Statistical Manual of Mental Disorders*, 3rd ed. Washington, D.C.: American Psychiatric Association, 1980.

Anyon, Jean. "Ideology and United States History Textbooks," *Harvard Educational Review* 49, 3 (August 1979): 361–386.

Appy, Christian. "Vietnam According to Oliver Stone: John Wayne Rides Again," *Commonweal* (March 23, 1990): 187–188.

Appy, Christian. *Working-Class War: American Combat Soldiers and Vietnam*. Chapel Hill: University of North Carolina Press, 1993.

Aronowitz, Stanley. *The Politics of Identity: Class, Culture, Social Movements*. New York: Routledge, 1992.

Ashley, Bob. *The Study of Popular Fiction: A Source Book*. London: Pinter, 1989.

Askeland, Lori. "Remaking the Model Home in *Uncle Tom's Cabin* and *Beloved*," *American Literature* 64, 4 (December 1992): 785–803.

Atkinson, Rick. *The Long Gray Line*. New York: Pocket Books, 1991.

Auster, Albert, and Leonard Quart. "Hollywood and Vietnam: The Triumph of the Will," *Cineaste* 9, 3 (Spring 1979): 4–9.

Auster, Albert, and Leonard Quart. *How the War Was Remembered: Hollywood and Vietnam*. New York: Praeger, 1988.

Baker, Carlos. *Hemingway: The Writer as Artist*. Princeton, N.J.: Princeton University Press, 1956.

Baker, Mark. *Nam: The Vietnam War in the Words of the Men and Women Who Fought There*. London: Abacus, 1982.

Balaban, John. *Remembering Heaven's Face: A Moral Witness in Vietnam*. New York: Poseidon Press, 1991.

Balaban, John. *Vietnam: The Land We Never Know*. San Francisco: Chronicle Books, 1989.

Bammer, Angelika. Editorial ("The Question of 'Home'"), *New Formations* 17 (Summer 1992): vii-xi.

Bao Ninh. *The Sorrow of War*. London: Minerva, 1994.

Baritz, Loren. *Backfire: A History of How American Culture Led Us Into Vietnam and Made Us Fight the Way We Did*. New York: Ballantine, 1985.

Barthes, Roland. "African Grammar," in *The Eiffel Tower: And Other Mythologies*. New York: Hill and Wang, 1979.

Barthes, Roland. *Mythologies*. New York: Hill and Wang, 1972.

Barthes, Roland. "Pax Culturalis," in *The Rustle of Language*. New York: Hill and Wang, 1986.

Barthes, Roland. "The Photographic Message," in *A Barthes Reader*, ed. S. Sontag. New York: Hill and Wang, 1982.

Barthes, Roland. "Writers, Intellectuals, Teachers," in *Image-Music–Text*. New York: Farrar, Straus and Giroux, 1977.

Bates, Milton. *The Wars We Took to Vietnam: Cultural Conflict and Storytelling*. Berkeley: University of California Press, 1996.

Bausch, Robert. *On the Way Home*. New York: Avon, 1983.

Baxter, John. *Hollywood in the Sixties*. New York: Tantivity Press, 1972.

BDM Corporation. *Strategic Lessons Learned in Vietnam*. Washington, D.C.: BDM Corporation, 1981.

Beesley, Stanley. *Vietnam: The Heartland Remembers*. New York: Berkley Books, 1989.

Beidler, Philip. *American Literature and the Vietnam Experience*. Athens: University of Georgia Press, 1982.

Bellah, Robert, et al. *Habits of the Heart: Individualism and Commitment in American Life*. New York: Harper and Row, 1985.

Belsey, Catherine. *Critical Practice*. London: Methuen, 1983.

Benjamin, Walter. "Theories of German Fascism: On the Collection of Essays *War and Warrior*, edited by Ernst Junger," *New German Critique* 17 (Spring 1979): 120–128.

Benjamin, Walter. "Theses on the Philosophy of History," in *Illuminations*. New York: Schocken Books, 1969.

Berg, Rick. "Losing Vietnam: Covering the War in an Age of Technology," *Cultural Critique*, 3 (Spring 1986): 92–125.

Bhabha, Homi. "The Other Question . . . ," *Screen* 24, 6 (November-December 1983): 18–36.

Bhabha, Homi. "The World and the Home," *Social Text* 31–32 (1992): 141–153.

Bloom, Alexander, and Winifred Brienes (eds.). *"Takin' It To The Streets": A Sixties Reader*. New York: Oxford University Press, 1995.

Bloom, Alice. Reprint of review of *In Country*, in D. Marowski and R. Matuz (eds.), *Contemporary Literary Criticism*, vol. 43. Detroit: Gale, 1987.

Bloom, Allan. *The Closing of the American Mind*. New York: Simon and Schuster, 1987.

Blumenthal, Michael. "Of Arms and Men," *New York Times* (January 11, 1981): section 4, 23.

Blumenthal, Sidney. *The Rise of the Counter Establishment: From Conservative Ideology to Political Power*. New York: Times Books, 1986.

Bly, Robert. *Iron John: A Book about Men*. Shaftesbury, U.K.: Element, 1990.

Bly, Robert. "The Vietnam War and the Erosion of Male Confidence," in Walter Capps (ed.), *The Vietnam Reader*. New York: Routledge, 1991.

Bodnar, John. *Remaking America: Public Memory, Commemoration, and Patriotism in the Twentieth Century*. Princeton, N.J.: Princeton University Press, 1992.

Bourdieu, Pierre. *Language and Symbolic Power*. Cambridge, Mass.: Harvard University Press, 1991.

Bowen, Kevin. "Seeking Reconciliation in Vietnam," *Christian Science Monitor* (November 10, 1988): 34–35.

Bowen, Kevin. "'Strange Hells': Hollywood in Search of America's Lost War," in L. Dittmar and G. Michaud (eds.), *From Hanoi to Hollywood: The Vietnam War in American Film*. New Brunswick, N.J.: Rutgers University Press, 1990.

Boyd, David. "Prisoner of the Night," *Film Heritage* 12, 2 (Winter 1976–1977): 24–30.

Brende, Joel, and Erwin Parson. *Vietnam Veterans: The Road to Recovery*. New York: New American Library, 1986.

Brennan, Matthew. *Headhunters: Stories from the 1st Squadron, 9th Cavalry in Vietnam, 1965–1971*. Novato, Calif.: Presidio Press, 1987.

Brienes, Wini. "Whose New Left?" *Journal of American History* 75, 2 (September 1988): 1071–1082.

Britton, Andrew. "Blissing Out: The Politics of Reaganite Entertainment," *Movie* 31–32 (Winter 1986): 1–42.

Broyles, Jr., William. *Brothers in Arms: A Journey from War to Peace*. New York: Knopf, 1986.

Broyles, Jr., William. "Remembering a War We Want to Forget: A Veteran Reflects on Healing the Wounds of War," *Newsweek*, (November 22, 1982): 82–83.

Broyles, Jr., William. "The Wall That Heals," *Reader's Digest*, 130 (May 1987): 70–76.

Broyles, Jr., William. "Why Men Love War," *Esquire* (November 1984): 55–65.

Bryan, C. D. B. "Barely Suppressed Screams," *Harper's* (June 1984): 67–72.

Bryan, C. D. B. *Friendly Fire*. New York: Putnam, 1976.

Buckley, Christopher. "Viet Guilt," *Esquire* (September 1983): 68–72.

Bui Phu. "The Seventh Goddess," *Framework* 25 (1984): 71–93.

Burns, J. (ed.). *To Heal and to Build: The Programs of President Lyndon B. Johnson*. New York: McGraw-Hill, 1968.

Bush, George. "Inaugural Address: A New Breeze is Blowing" (January 20 1989), *Vital Speeches of the Day* 40, 9 (February 15, 1989).

Butler, Deborah. *American Women Writers on Vietnam: Unheard Voices: A Selected Annotated Bibliography*. New York: Garland, 1990.

Butterfield, Fox. "The New Vietnam Scholarship," *New York Times Magazine* (February 13, 1983): 26, 28–35, 45–46, 50–57, 60–61.

Byron, Stuart. "*The Searchers*: Cult Movie of the New Hollywood," *New York Magazine* (March 5, 1979): 45–48.

Cagin, Seth, and Philip Dray. *Hollywood Films of the Seventies*. New York: Harper and Row, 1984.

Camacho, Paul. "The Future of Patriotism: The War Film, the Cinema Industry, and the Vietnam Veteran Movement," *New England Journal of History* 47, 1 (1990): 32–42.

Cameron, Ian, and Douglas Pye (eds.). *The Movie Book of the Western*. London: Studio Vista, 1996.

Capps, Walter. *The Unfinished War: Vietnam and the American Conscience*, 2nd ed. Boston: Beacon Press, 1990.

Caputo, Philip. *Indian Country*. London: Century, 1987.

Caputo, Philip. *A Rumor of War*. London: Arrow Books, 1978.

Carby, Hazel. "Genealogies of Race and Nation: *Grand Canyon*, a Narrative for Our Times," in D. Bennett (ed.), *Cultural Studies: Pluralism and Theory*. Melbourne: University of Melbourne, 1993.

Carroll, Peter. *It Seemed Like Nothing Happened: America in the 1970s*. New Brunswick, N.J.: Rutgers University Press, 1990.

Carroll, Tod, and P. J. O'Rourke. "Born Again on the Fourth of July: Vietnam Combat Veterans Simulator Kit," *National Lampoon* (July 1978): 65–70, 96.

Carter, Jimmy. "Report on Progress of Veterans of the Vietnam Era," *Congressional Record*, 95th Cong., 2nd sess., October 10, 1978.

Cembalest, Robin. "Sensitivity or Censorship?" *Artnews* 92 (November 1993): 49.

Chafe, William. *The Unfinished Journey: America Since World War II*. New York: Oxford University Press, 1986.

Charlé, Suzanne. "Good Morning Vietnam," *Harper's Bazaar* (May 1993): 60–61, 82.

Charlot, John. "Vietnam, the Strangers Meet: The Vietnam Film Project," in The East-West Center, *The 8th Hawai'i International Film Festival, 1988*. Honolulu: The Center, 1988.

Charlot, John. "Vietnam Cinema: First Views," *Journal of Southeast Asian Studies* (March 1991): 33–62.

Charlot, John. "Vietnam Cinema: The Power of the Past," *Journal of American Folklore* 102 (October-December 1989): 442–452.

Charyn, Jerome. *War Cries over Avenue C*. New York: Penguin, 1986.

Chomsky, Noam. "The Remaking of History," in *Toward a New Cold War: Essays on the Current Crisis and How We Got There*. New York: Pantheon Books, 1982.

Chomsky, Noam. "The United States and Indochina: Far from an Aberration," *Bulletin of Concerned Asian Scholars* 21, 2–4 (1989): 76–92.

Christensen, Terry. *Reel Politics: American Political Movies from Birth of a Nation to Platoon*. New York: Blackwell, 1987.

Christopher, Renny. *The Viet Nam War/The American War: Images and Representations in Euro-American and Vietnamese Exile Narratives*. Amherst: University of Massachusetts Press, 1995.

Cixous, Hélène. "Castration or Decapitation?" *Signs* 7, 1 (Autumn 1981): 41–55.

Clark, Michael. "Remembering Vietnam," *Cultural Critique* 3 (Spring 1986): 46–78.

Clarke, Stuart. "Fear of a Black Planet," *Socialist Review* 21, 3–4 (1991): 37–59.

Clines, Francis. "Tribute to Vietnam: Words, a Wall," *New York Times* (November 11, 1982): B15.

Clinton, William J. "Remarks at Memorial Day Ceremony at the Vietnam Veterans Memorial, May 31, 1993," *Public Papers of the Presidents of the United States: William J. Clinton, 1993*. Washington, D.C.: Government Printing Office, 1994.

Cockburn, Alexander. *Corruptions of Empire: Life Studies and the Reagan Era*. London: Verso, 1987.

Cohen, Stanley. *Folk Devils and Moral Panics: The Creation of Mods and Rockers*. London: MacGibbon and Kee, 1972.

Coleman, Charles. *Sergeant Back Again*. New York: Harper and Row, 1980.

Collier, Peter, and David Horowitz (eds.). *Destructive Generation: Second Thoughts about the Sixties*. New York: Summit Books, 1990.

Comaroff, Jean. "Medicine and Culture: Some Anthropological Perspectives," *Social Science and Medicine* 12B (1978): 247–254.

Conlin, Joseph. *The Troubles: A Jaundiced Glance Back at the Movement of the Sixties*. New York: Franklin Watts, 1982.

Cooper, David. *Metaphor*. Oxford: Basil Blackwell, 1986.

Corliss, Richard. "You Get What You Need," *Time* (September 12, 1983): 72.

Crimp, Douglas. "Mourning and Militancy," *October* 51 (Winter 1989): 3–18.

Crowley, Tony. "Language and Hegemony: Principles, Morals and Pronunciation," *Textual Practice* 1, 3 (Winter 1982): 277–294.

Davidson, Joanne, and John Lang. "Vietnam's Sad Legacy: Vets Living in the Wild," *U.S. News and World Report* (March 12, 1984): 38–39.

Davis, George. *Coming Home*. New York: Random House, 1971.

Davis, Mike. *City of Quartz: Excavating the Future in Los Angeles*. London: Vintage, 1990.

DeBenedetti, Charles, and C. Chatfield. *An American Ordeal: The Antiwar Movement of the Vietnam Era*. Syracuse, N.Y.: Syracuse University Press, 1990.

Debord, Guy. *Society of the Spectacle*. Detroit: Black and Red, 1983.

Deutsch, James. "Piercing the Penelope Syndrome: The Depiction of World War II Veterans' Wives in 1940s Hollywood Films," *Humboldt Journal of Social Relations,* 16, 1 (1990): 31–42.

Devi, Mashasweta. *Imaginary Maps,* translated and introduced by G. Spivak. New York: Routledge, 1994.

DiFusco, John, et al. *Tracers.* New York: Hill and Wang, 1986.

Dickstein, Morris. *Gates of Eden: American Culture in the Sixties.* New York: Penguin, 1989.

Doherty, Thomas. "Rambo: First Blood Part II," *Film Quarterly,* 39, 3 (Spring 1986): 50–54.

Donahue, Suzanne. *American Film Distribution: The Changing Marketplace.* Ann Arbor, Mich.: UMI, 1987.

Douglas, Mary. "The Healing Rite," in *Implicit Meanings: Essays in Anthropology.* London: Routledge and Kegan Paul, 1975.

Douglas, Mary. *Natural Symbols: Explorations in Cosmology.* Harmondsworth, Middlesex, U.K.: Penguin, 1973.

Douglas, Mary. *Purity and Danger: An Analysis of Concepts of Pollution and Taboo.* Harmondsworth, Middlesex, U.K.: Penguin, 1970.

Downs, Frederick. *The Killing Zone: My Life in Vietnam.* New York: Berkley Books, 1983.

Downs, Frederick. *No Longer Enemies, Not Yet Friends.* New York: Norton, 1991.

Dunn, Geoffrey. "Vietnam: The Strangers Meet," *San Francisco Review of Books* 14, 1 (Summer 1989): 29–31.

Dunn, Joe. "Texts and Auxiliary Resources," in M. J. Gilbert (ed.), *The Vietnam War: Teaching Approaches and Resources.* New York: Greenwood Press, 1991.

Duong Thu Huong. *Novel Without a Name.* New York: Morrow, 1995.

Durden, Charles. *No Bugles, No Drums.* New York: Charter, 1978.

Ehrenhaus, Peter. "Commemorating the Unwon War: On *Not* Remembering Vietnam," *Journal of Communication* 39, 1 (Winter 1989): 96–107.

Ehrhart, William D. (ed.). *Carrying the Darkness: The Poetry of the Vietnam War.* Lubbock: Texas Tech University Press, 1989.

Ehrhart, William D. "A Common Language," *Virginia Quarterly Review* 67, 3 (Summer 1991): 377–396.

Ehrhart, William D. *Going Back: An Ex-Marine Returns to Vietnam.* Jefferson, N.C.: McFarland, 1987.

Ehrhart, William D. "The Invasion of Grenada," *Cultural Critique* 3 (Spring 1980): 91.

Ehrhart, William D. (ed.). *Unaccustomed Mercy: Soldier-Poets of the Vietnam War.* Lubbock: Texas Tech University Press, 1988.

Ellis, John. *Visible Fictions: Cinema, Television, Radio.* London: Routledge, 1982.

Engelmann, Larry. *Tears Before the Rain: An Oral History of the Fall of South Vietnam*. New York: Oxford University Press, 1990.

Erdrich, Louise. *Love Medicine*. New York: Holt, Rinehart and Winston, 1984.

Erickson, Paul D. *Reagan Speaks: The Making of American Myth*. New York: New York University Press, 1985.

Evans, Sara, and Roy Rosenzweig. "Textbooks and Teaching," *Journal of American History* 78, 4 (March 1992): 1377–1379.

"Excerpts from Ford Address at Tulane," *New York Times* (April 24, 1975): 19.

Fallows, James. "No Hard Feelings," *Atlantic Monthly* 262, 6 (December 1988): 71–78.

Faludi, Susan. *Backlash: The Undeclared War Against Women*. London: Chatto and Windus, 1991.

Farmanfarmaian, Abouali. "Sexuality in the Gulf War: Did You Measure Up?" *Genders* 13 (Spring 1992): 1–29.

Featherstone, Mike. "The Body in Consumer Culture," *Theory, Culture and Society* 1, 1 (Spring 1982): 18–33.

Findlay, John. *Hegel: A Re-examination*. London: Allen and Unwin, 1958.

Fiske, John. "Cultural Studies and the Culture of Everyday Life," in L. Grossberg, C. Nelson, and P. Treichler (eds.), *Cultural Studies*. New York: Routledge, 1992.

Fiske, John. *Reading the Popular*. Boston: Unwin Hyman, 1989.

Fiske, John. *Understanding Popular Culture*. Boston: Unwin Hyman, 1989.

FitzGerald, Frances. *America Revised: History Schoolbooks in the Twentieth Century*. New York: Vintage, 1980.

FitzGerald, Frances. *Fire in the Lake: The Vietnamese and the Americans in Vietnam*. New York: Vintage, 1972.

Ford, Gerald. *A Time to Heal*. New York: Harper and Row, 1979.

Foster, Gaines M. "Coming to Terms with Defeat: Post–Vietnam America and the Post–Civil War South," *Virginia Quarterly Review* 66, 1 (Winter 1990): 17–35.

Foucault, Michel. *The Archaeology of Knowledge*. New York: Pantheon Books, 1972.

Foucault, Michel. *The Birth of the Clinic*. London: Tavistock, 1973.

Foucault, Michel. *Discipline and Punish: The Birth of the Prison*. London: Tavistock, 1977.

Foucault, Michel. *The History of Sexuality*, vol. 1. London: Tavistock, 1977.

Foucault, Michel. "Interview," *Edinburgh '77 Magazine* (1977): 22–28.

Frank, Lawrence. *Society as the Patient: Essays on Culture and Personality*. Port Washington, N.Y.: Kennikat Press, 1948.

Franklin, Ben. "President Accepts Vietnam Memorial: Crowd of Veterans and Others Hear Call for Healing," *New York Times* (November 12, 1984): 10.

Franklin, H. Bruce. "From Realism to Virtual Reality: Images of America's Wars," in S. Jeffords and L. Rabinovitz (eds.), *Seeing Through the Media: The Persian Gulf War*. New Brunswick, N.J.: Rutgers University Press, 1994.

Franklin, H. Bruce. *M.I.A, or Mythmaking in America*. New Brunswick, N.J.: Rutgers University Press, 1993.

Freeman, Dan, and Jacqueline Rhoads. *Nurses in Vietnam: The Forgotten Veterans*. Austin: Texas Monthly Press, 1989.

French, Marilyn. *The War Against Women*. New York: Summit, 1992.

Fussell, Paul. *Wartime: Understanding and Behavior in the Second World War*. New York: Oxford University Press, 1989.

Garfield, S. "Problems in Diagnostic Classification," in T. Millon and G. Klerman (eds.), *Contemporary Directions in Psychopathology, Toward the DSM-IV*. New York: Guilford Press, 1986.

Gaspar, Charles. "Searching for Closure: Vietnam War Literature and the Veterans Memorial," *War, Literature and the Arts* 1, 1 (Spring 1989): 19–33.

Gelb, Leslie, and Richard K. Betts. *The Irony of Vietnam: The System Worked*. Washington, D.C.: Brookings Institute, 1978.

Gilbert, Scott. "The Metaphorical Structuring of Social Perceptions," *Soundings* 62, 2 (Summer 1979): 166–185.

Gilman, Jr., Owen, and Lorrie Smith. *America Rediscovered: Critical Essays on Literature and Film of the Vietnam War*. New York: Garland, 1990.

Gitlin, Todd. *The Sixties: Years of Hope, Days of Rage*. New York: Bantam, 1989.

Gitlin, Todd. *The Whole World Is Watching: Mass Media in the Making and Unmaking of the New Left*. Berkeley: University of California Press, 1980.

Goff, Stanley, Robert Sanders, and Clark Smith. *Brothers: Black Soldiers in the Nam*. Novato, Calif.: Presidio Press/Arms and Armour Press, 1982.

Goldman, Peter, and Tony Fuller. *Charlie Company: What Vietnam Did to Us*. New York: Ballantine, 1983.

Goldstein, Jonathan. "Using Literature in a Course on the Vietnam War," *College Teaching* 37, 3 (Summer 1989): 91–95.

Goodgame, Dan. "How the War Was Won," *Time* (January 26, 1987): 56.

Graetz, Rick. *Vietnam: Opening Doors to the World*. Helena, Mont.: American Geographic Publishing, 1988.

Gramsci, Antonio. *Selections from the Prison Notebooks*. London: Lawrence and Wishart, 1971.

Greene, Bob. *Homecoming: When the Soldiers Returned from Vietnam*. New York: Ballantine, 1989.

Greene, Graham. *The Quiet American*. London: Reprint Society, 1955.

Grey, Anthony. *Saigon*. Boston: Little, Brown, 1982.

Griffen, William, and John Marciano. *Teaching the Vietnam War: A Critical Examination of School Texts and an Interpretative History Utilizing the Pentagon Papers and Other Documents*. Montclair, N.J.: Allenheld, Osmun, 1979.

Griswold, Charles. "The Vietnam Veterans Memorial and the Washington Mall: Philosophical Thoughts on Political Iconography," *Critical Inquiry* 12, 4 (Summer 1986): 688–719.

Grossberg, Lawrence. "It's a Sin: Politics, Post-modernity and the Popular," in L. Grossberg, T. Fry, A. Curthoys, and P. Patton, *It's a Sin: Essays on Postmodernism, Politics and Culture.* Sydney: Power Publications, 1988.

Grumwald, Lisa. "Facing the Wall," *Life* (November 1992): 24–36.

Gruner, Elliott. *Prisoners of Culture: Representing the Vietnam POW.* New Brunswick, N.J.: Rutgers University Press, 1993.

Haines, Harry. "Disputing the Wreckage: Ideological Struggle at the Vietnam Veterans Memorial," *Vietnam Generation* 1, 1 (Winter 1989): 141–156.

Haines, Harry. "Hegemony and the GI Resistance: Introductory Notes," *Vietnam Generation* 2, 1 (1990): 3–7.

Haines, Harry. "The Pride Is Back: *Rambo, Magnum, P.I.*, and the Return Trip to Vietnam," in R. Morris and P. Ehrenhaus (eds.), *Cultural Legacies of Vietnam: Uses of the Past in the Present.* Norwood, N.J.: Ablex, 1990.

Haines, Harry. "'They Were Called and They Went': The Political Rehabilitation of the Vietnam Veteran," in L. Dittmar and G. Michaud (eds.), *From Hanoi to Hollywood: The Vietnam War in American Film.* New Brunswick, N.J.: Rutgers University Press, 1990.

Haines, Harry. "'What Kind of War?': An Analysis of the Vietnam Veterans Memorial," *Critical Studies in Mass Communication* 3, 1 (March 1986): 1–20.

Halberstam, David. "The Vietnamization of America," in J. Livingstone and R. Thompson (eds.), *The Dissent of the Governed: Readings on the Democratic Process.* New York: Macmillan, 1972.

Hall, Stuart. "Culture, Media and the 'Ideological Effect,'" in J. Curran, M. Gurevitch, and J. Woollacott (eds.), *Mass Communication and Society.* London: Edward Arnold, 1977.

Hall, Stuart. "Gramsci and Us," in *The Hard Road to Renewal.* London: Verso, 1988.

Hall, Stuart. "New Ethnicities," in *Black Film, British Cinema*, ICA Documents 7. London: Institute of Contemporary Art, 1988.

Hall, Stuart. "On Postmodernism and Articulation: An Interview with Stuart Hall," *Journal of Communication Inquiry* 10, 2 (Summer 1986): 45–60.

Hall, Stuart "The Problem of Ideology—Marxism Without Guarantees," *Journal of Communication Inquiry* 10, 2 (1986): 28–44.

Hall, Stuart. "The Toad in the Garden: Thatcherism Among the Theorists," in C. Nelson and L. Grossberg (eds.), *Marxism and the Interpretation of Culture.* London: Macmillan, 1988.

Hall, Stuart, Bob Lumley, and Gregor McLennan. "Politics and Ideology: Gramsci," in Centre for Contemporary Cultural Studies, *On Ideology.* London: Hutchinson, 1978.

Hamamoto, Darrell. *Monitored Peril: Asian Americans and the Politics of TV Representation*. Minneapolis: University of Minnesota, 1994.

Hammer, Richard. *One Morning in the War: The Tragedy at Son My*. New York: Coward, McCann and Geoghegan, 1970.

Hanley, Lynne. *Writing War: Fiction, Gender, and Memory*. Amherst: University of Massachusetts Press, 1991.

Hartz, Louis. *The Liberal Tradition: An Interpretation of American Political Thought Since the Revolution*. New York: Harcourt, Brace, 1955.

Hayslip, Le Ly, with Jay Wurts. *When Heaven and Earth Changed Places: A Vietnamese Woman's Journey from War to Peace*. New York: Plume, 1990.

Hebdige, Dick. *Subculture: The Meaning of Style*. London: Methuen, 1979.

Heinemann, Larry. "'Just Don't Fit': Stalking the Elusive 'Tripwire' Veteran," *Harper's* (April 1985): 55–63.

Heinemann, Larry. *Paco's Story*. New York: Penguin, 1987.

Heinemann, Larry. "Syndromes," *Harper's* (July 1991): 68–76.

Hellmann, John. *American Myth and the Legacy of Vietnam*. New York: Columbia University Press, 1986.

Hellmann, John. *Fables of Fact: The New Journalism as New Fiction*. Urbana: University of Illinois Press, 1981.

Helmer, John. *Bringing the War Home: The American Soldier in Vietnam and After*. New York: Free Press, 1974.

Hemingway, Ernest. *A Farewell to Arms*. London: Jonathan Cape, 1958.

Herr, Michael. *Dispatches*. London: Picador, 1978.

Herring, George. "Vietnam Remembered," *Journal of American History* 73, 1 (June 1986): 152–164.

Hersh, Seymour. *My Lai 4: A Report of the Massacre and Its Aftermath*. New York: Random House, 1970.

Herzog, Tobey. *Vietnam War Stories: Innocence Lost*. New York: Routledge, 1992.

Hess, Elizabeth. "An Interview with Maya Lin/Frederick Hart," in R. Williams (ed.), *Unwinding from the War: From War into Peace*. Seattle: Real Comet Press, 1987.

Hess, Martha. *Then the Americans Came: Voices from Vietnam*. New York: Four Walls/Eight Windows, 1993.

Higgins, John. "The Big Chill," in M. Davis, F. Pfeil, and M. Sprinker (eds.), *The Year Left: An American Socialist Yearbook*. London: Verso, 1985.

Hirsch, Jr., E. D. *Cultural Literacy: What Every American Needs to Know*. New York: Bantam/Schwartz. 1989.

Hoberman, John. "Vietnam: The Remake," in B. Kruger and P. Mariani (eds.), *Remaking History*. Seattle: Bay Press, 1989.

Hodgson, Godfrey. *America in Our Time*. New York: Vintage, 1978.

Hofstadter, Richard. "The Age of Rubbish," *Newsweek* (July 6, 1970): 12–15.

Hoggart, Richard. *The Uses of Literacy: Aspects of Working-Class Life with Special Reference to Publications and Entertainments.* Harmondsworth, Middlesex, U.K.: Penguin, 1977.

Holmes, Richard. *Acts of Battle: The Behavior of Men in Battle.* New York: Free Press, 1985.

hooks, bell. "Talking Back," in R. Ferguson, M. Gever, Trinh T. Minh-ha, and C. West (eds.), *Out There: Marginalization and Contemporary Culture.* New York: New Museum of Art, 1990.

hooks, bell. *Yearning: Race, Gender, and Cultural Politics.* Boston: South End Press, 1990.

Horne, A. D. (ed.). *The Wounded Generation: America After Vietnam.* Englewood Cliffs, N.J.: Prentice-Hall, 1981.

"How Should Americans Feel?" *Time* (April 14, 1975): 27.

Institute of Medicine (U.S.), Committee to Review the Health Effects in Vietnam Veterans of Exposure to Herbicides. *Veterans and Agent Orange: Health Effects of Herbicides used in Vietnam.* Washington, D.C.: National Academy Press, 1994.

Irving, John. *A Prayer for Owen Meany.* London: Corgi, 1989.

"Ivan Passer." *American Film* 14, 2 (November 1988): 14–17.

Jacoby, Russell. *Social Amnesia: A Critique of Conformist Psychology from Adler to Laing.* Boston: Beacon Press, 1975.

Jacoby, Susan. "Women and the War," in A. D. Horne (ed.), *The Wounded Generation: America After Vietnam.* Englewood Cliffs, N.J.: Prentice-Hall, 1981.

Jaehne, Karen. "Cinema in Vietnam: When the Shooting Stopped," *Cineaste* 17, 2 (1989): 32–37.

Jaehne, Karen. "Company Man," *Film Comment* 25, 2 (March-April 1985): 11–15.

James, David. "Presence of Discourse/Discourse of Presence: Representing Vietnam," *Wide Angle* 7, 4 (1985): 41–52.

James, David. *To Take the Glamour out of War: American Film Against the War in Vietnam.* New York: Whitney Museum of Modern Art, 1990.

James, David, and Rick Berg. "College Course File: Representing the Vietnam War," *Journal of Film and Video* 41, 4 (Winter 1989): 60–74.

Jameson, Fredric. *The Geopolitical Aesthetic: Cinema and Space in the World System.* Bloomington: Indiana University Press, and London: BFI Publishing, 1992.

Jameson, Fredric. *The Political Unconscious: Narrative as a Socially Symbolic Act.* New York: Routledge, 1989.

Jameson, Fredric. "Third-World Literature in the Era of Multinational Capitalism," *Social Text* 15 (Fall 1986): 65–88.

Jameson, Richard. "Passer's Way," *Film Comment* (July/August 1981): 18–23.

Jay, Martin. "Anamnestic Totalization: Reflections on Marcuse's Theory of Remembrance," *Theory and Society* 11, 1 (January 1982): 1–15.

Jeffords, Susan. "Point Blank: Shooting Vietnamese Women," *Vietnam Generation* 1, 3–4 (Summer-Fall 1989): 152–167.

Jeffords, Susan. "Rape and the New World Order," *Cultural Critique* 19 (Fall 1991): 203–216.

Jeffords, Susan. *The Remasculinization of America: Gender and the Vietnam War*. Bloomington: Indiana University Press, 1989.

Jeffords, Susan. "Reproducing Fathers: Gender and the Vietnam War in American Culture," in R. Morris and P. Ehrenhaus (eds.), *Cultural Legacies of Vietnam: Uses of the Past in the Present*. Norwood, N.J.: Ablex, 1990.

Jeffords, Susan. "Women, Gender, and the War," *Critical Studies in Mass Communication* 6, 1 (1989): 83–90.

Johnson, Leslie. "The Study of Popular Culture: The Need for a Clear Agenda," *Australian Journal of Cultural Studies* 4, 1 (June 1986): 2–14.

Kaiser, Charles. *1968 in America: Music, Politics, Chaos, Counterculture, and the Shaping of a Generation*. New York: Weidenfeld and Nicolson, 1988.

Karlin, Wayne, Basil Parquet, and Larry Lee Rottmann (eds.). *Free Fire Zone: Short Stories by Vietnam Veterans*. Brooklyn: 1st Casualty Press, 1973.

Karnow, Stanley. *Vietnam: A History*. New York: Viking Press, 1983.

Kattenburg, Paul. "Reflections on Vietnam: Of Revisionism and Lessons Yet to Be Learned," *Parameters* 14 (Autumn 1984): 42–50.

Kauffmann, Stanley. "Fact-Facing," *New Republic* (April 24, 1989): 24.

Kauffmann, Stanley. "Now About Rambo . . . ," *New Republic* (July 1, 1985): 16.

Kelly, Mary Pat. *Martin Scorsese: A Journey*. London: Secker and Warburg, 1992.

Kendrick, Alexander. *The Wound Within: America in the Vietnam Years, 1945–1974*. Boston: Little, Brown, 1974.

Kerry, John, and Vietnam Veterans Against the War. *The New Soldier*, ed. D. Thorne and G. Butler. New York: Collier Books, 1971.

Ketwig, John. *. . . And a Hard Rain Fell*. New York: Pocket Books, 1985.

Kimball, Jeffrey. "The Stab-in-the-Back Legend and the Vietnam War," *Armed Forces and Society* 14, 3 (Spring 1988): 433–457.

Kingston, Maxine Hong. *China Men*. London: Picador, 1981.

Kinney, Judy Lee. "*Gardens of Stone, Platoon,* and *Hamburger Hill*: Ritual and Remembrance," in M. Anderegg (ed.), *Inventing Vietnam: The War in Film and Television*. Philadelphia: Temple University Press, 1991.

Klinkowitz, Jerome. *The American 1960s: Imaginative Acts in a Decade of Change*. Ames: Iowa State University Press, 1980.

Kolker, Robert Phillip. *A Cinema of Loneliness: Penn, Kubrick, Scorsese, Spielberg, Altman*, 2nd ed. New York: Oxford University Press, 1988.

Kopit, Arthur. *Indians*. New York: Bantam, 1971.

Kovic, Ron. *Born on the Fourth of July*. New York: Pocket Books, 1977.

Krebs, Albin. "Paley, C.B.S Chairman, Personally Vetoed Showing 'Sticks and Bones,'" *New York Times* (March 20, 1973): 76.

Kuenning, Dolores. *Life After Vietnam: How Veterans and Their Loved Ones Can Heal the Psychic Wounds of War.* New York: Paragon House, 1991.

Kunen, James Simon. *The Strawberry Statement: Notes of a College Age Revolutionary.* New York: Avon, 1970.

Laclau, Ernesto. *Politics and Ideology in Marxist Theory.* London: New Left Books, 1977.

Laclau, Ernesto, and Chantal Mouffe. *Hegemony and Socialist Strategy: Toward a Radical Democratic Politics.* London: Verso, 1989.

LaFeber, Walter. "The Last War, the Next War, and the New Revisionists," *Democracy* (January 1981): 93–103.

Lakoff, George, and Mark Johnson. *Metaphors We Live By.* Chicago: University of Chicago Press, 1980.

Lang, John. "A Memorial Wall That Healed Our Wounds," *U.S. News and World Report* (November 21, 1983): 68–70.

Lasch, Christopher. *The Culture of Narcissism: American Life in an Age of Diminishing Expectations.* New York: Warner Books, 1979.

Lasch, Christopher. *Haven in a Heartless World: The Family Besieged.* New York: Basic Books, 1977.

Lears, T. J. Jackson. *No Place of Grace: Antimodernism and the Transformation of American Culture, 1880–1920.* New York: Pantheon Books, 1981.

Lears, T. J. Jackson. "Power, Culture, and Memory," *Journal of American History* 75, 1 (June 1988): 137–140.

LeClair, Tom, and Larry McCaffery (eds.). *Anything Can Happen: Interviews with Contemporary American Novelists.* Urbana: University of Illinois Press, 1983.

Lederer, Walter, and Eugene Burdick. *The Ugly American.* New York: Norton, 1958.

Leed, Eric. *No Man's Land: Combat and Identity in World War I.* Cambridge, U.K.: Cambridge University Press, 1979.

Lehman, Peter. "'Well, What's It Like Over There? Can You Tell Us Anything?': Looking for Vietnam in *The Deer Hunter*," *North Dakota Quarterly* 5 (Summer 1983): 131–140.

Levi, Jonathan. "Norman Podhoretz: Impotence," *Granta* 15 (Spring 1985): 125–128.

Lévi-Strauss, Claude. *The Raw and the Cooked: Introduction to a Science of Mythology.* New York: Harper and Row, 1969.

Lévi-Strauss, Claude. *Structural Anthropology.* New York: Harper and Row, 1963.

Lewis, Lloyd. *The Tainted War: Culture and Identity in Vietnam War Narratives.* Westport, Conn.: Greenwood Press, 1985.

Lewy, Guenter. *America in Vietnam.* New York: Oxford University Press, 1978.

Lindberg, Tod. "Of Arms, Men and Monuments," *Commentary* 68, 4 (October 1984): 56.

Lipsitz, George. "Listening to Learn and Learning to Listen: Popular Culture, Cultural Theory, and American Studies," *American Quarterly* 42, 4 (December 1990): 615–636.

Lomperis, Tomothy. *Reading the Wind: The Literature of the Vietnam War—An Interpretative Critique.* Durham, N.C.: Duke University Press, 1987.

London, Bette. *The Appropriated Voice: Narrative Authority in Conrad, Forster, and Woolf.* Ann Arbor: University of Michigan Press, 1990.

Louvre, Alf, and Jeffrey Walsh (eds.). *Tell Me Lies about Vietnam: Cultural Battles for the Meaning of the War.* Milton Keynes, U.K.: Open University Press, 1988.

Luke, Tim. *Screens of Power: Ideology, Domination, and Resistance in Informational Society.* Urbana: University of Illinois Press, 1989.

Macherey, Pierre. *A Theory of Literary Production.* London: Routledge and Kegan Paul, 1978.

MacPherson, Myra. *Long Time Passing: Vietnam and the Haunted Generation.* New York: Signet, 1984.

Mahedy, William. *Out of the Night: The Spiritual Journey of Vietnam Vets.* New York: Ballantine, 1986.

Mailer, Norman. *Advertisements for Myself.* New York: Putnam, 1959.

Mailer, Norman. *The Armies of the Night: History as a Novel, the Novel as History.* Harmondsworth, Middlesex, U.K.: Penguin, 1968.

Mailer, Norman. "In the Red Light: A History of the Republican Convention in 1964," in *Cannibals and Christians.* New York: Delta, 1966.

Mailer, Norman. "Mailer's Reply," in *Cannibals and Christians.* New York: Delta, 1966.

Mailer, Norman. *Why Are We in Vietnam?* London: Panther, 1970.

Maland, Charles. "Synthetic Criticism and American Movies," *American Quarterly* 41, 1 (March 1989): 676–679.

Marchetti, Gina. "Excess and Understatement: War, Romance, and Melodrama in Contemporary Vietnamese Cinema," *Genders* 10 (Spring 1991): 47–74.

Marshall, Kathryn. *In the Combat Zone: An Oral History of American Women in Vietnam, 1966–1975.* Boston: Little, Brown, 1987.

Martin, Andrew. *Receptions of War: Vietnam in American Culture.* Norman: University of Oklahoma Press, 1993.

Mason, Bobbie Ann. "Big Bertha Stories," *Love Life.* London: Vintage, 1990.

Mason, Bobbie Ann. *In Country.* London: Flamingo, 1987.

Mason, Patience. *Recovering from the War: A Woman's Guide to Helping Your Vietnam Veteran, Your Family, and Yourself.* New York: Penguin, 1990.

Massey, Doreen. "A Place Called Home?" *New Formations* 17 (Summer 1992): 3–15.

Maurer, Harry. *Strange Ground: An Oral History of Americans in Vietnam, 1945–1975.* New York: Avon, 1990.

Mayo, James. *War Memorials as Political Landscape: The American Experience and Beyond*. New York: Praeger, 1988.

McCabe, Colin. "Theory and Film: Principles of Realism and Pleasure," in *Theoretical Essays: Film, Linguistics, Literature*. Manchester, U.K.: Manchester University Press, 1985.

McCloud, Bill (ed.). *What Should We Tell Our Children about Vietnam?*. Norman: University of Oklahoma Press, 1989.

McFadden, Robert. "Thousands Here Honor Vietnam Veterans," *New York Times* (April 1, 1973): 1, 76.

McNeill, William. "The Care and Repair of Public Myth," *Foreign Affairs*, 61 (Fall 1982): 1–13.

McQuaid, Kim. *The Anxious Years: America in the Vietnam-Watergate Era*. New York: Basic Books, 1989.

Melling, Philip. *Vietnam in American Literature*. Boston: Twayne, 1990.

Mercer, Kobena. "'1968': Periodizing Politics and Identity," in L. Grossberg, C. Nelson, and P. Treichler (eds.), *Cultural Studies*. New York: Routledge, 1992.

Modleski, Tania. "A Father Is Being Beaten: Male Feminism and the War Film," *Discourses: A Journal for Theoretical Studies in Media and Culture* 10, 2 (Spring-Summer 1988): 62–77.

Moeller, S. *Shooting War: Photography and the American Experience of Combat*. New York: Basic Books, 1989.

"Monumental Talent." *U.S. News and World Report* (November 6, 1989): 18.

Moore, Robin. *The Green Berets*. New York: Crown, 1965.

Morgan, Philip (ed.). *Diversity and Unity in Early North America*. London: Routledge, 1993.

Morganthau, Tom, and Mary Lord. "Honoring Vietnam Veterans—At Last," *Newsweek* (November 22, 1982): 32–33, 36.

Morrow, Lance. "A Bloody Rite of Passage," *Time* (April 15, 1985): 20–31.

Morrow, Lance. "An Elegy for the New Left," *Time* (August 15, 1977): 43.

Morrow, Lance. "The Forgotten Warriors," *Time* (July 13, 1981): 18–25.

Mouffe, Chantal. "Citizenship and Political Identity," *October* 61 (Summer 1992): 28–32.

Mouffe, Chantal. "Hegemony and the Integral State in Gramsci: Toward a New Concept of Politics," in G. Bridges and R. Brunt (eds.), *Silver Linings: Some Strategies for the Eighties*. London: Lawrence and Wishart, 1981.

Murolo, Priscilla. "Remembering Vietnam," *Radical History Review* 33 (1985): 182–185.

Myers, Thomas. *Walking Point: American Narratives of Vietnam*. New York: Oxford University Press, 1988.

Ngo Phong Lan. "Vietnam: Witness to History," *Cinemaya* 28–29 (Summer 1995): 4–7.

Nicholls, John. *American Blood*. London: Grafton Books, 1990.

Nichols, Bill. "Questions of Magnitude," in J. Corner (ed.), *Documentary and the Mass Media*. London: Edward Arnold, 1986.

Nichols, Bill. "The Voice of Documentary," in B. Nichols (ed.), *Movies and Methods: An Anthology, vol. 2.* Berkeley: University of California Press, 1985.

"1968: The Year That Shaped a Generation" (cover). *Time* (January 11, 1988).

"The Nintendo Issue." *Washington Post* (February 23, 1991): A16.

Nixon, Richard. *Beyond Peace*. New York: Random House, 1994.

Norden, Martin. *The Cinema of Isolation: A History of Physical Disability in the Movies*. New Brunswick, N.J.: Rutgers University Press, 1994.

Norman, Elizabeth. *Women at War: The Story of Fifty Military Nurses Who Served in Vietnam*. Philadelphia: University of Pennsylvania Press, 1990.

Norris, Margot. "Military Censorship and the Body Count in the Persian Gulf War," *Cultural Critique* 19 (Fall 1991): 223–229.

Norton, M. "Wound That Will Not Heal," *New York Times Magazine*, (November 11, 1979): 134–141.

Nowell-Smith, Geoffrey. "Common Sense," *Radical Philosophy* (Spring 1974): 16–19.

Nowell-Smith, Geoffrey. "Minnelli and Melodrama," in C. Gledhill (ed.), *Home Is Where the Heart Is: Studies in Melodrama and the Women's Film*. London: BFI Publishing, 1987.

O'Brien, Tim. *Going After Cacciato*. London: Triad/Granada, 1980.

O'Brien, Tim. *If I Die in a Combat Zone*. London: Granada, 1980.

O'Brien, Tim. *The Things They Carried*. New York: Penguin, 1991.

O'Brien, Tim. "The Violent Vet," *Esquire*, (December 1979): 96–104.

O'Brien, Tim. "We've Adjusted Too Well," in A. D. Horne (ed.), *The Wounded Generation: America After Vietnam*. Englewood Cliffs, N.J.: Prentice-Hall, 1981.

O'Hara, John. "The Narrative Construction of Reality: An Interview with Stuart Hall," *Southern Review* [Australia] 17, 1 (March 1984): 9–15.

O'Neill, William. *Coming Apart: An Informal History of America in the 1960's*. New York: Times Books, 1971.

O'Sullivan, Tim, John Hartley, Danny Saunders, and John Fiske. *Key Concepts in Communication*. London: Routledge, 1989.

Ong, Aihwa. "Southeast Asian Refugees and Investors in Our Midst," *Positions* 3, 3 (Winter 1995): 806–813.

Ono, Shin'ya. "You Do Need a Weatherman," originally published in *Leviathan*, December 1969, reprinted in J. Alpert and S. Alpert (eds.), *The Sixties Papers: Documents of a Rebellious Decade*. New York: Praeger, 1984.

Phelan, Shane. *Identity Politics*. Philadelphia: Temple University Press, 1989.

Plath, Sylvia. "Daddy," in *Sylvia Plath's Selected Poems*, selected by T. Hughes. London: Faber and Faber, 1985.

Polan, Dana. "'Above All Else to Make You See': Cinema and the Ideology of Spectacle," in J. Arac (ed.), *Postmodernism and Politics*. Manchester, U.K.: Manchester University Press, 1986.

Popular Culture Association. Program, Twentieth Annual Meeting, Toronto, Ontario, Canada, March 7–10, 1990. Bowling Green, Ohio: Bowling Green State University, 1990.

Powell, Stewart. "The Healing Nation," *U.S. News and World Report* (April 15, 1985): 35–37.

Pratt, John Clark. *Vietnam Voices: Perspectives on the War Years, 1941–1982*. New York: Viking, 1984.

"Propaganda Films about the War in Vietnam." *Film Comment* 4, 1 (Fall 1966): 4–13.

Quart, Leonard, and Albert Auster. "The Working Class Goes to Hollywood," in P. Davies and B. Neve (eds), *Cinema, Politics and Society in America*. New York: St. Martin's Press, 1981.

Quart, Leonard, and Albert Auster. "The Wounded Vet in Postwar Film," *Social Policy* 13, 2 (Fall 1982): 24–31.

Rabe, David. *The Vietnam Plays, vol. 1, "The Basic Training of Pavlo Hummel"* and *"Sticks and Bones."* New York: Grove Press, 1993.

Ray, Robert. *A Certain Tendency of the Hollywood Cinema, 1930–1980*. Princeton, N.J.: Princeton University Press, 1985.

Reagan, Ronald. "Veterans Day Ceremony: Vietnam Veterans Memorial, November 11, 1988," in *Speaking My Mind: Selected Speeches*. London: Hutchinson, 1990.

Ricoeur, Paul. *The Rule of Metaphor*. London: Routledge and Kegan Paul, 1978.

Rieff, Philip. *The Triumph of the Therapeutic: Uses of Faith After Freud*. New York: Harper and Row, 1966.

Ringnalda, Donald. *Fighting and Writing the Vietnam War*. Jackson: University Press of Mississippi, 1994.

Ringnalda, Donald. "Unlearning to Remember," in O. Gilman, Jr., and L. Smith (eds.), *America Rediscovered: Critical Essays on Literature and Film of the Vietnam War*. New York: Garland, 1990.

Robertson, James Oliver. *American Myth, American Reality*. New York: Hill and Wang, 1980.

Robertson, Roland. "After Nostalgia? Wilful Nostalgia and the Phases of Globalization," in B. Turner (ed.), *Theories of Modernity and Postmodernity*. London: Sage, 1990.

Rodowick, David N. *The Difficulty of Difference: Psychoanalysis, Sexual Difference and Film Theory*. New York: Routledge, 1991.

Rogers, Kenny, and the First Edition. "Ruby, Don't Take Your Love to Town" (Reprise, 1969).

Rogin, Michael. "'Make My Day!': Spectacle as Amnesia in Imperial Politics," *Representations* 29 (Winter 1990): 99–123.

Rollyson, Carl. *The Lives of Norman Mailer: A Biography*. New York: Paragon House, 1991.

"Ronald Reagan Calls Vietnam a Noble and Just Cause, 1988," in M. McMahon (ed.), *Major Problems in the History of the Vietnam War: Documents and Essays*. Lexington, Mass.: Heath, 1990.

Ross, Andrew. "Cowboys, Cadillacs and Cosmonauts: Families, Film Genres, and Technocultures," in J. Boone and M. Cadden (eds.), *Engendering Men: The Question of Male Feminist Criticism*. New York: Routledge, 1990.

Roth, Philip. "Writing American Fiction," in M. Bradbury (ed.), *The Novel Today: Contemporary Writers on Modern Fiction*. London: Fontana, 1977.

Rottmann, Larry Lee. "A Hundred Happy Sparrows: An American Veteran Returns to Vietnam," *Vietnam Generation* 1, 1 (1989): 113–139.

Rottmann, Larry Lee, Jan Barry, and Basil Parquet (eds.). *Winning Hearts and Minds: War Poems by Vietnam Veterans*. Brooklyn: 1st Casualty Press, 1972.

Rowe, John Carlos. "'Bringing It All Back Home': American Recyclings of the Vietnam War," in N. Armstrong and L. Tennenhouse (eds.), *The Violence of Representation: Literature and the History of Violence*. London: Routledge, 1989.

Rowe, John Carlos. "Eye-Witness: Documentary Styles in the American Representations of Vietnam," *Cultural Critique* 3 (1986): 126–150.

Rowe, John Carlos. "From Documentary to Docudrama: Vietnam on Television in the 1980's," *Genre* 21, 4 (Winter 1988): 451–478.

Rowe, John Carlos. "Vietnam and American Literary Historiography," in D. Nye and C. Thomsen (eds.), *American Studies in Transition*. Odense, Denmark: Odense University Press, 1985.

Rowe, John Carlos, and Rick Berg (eds.). *The Vietnam War and American Culture*. New York: Columbia University Press, 1991.

Ryan, Michael. *Politics and Culture: Working Hypotheses for a Post-Revolutionary Society*. Houndsmill, Basingstoke, U.K.: Macmillan, 1989.

Ryan, Michael, and Douglas Kellner. *Camera Politica: The Politics and Ideology of Contemporary Hollywood Film*. Bloomington: Indiana University Press, 1988.

Santoli, Al. *Everything We Had: An Oral History of the Vietnam War by Thirty-three American Soldiers Who Fought It*. New York: Ballantine, 1982.

Santoli, Al. *To Bear Any Burden: The Vietnam War and Its Aftermath in the Words of Americans and Southeast Asians*. London: Sphere, 1986.

Sato, Tadao. "Voice of Vietnam," *Cinemaya* 16 (1992): 46–67.

Sayres, Sonya, Anders Stephanson, Stanley Aronowitz, and Fredric Jameson (eds.). *The 60s Without Apology*. Minneapolis: University of Minnesota Press, 1984.

Scarry, Elaine. *The Body in Pain: The Making and Unmaking of the World*. New York: Oxford University Press, 1995.

Scarry, Elaine. "Injury and the Structure of War," *Representations* 10 (Spring 1985): 1–51.

Schaeffer, Susan Fromberg. *Buffalo Afternoon*. New York: Knopf, 1989.

Scruggs, Jan, and Joel Swerdlow. *To Heal a Nation*. New York: Harper and Row, 1986.

Searle, William. J. "The Vietnam War Novel and the Reviewers," *Journal of American Culture* 42, 2 (Summer 1981): 83–94.

Searle, William J. "Walking Wounded: Vietnam War Novels of Return," in W. J. Searle (ed.), *Search and Clear: Critical Responses to Selected Literature and Films of the Vietnam War*. Bowling Green, Ohio: Bowling Green State University Popular Press, 1988.

Sekula, Alan. "War Without Bodies," *Artforum* (November 1991): 107–110.

Sennett, Richard, and Jonathan Cobb. *The Hidden Injuries of Class*. New York: Vintage, 1973.

Severo, Richard, and Lewis Milford. *The Wages of War: When America's Soldiers Came Home—From Valley Forge to Vietnam*. New York: Simon and Schuster, 1990.

Shklovsky, Victor. "Art as Technique," in L. Leman and M. Reis (eds.), *Russian Formalist Criticism: Four Essays*. Lincoln: University of Nebraska Press, 1965.

Silkin, Jon (ed.). *The Penguin Book of First World War Poetry*, 2nd ed. Harmondsworth, Middlesex, U.K.: Penguin, 1981.

Silverman, Kaja. "Historical Trauma and Male Subjectivity," in E. Kaplan (ed.), *Psychoanalysis and Cinema*. New York: Routledge, 1990.

Skolnick, Arlene. *Embattled Paradise: The American Family in an Age of Uncertainty*. New York: Basic Books, 1991.

Slater, Philip. *The Pursuit of Loneliness: American Culture at Breaking Point*. Boston: Beacon Press, 1990.

Sloan, Irving (ed.). *Ronald Reagan, 1911– : Chronology–Documents–Bibliographical Aids*. Dobbs Ferry, N.Y.: Oceana, 1990.

Slotkin, Richard. *The Fatal Environment: The Myth of the Frontier in the Age of Industrialization, 1800–1890*. New York: Atheneum, 1985.

Slotkin, Richard. *Gunfighter Nation: The Myth of the Frontier in Twentieth-Century America*. New York: Harper and Row, 1993.

Slotkin, Richard. *Regeneration Through Violence: The Mythology of the American Frontier, 1600–1860*. Middletown, Conn.: Wesleyan University Press, 1973.

Smith, Julian. *Looking Away: Hollywood and Vietnam*. New York: Scribners, 1975.

Smith, Lorrie. "Back Against the Wall: Anti-Feminist Backlash in Vietnam War Literature," *Vietnam Generation* 1, 3–4 (Summer-Fall,1989): 115–126.

Sobchack, Vivian (ed.). *The Persistence of History: Cinema, Television, and the Modern Event*. New York: Routledge, 1996.

Sommer, Dorris. "Cortez in the Courts: The Traps of Translation from Newsprint to Film," in M. Garber, J. Matlock, and R. Walkowitz (eds.), *Media Spectacles*. New York: Routledge, 1993.

Sontag, Susan. *Illness as Metaphor*. Harmondsworth, Middlesex, U.K.: Penguin, 1983.

Spivak, Gayatri. "Can the Subaltern Speak?" in C. Nelson and L. Grossberg (eds.), *Marxism and the Interpretation of Culture*. Urbana: University of Illinois Press, 1988.

Springer, Claudia. "*Vietnam: A Television History* and the Equivocal Nature of Objectivity," *Wide Angle* 7, 4 (1985): 53–60.

Springsteen, Bruce. "Born in the U.S.A.," on *Born in the U.S.A.* (CBS, 1984).

Stanley, Alexander. "Healing Viet Nam's Wounds," *Time* (November 26, 1984): 44.

Stevenson, W. Taylor. "The Experience of Defilement: A Response to John Wheeler," *Anglican Theological Review* 64, 1 (January 1982): 15–36.

Stewart, Catherine. *On Longing: Narratives of the Miniature, the Gigantic, the Souvenir, the Collection*. Baltimore: Johns Hopkins University Press, 1984.

Stone, Oliver. "The Killing of JFK: A Very American Coup," *Weekend Australian* (December 28–29, 1991), Review, 3.

Stone, Oliver. *Platoon / Salvador: The Screenplays*. London: Ebury Press, 1987.

Stone, Robert. *Children of Light*. London: Andre Deutsch, 1986.

Stone, Robert. *Dog Soldiers*. London: Wyndham, 1976.

Stone, Robert. *A Flag for Sunrise*. London: Picador, 1983.

Stone, Robert. *A Hall of Mirrors*. Harmondsworth, Middlesex, U.K.: Penguin, 1968.

Stone, Robert. *Outerbridge Reach*. Harmondsworth, Middlesex, U.K.: Penguin, 1992.

Students for a Democratic Society. "Bringing the War Home," reprinted in J. Alpert and S. Alpert (eds.), *The Sixties Papers: Documents of a Rebellious Decade*. New York: Praeger, 1984.

Sturken, Marita. *Tangled Memories: The Vietnam War, the AIDS Epidemic, and the Politics of Remembering*. Berkeley: University of California Press, 1997.

Sturken, Marita. "The Wall, the Screen, and the Image: The Vietnam Veterans Memorial," *Representations* 35 (Summer 1991): 118–142.

Suid, Lawrence. "Hollywood and Vietnam," *Journal of American Culture* 4, 2 (Summer 1981): 136–148.

Summers, Harry. *On Strategy: The Vietnam War in Context*. Novato, Calif.: Presidio Press, 1982.

Swiers, George. "'Demented Vets' and Other Myths: The Moral Obligation of Veterans," in H. Salisbury (ed.), *Vietnam Reconsidered: Lessons from a War*. New York: Harper and Row, 1984.

Tal, Kali. "When History Talks Back: The Voice of the Veteran," in M. J. Gilbert (ed.), *The Vietnam War: Teaching Approaches and Resources*. New York: Greenwood Press, 1991.

Tal, Kali. *Worlds of Hurt: Reading the Literature of Trauma*. Cambridge, U.K.: Cambridge University Press, 1996.

Talbott, Strobe. "The War That Will Not End," *Time* (September 9, 1992): 57.

Terry, Wallace. *Bloods: An Oral History of the Vietnam War by Black Veterans.* New York: Random House, 1984.

Thelen, David. "Memory and American History," *Journal of American History* 75, 4 (March 1989): 1117–1129.

Thompson, W. Scott, and Donald D. Frizzel (eds.). *The Lessons of Vietnam.* New York: Crane, Russak, 1977.

Thorburg, Newton. *Cutter and Bone.* London: William Heinemann, 1978.

Trinh T. Minh-ha. "Why a Fish Pond? Fiction at the Heart of Documentation," an interview conducted by L. Jayamanne and A. Rutherford, *Filmnews* [Sydney] (November 1990): 10–13.

Turner, Frederick Jackson. "The Significance of the Frontier in American History," in *The Frontier in American History.* New York: Holt, Rinehart, 1958.

Van Devanter, Lynda, with Christopher Morgan. *Home Before Morning: The Story of an Army Nurse in Vietnam.* New York: Warner Books, 1984.

"Viet Nam as It Really Was" (cover). *Time* (January 26, 1987).

"Vietnam—Will There Be a Collective Healing?" *Center Magazine* 14, 4 (July-August 1981): 14–28.

"Vietnam as Unending Trauma." *Society* 21 (November-December 1983): 4–33.

Vietnam Veterans Against the War. *The Winter Soldier Investigation: An Inquiry into American War Crimes.* Boston: Beacon Press, 1972.

Vogelsang, Sandy. *The Long Dark Night of the Soul: The American Intellectual Left and the Vietnam War.* New York: Harper and Row, 1974.

Vonnegut, Kurt. *Hocus Pocus.* New York: Berkley Books, 1991.

Wagner-Pacifici, Robin, and Barry Schwartz. "The Vietnam Veterans Memorial: Commemorating a Difficult Past," *American Journal of Sociology* 97, 2 (September 1991): 376–420.

Walker, Keith. *A Piece of My Heart: The Stories of Twenty-six American Women Who Served in Vietnam.* Novato, Calif.: Presidio Press, 1985.

Walker, Mark. *Vietnam Veteran Films.* Metuchen, N.J.: Scarecrow Press, 1991.

Warner, Dennis. *Certain Victory.* Mission, Kans.: Sheed, Andrews, and McNeel, 1977.

Washington Project for the Arts. *War and Memory: In the Aftermath of Vietnam.* Washington, D.C.: The Project, 1987.

Webb, James. *Fields of Fire.* New York: Bantam, 1979.

Wheeler, John. "Coming to Grips with Vietnam," *Foreign Affairs* 63, 4 (Spring 1985): 747–758.

Wheeler, John. *Touched with Fire: The Future of the Vietnam Generation.* New York: Avon Books, 1984.

Wheeler, John. "The Vietnam Generation," in R. Bremner, G. Reichard and R. Hopkins (eds.), *American Choices: Social Dilemmas and Public Policy Since 1960.* Columbus: Ohio State University Press, 1986.

Wiebe, Robert. *The Segmented Society.* London: Oxford University Press, 1975.

Wiener, Jon. "The Sixties and Popular Memory," *Radical America* 21, 6 (November-December 1987): 24–25.

Willenson, Kim, with the correspondents of *Newsweek*. *The Bad War: An Oral History of the Vietnam War*. New York: New American Library, 1987.

Williams, John. *Captain Blackman*. New York: Thunder's Mouth Press, 1988.

Williams, Raymond. *The Long Revolution*. Harmondsworth, Middlesex, U.K.: Penguin, 1965.

Williams, Raymond. *Marxism and Literature*. Oxford: Oxford University Press, 1977.

Wilson, James. *Landing Zones: Southern Veterans Remember Vietnam*. Durham, N.C.: Duke University Press, 1990.

Wolf, Naomi. *The Beauty Myth: How Images of Beauty Are Used Against Women*. London: Vintage, 1991.

Wolfe, Tom. *Radical Chic, and Mau-Mauing the Flak Catchers*. New York: Bantam, 1971.

Wood, Robin. "80s Hollywood: Dominant Tendencies," *CineAction!* (Spring 1985): 2–5.

Wood, Robin. *Hollywood from Vietnam to Reagan*. New York: Columbia University Press, 1986.

Woodward, C. Vann. "The Fall of the American Adam: Myths of Innocence and Guilt," *New Republic* (December 2, 1981): 14–15.

Woodward, K., et al. "Saving the Family," *Newsweek* (May 15, 1978): 49–54.

"Wounds That Will Not Heal." *Time* (July 13, 1981): 22.

Wright, Robert. "'History's Heavy Attrition': Literature, Historical Consciousness and the Impact of Vietnam," *Canadian Review of American Studies* 17, 3 (Fall 1986): 301–316.

Wright, Stephen. *Meditations in Green*. London: Abacus, 1985.

Yardley, Jonathan. Reprint of review of *In Country*, in D. Marowski and R. Matuz (eds.), *Contemporary Literary Criticism*, vol. 43. Detroit: Gale, 1987.

Zahn, Gordon. "Memories in Stone," *America* 149, 11 (October 15, 1983): 213.

Zinn, Howard. *A People's History of the United States*. New York: Harper Perennial, 1990.

FILM AND TELEVISION SERIES

(The form of the following entries, for films: title; year of release; director; production and/or distribution company; for television series: title; network; year of premier.)

The A-Team, NBC, 1983

The Abandoned Field—Free Fire Zone, 1979, Hong Sen, Vietnam Feature Film Studios

Airport, 1970, George Seaton, Universal

Alamo Bay, 1985, Louis Malle, Tri-Star

Ambush, 1992, Joseph Gray, Artists' Kentucky Project

American Graffiti, 1973, George Lucas, Universal

The Anderson Platoon, 1967, Pierre Schoendorffer, Schoendorffer Films Inc.

Angels From Hell, 1968, Bruce Kessler, American International

The Angry Breed, 1968, David Commons, Commonwealth United

Animal House (aka *National Lampoon's Animal House*), 1979, John Landis, Universal

Apocalypse Now, 1979, Francis Ford Coppola, United Artists

Ashes and Embers, 1982, Haile Gerima, Mypheduh Films

Author! Author!, 1982, Arthur Hiller, Twentieth Century Fox

The Best Years of Our Lives, 1946, William Wyler, Samuel Goldwyn

Beyond the Law, 1967, Norman Mailer

The Big Chill, 1983, Lawrence Kasdan, Columbia

Billy Jack, 1971, T. C. Frank (Tom Laughlin), Warner Brothers

Billy Jack Goes to Washington, 1977, Tom Laughlin, Taylor-Laughlin

Black Cactus, 1991, Le Dan, Vietnam Feature Film Studios

Black Sunday, 1976, John Frankenheimer, Paramount

Blood of Ghastly Horror, 1971, Al Adamson, Hemisphere Productions

Bobby Deerfield, 1977, Sydney Pollack, Columbia

The Born Losers, 1967, T. C. Frank (Tom Laughlin), American International

Born on the Fourth of July, 1989, Oliver Stone, Universal

Braddock: Missing in Action III, 1988, Aaron Norris, Cannon

Brothers and Relations, 1986, Tran Vu and Nguyen Huu Luyen, Vietnam Feature Film Studios

Bus Riley's Back in Town, 1965, Harvey Hart, Universal

Casualties of War, 1989, Brian DePalma, Columbia

Cease Fire, 1984, David Nutter, Cineworld Enterprises

The Champ, 1979, Franco Zeffirelli, United Artists/MGM

China Beach, ABC, 1988

Christmas in Vietnam, 1965, Joe Gorsuch, CBS News

Chrome and Hot Leather, 1971, Lee Frost, American International

Coming Home, 1978, Hal Ashby, United Artists

The Cosby Show, NBC, 1984

The Crazy World of Julius Vrooder, 1974, Arthur Hiller, Twentieth Century Fox

Cu Chi Guerrilla, 1967, Vietnam Central Newsreel and Documentary Film Studio

Cutter's Way (aka *Cutter and Bone*), 1981, Ivan Passer, United Artists

Deathdream (aka *Dead of Night* and *The Night Walk*), 1972, Bob Clark, Bob Clark/Europix Consolidated

The Deer Hunter, 1978, Michael Cimino, EMI/Columbia/Warner

Desert Shield, 1991, Shimon Dotan, Twentyfirst Century Productions

Distant Thunder, 1988, Rick Rosenthal, Paramount

Earthquake, 1975, Mark Robson, Universal

The Edge, 1967, Robert Kramer, Blue Van Productions-Alpha 60
84 Charlie Mopic, 1989, Patrick Duncan, New Century-Vista
E.T.: The Extraterrestrial, 1982, Steven Spielberg, Universal
A Face of War, 1968, Eugene Jones, International Historic Films
Family Ties, NBC, 1982
First Blood, 1982, Ted Kotcheff, Orion
Forrest Gump, 1994, Robert Zemeckis, Paramount
Frank: A Vietnam Veteran, 1981, Fred Simon, Fanlight Productions
Full Metal Jacket, 1987, Stanley Kubrick, Warner Brothers
Getting Straight, 1970, Richard Rush, Columbia
GI Jose, 1975, Norberto Lopez, Third World Newsreel
The Girl on the River, 1987, Dang Nhat Minh, Vietnam Feature Film Studios
Going Back: A Return to Vietnam, 1982, David Munro, Bullfrog Films
Good Bye and Good Luck, 1969, WNET Boston
Good Guys Wear Black, 1977, Ted Post, Mar Vista
Grand Canyon, 1992, Lawrence Kasdan, Twentieth Century Fox
The Green Berets, 1968, John Wayne and Ray Kellogg, Warner Brothers/Seven Arts
Growing Pains, ABC, 1985
Hamburger Hill, 1987, John Irvin, RKO
Hanoi Hilton, 1987, Lionel Chetwynd, Golan-Globus
Happy Days, ABC, 1974
The Hard Ride, 1971, Bruce Topper, American International
Hardcore, 1978, Paul Schrader, Columbia/A-Team
Heartbreak Ridge, 1986, Clint Eastwood, Malpaso/Weston
Heroes, 1977, Jeremy Paul Kagan, Universal
Hot Shots II, 1992, Jim Abrahams, Twentieth Century Fox
Ice Castles, 1979, Donald Wrye, Columbia
In Country, 1989, Norman Jewison, Warner Brothers
Interviews with My Lai Veterans, 1972, Joseph Strick, Films Inc
Intimate Strangers, 1986, Robert Ellis Miller, Telepictures
Jacknife, 1989, David Jones, Vestron
Johnny Firecloud, 1975, W. A. Castleman, American National
Journey through Rosebud, 1972, Tom Gries, GSF Video
Karma, 1986, Ho Quang Minh, Vietnam Feature Film Studios
Kramer vs. Kramer, 1979, Robert Benton, Columbia
The Lady from Yesterday, 1985, Robert Day, Comworld Productions
Latino, 1985, Haskell Wexler, Lucasfilms
Laverne and Shirley, ABC, 1975
Lethal Weapon, 1987, Richard Donner, Warner Brothers
Lethal Weapon II, 1989, Richard Donner, Warner Brothers
Lethal Weapon III, 1992, Richard Donner, Warner Brothers
Little Big Man, 1971, Arthur Penn, Cinema Center
Long Shadows, 1987, Ross Spears, James Agee Film Project

Lords of Discipline, 1983, Franc Roddom, Paramount
The Losers, 1970, Jack Starrett, Fanfare Films
Magnum, P.I., CBS, 1980
Maidstone, 1968, Norman Mailer
Medium Cool, 1969, Haskell Wexler, Paramount
Meet Me in St. Louis, 1944, Vicente Minnelli, MGM
The Men, 1951, Fred Zinnemann, United Artists
Miami Vice, NBC, 1984
Missing in Action, 1984, Joseph Zitto, Cannon
Missing in Action II: The Beginning, 1985, Lance Hool, Cannon
Motor Psycho, 1965, Russ Meyer, Eve Productions
Mr. Mom, 1983, Stan Dragoti, Paramount
The Most Dangerous Situation, 1967, Vietnam Central Newsreel and Documentary Film Studio
Mr. Smith Goes To Washington, 1939, Frank Capra, Columbia
My Old Man's Place (aka *Glory Boy)*, 1972, Edwin Sherin, Cinerama
Ngu Thuy Girls, 1969, Vietnam Central Newsreel and Documentary Film Studio
No Game, 1968, The Newsreel, Third World Newsreel
No Vietnamese Ever Called Me Nigger, 1968, David Weiss, Paradigm Films
An Officer and a Gentlemen, 1982, Taylor Hackford, Lorimer
Operation Nam, 1985, Larry Ludman, Imperial Entertainment
Ordinary People, 1980, Robert Redford, Paramount/Wildwood
The Other Side of Midnight, 1977, Charles Jarrott, Twentieth Century Fox
P.O.W.: The Escape, 1986, Gideon Amir, Golan/Globus
Platoon, 1986, Oliver Stone, Hemdale
The Poseidon Adventure, 1972, Ronald Neame, Twentieth Century Fox
Powwow Highway, 1989, Joanelle Romero and Jonathan Wacks, Warner Brothers
Pride of the Marines, 1945, Delmer Daves, Warner Brothers
Private Benjamin, 1980, Howard Zieff, Warner Brothers
Rambo: First Blood, II, 1985, George Cosmatos, Tri-Star
Riders of the Storm (aka *The American Way)*, 1986, Maurice Phillips, Miramax
Riptide, NBC, 1984
Riverbend, 1990, Sam Firstenberg, Prism
Rolling Thunder, 1977, John Flynn, AIP
Roots, ABC, 1977
Salvador, 1986, Oliver Stone, Hemdale
Sands of Iwo Jima, 1949, Allan Dwan, Republic
Satan's Sadists, 1969, Al Adamson, Independent International
The Searchers, 1956, John Ford, Whitney/Warner Brothers
The Secret Agent, 1983, Jacki Ochs and Daniel Keller, Green Mountain Post Films
Shoot the Moon, 1982, Alan Parker, MGM/United Artists
Slow Dancing in the Big City, 1978, John Avildsen, United Artists
Soldier Blue, 1970, Ralph Nelson, Avco Embassy

Some Kind of Hero, 1982, Michael Pressman, Paramount
The Strawberry Statement, 1970, Stuart Hagmann, MGM
Stripes, 1981, Ivan Reitman, Columbia
The Strolling Singers, Chau Hue, 1991, Vietnam Feature Film Studios
The Stunt Man, 1978, Richard Rush, Twentieth Century Fox
Surname Viet, Given Name Nam, 1989, Trinh T. Minh-ha, Women Make Film
Summer of '68, 1968, The Newsreel, Third World Newsreel
Taps, 1981, Harold Becker, Twentieth Century Fox
Taxi Driver, 1976, Martin Scorsese, Columbia
Terms of Endearment, 1983, James Brooks, Paramount
To Kill a Clown, 1972, George Bloomfield, Twentieth Century Fox
To Heal a Nation, 1987, Michael Pressman, Lionel Chetwynd Productions/Orion
    Pictures Television
Top Gun, 1986, Tony Scott, Paramount
Tour of Duty, CBS, 1987
Towering Inferno, 1975, John Guillermin, Twentieth Century Fox/ Warner Brothers
Tracks, 1976, Henry Jaglom, Rainbow Pictures
The Trial of Billy Jack, 1974, Frank Laughlin, Taylor-Laughlin
True Romance, 1993, Tony Scott, Warner Brothers
Twilight's Last Gleaming, 1977, Robert Aldrich, Lorimar/Geria
Ulzana's Raid, 1972, Robert Aldrich, Columbia
Uncommon Valor, 1983, Ted Kotcheff, Paramount
Vietnam Requiem: Vets in Prison, 1982, Jonas McCord, Direct Cinema
Vietnam Veterans: Dissidents for Peace, 1988, Ying Ying Wu, Filmakers Library
Vinh Linh Fortress, 1970, Vietnam Central Newsreel and Documentary Film Studio
The Visitors, 1972, Elia Kazan, United Artists
Wall Street, 1987, Oliver Stone, Twentieth Century Fox
The War in El Cedro, 1988, Don North, Northstar Productions
Weekend, 1967, Jean-Luc Godard, Films Copernic
Welcome Home, 1989, Franklin Schaffer, Columbia/Rank
Welcome Home, Soldier Boys, 1972, Richard Compton, Twentieth Century Fox
When the Tenth Month Comes, 1984, Dang Nhat Minh, Vietnam Feature Film
    Studios
Who'll Stop the Rain? 1978, Karel Reisz, United Artists
Who's the Boss? ABC, 1984
Wild 90, 1968, Norman Mailer
The Wild Bunch, 1969, Sam Peckinpah, Warner Brothers/Seven Arts
The Wonder Years, ABC, 1988
The World According to Garp, 1983, George Roy Hill, Warner Brothers
Zabriskie Point, 1970, Michelangelo Antonioni, MGM

Index

About the Author

Keith Beattie is the editor of the *Australasian Journal of American Studies*, and a member of the editorial collective of *Sites: A Journal of South Pacific Cultural Studies*. He is the author of numerous articles on cultural theory and American culture and has won various grants and awards, including a scholarship from the National Endowment for the Humanities. He received his doctorate from the University of New South Wales, Sydney, Australia, where he taught for a number of years before his current position of lecturer in media studies and American cultural studies at Massey University, New Zealand.